WALTER BENJAMIN AND

THE AESTHETICS OF POWER

Modern
German Culture
and Literature

WALTER BENJAMIN
AND THE AESTHETICS
OF POWER

LUTZ KOEPNICK

University of Nebraska Press
Lincoln and London
1999

Acknowledgments for the
use of previously published
material appear on page vii.
© 1999 by the University of
Nebraska Press. All rights
reserved. Manufactured in the
United States of America
♾ Library of Congress
Cataloging-in-Publication
Data. Koepnick, Lutz, 1963–
Walter Benjamin and the
aesthetics of power / Lutz
Koepnick. p. cm. –
(Modern German culture and
literature) Includes biblio-
graphical references and index.
ISBN 0-8032-2744-2 (cl.: alk.
paper) 1. Benjamin, Walter,
1892–1940 – Political and social
views. 2. Benjamin, Walter,
1892–1940 – Aesthetics.
3. National socialism and art.
4. Fascism and art. 5. Mass
society. 6. Popular culture.
7. Aesthetics, Modern – 20th
century. I. Title. II. Series.
PT2603.E455Z6994 1999
838'.91209 – dc21
99-12013 CIP

CONTENTS

Acknowledgments

This book is the result of extended attempts to theorize the role of modern mass culture and the aesthetic in German National Socialism. I would like to express my gratitude to the many colleagues and friends whose encouragement and criticism have been essential to the completion of this project. In particular I am indebted to Russell Berman for his intellectual guidance throughout the first stages of this enterprise. I would also like to thank Leslie Adelson, Karen Fiss, Peter Hohendahl, Martin Jay, Michael Jennings, Kurt Mueller-Vollmer, David Pan, Eric Rentschler, and Paul Robinson – all of whom have been helpful beyond measure to rethink half-baked premises and sharpen individual arguments. Thanks are also due to Douglas Clayton, formerly at the University of Nebraska Press, for his patience and persistent support throughout the process of getting this book finished, and to Dennis Marshall, who carefully copyedited the book for publication.

Several institutions have contributed to this project. During the earlier stages, both the Stanford Humanities Center (1992–93) and the Whiting Foundation (1993–94) provided important resources for my research. I also owe gratitude to the German Department and the Graduate School of Arts and Sciences at Washington University for the support that made the writing and rewriting of this book possible.

Portions of this project appeared in embryonic form in previously published articles. For their permission to make use of these materials, I would like to acknowledge *Critical Inquiry*, for "The Spectacle, the *Trauerspiel*, and the Politics of Resolution: Benjamin Reading the Baroque Reading Weimar," 22.2 (1996): 268–91; and *Soundings: An Interdisciplinary Journal*, for "Allegory and Power: Walter Benjamin and the Politics of Representation," 79.1–2 (1996): 59–78.

Christa Johnson has read and commented on every line of the many drafts of this project. Without her unswerving support – intellectual and otherwise – *Walter Benjamin and the Aesthetics of Power* would simply not have been possible.

I dedicate this book to my parents, Eva-Maria and Horst Köpnick.

ABBREVIATIONS

References to Benjamin's work appear as parenthetical notations within the text. For the reader's convenience I have included references for both Benjamin's *Gesammelte Schriften* and the existing English translations (e.g., ILL 242; GS 1:507). For references not yet translated, I provide my own translations of the German original.

CP "Central Park." Trans. Lloyd Spencer. *New German Critique* 34 (winter 1985): 1–27.

GS *Gesammelte Schriften*. Ed. Rolf Tiedemann and Hermann Schweppenhäuser. Frankfurt am Main: Suhrkamp, 1972–89.

ILL *Illuminations: Essays and Reflections*. Trans. Harry Zohn, ed. Hannah Arendt. New York: Schocken, 1969.

OTD *The Origin of German Tragic Drama*. Trans. John Osborne. London: NLB, 1977.

REF *Reflections: Essays, Aphorisms, Autobiographical Writings*. Trans. Edmund Jephcott, ed. Peter Demetz. New York: Schocken, 1986.

SW *Selected Writings*. Ed. Marcus Bullock and Michael W. Jennings. Cambridge: Harvard University Press, 1996–.

TGF "Theories of German Fascism: On the Collection of Essays *War and Warrior*, edited by Ernst Jünger." Trans. Jerolf Wikoff. *New German Critique* 17 (spring 1979): 120–28.

INTRODUCTION

FASCISM, MASS CULTURE, AND THE AVANT-GARDE

It has become commonplace for scholars of modern German culture to say that National Socialism cannot be understood without considering the role of Nazi culture and aesthetics. According to this view, the stage-managing of political action and the coordination of all cultural expressions during the Nazi period served the decisively antimodern goal of dedifferentiation and false reconciliation. National Socialism infused aesthetics into the political sphere in order to turn life into a unified work of art. As a perverse continuation of certain avant-garde projects, Nazi aesthetics revoked peculiarly modern boundaries between modes of cognition, experience, and expression. It recast the political as a realm of the beautiful so as to compensate for the costs of modern disenchantment and to suture disenfranchised individuals into an all-encompassing spectacle of homogenization, an aesthetic simulation of community. Don DeLillo's 1985 novel *White Noise* neatly summarizes what has become standard fare among historians and theorists of National Socialism. The novel's protagonist, Jack Gladney, a professor of Hitler studies at a small midwestern college, regularly screens a self-edited documentary that features military parades, mass rallies, and other highly choreographed crowd scenes: "Close-up jostled shots of thousands of people outside a stadium after a Goebbels speech, people surging, massing, bursting through the traffic. Halls hung with swastika banners, with mortuary wreaths and death's-head insignia. Ranks of thousands of flagbearers arrayed before columns of frozen light, a hundred and thirty aircraft searchlights aimed straight up – a scene that resembled a geometric longing, the formal notation of some powerful mass desire."[1]

Deeply engrossed in the power of the visual, the postmodern imagination remains haunted by the operatic extravaganzas of Nazi culture and aesthetics. Contemporary entertainment industries, in fact, utilize images such as those of Gladney – political spectacles, the Nazi cult of death, and the geometrical organization of the crowd – as one of the most powerful and enduring cultural commodities of the twentieth century. For some, this fascination speaks for the particular erosion of historical depth often attributed to the postmodern condition. It brings into view the precarious ways in which contemporary culture puts distant traditions and disparate objects on a single plane of instant availability and mass consumption. For others, however, the persistent currency of Nazi aesthetics more than half a century after the end of World War II reveals a much darker truth about the visual turn of twentieth-century culture. In its endeavor to supplant direct experience and exchange reality for illusion, Nazi culture "granted a preview of postmodern attractions."[2] Nazi aesthetics remains fascinating today because postmodern culture similarly desires spectacles and mass-produced representations. An uncanny soulmate of the Nazi spectacle, postmodernism incessantly recycles images of the Third Reich as it seeks in its own ways to break down modern boundaries between politics and aesthetics and to turn life into a fantastic work of art.

It is understandable, then, that many critics embrace Walter Benjamin's thesis about the aestheticizing nature of fascism as a tool not only to shed light on the staging of political action in Nazi Germany but also, by analogy, on the postmodern blurring of culture and politics, media and power. Benjamin's legendary formula has led us to believe that aesthetic politics reintegrates autonomous art into the realms of political action and everyday life, a project that fascist imagemakers share with postmodern media czars. Though operating under different auspices indeed, both the Third Reich and the postmodern spectacle aestheticize politics with the hope of annulling the complexity of modern society – of reconciling incompatible practices, discourses, value spheres, and social subsystems. Whether Nazi or postmodern in origin, aesthetic politics turns political values into aesthetic experiences in order to do away with what Kant, Weber, Habermas, or Luhmann, each in his own way, understands as the hallmark of the modern condition – namely, cognitive, normative, or functional differentiation.

As it revisits Walter Benjamin's seminal critique of fascism, this book argues against the understanding of aesthetic politics as a full-blown attack on modern differentiation, and in so doing, it intends not only to give new momentum to contemporary debates about the cultural politics of fascism, but also to rethink the relation between Nazi aesthetics and the postmodern spectacle. Benjamin's aestheticization thesis, I argue, instead of simply theorizing Nazi politics as a quasi-Wagnerian total work of art, sharpens our awareness for the pernicious complicity between fascism and the refraction of modern society into competing spheres of value, knowledge, and action. Benjamin's notion of aesthetic politics brings into view what interwar intellectuals of the extreme Right envisioned as the autonomy of the political. It employs the modalities of industrial mass culture with the intention of giving twentieth-century politics the appearance of unified, heroic action; it recycles decadent notions of artistic practice so as to refashion politics as a space of authenticity and existential self-assertion. Similar to the way in which the *l'art pour l'art*, in its protest against the commodification of nineteenth-century art, cut all links between art and social life, the aim of aesthetic politics is to redefine the political as an autonomous realm of absolute self-referentiality privileging cultic forms over ethical norms. Although explicitly directed against the institutionalization of multiple centers of domination in modernity, aesthetic politics thus pursues its own project of differentiation, autonomization, and modernization. Driven by the idea of pure politics, of Great Politics, fascist aestheticization proposes to recenter the state against the ever-increasing diffusion of power, to unchain political action from normative debates, and to undo the emasculating effects of procedural politics. Aesthetic politics attempts to move the state beyond bourgeois-democratic codes of legality, morality, and political emancipation. It seeks to redefine the political as the site at which nothing less than authenticity comes into being.

Walter Benjamin and the Aesthetics of Power argues, contrary to common assumption, that Benjamin did not simply develop one but in fact three different versions of the aestheticization thesis. The first version is a by-product of Benjamin's early treatise on the baroque *Trauerspiel* (chapter 1). It is inextricably bound up with theoretical traditions that Benjamin himself revokes in his later work. Reading Weimar constellations into the seventeenth century, this initial theory of aesthetic politics insists on the absolute autonomy of aesthetic expressions. In a quasi-Kantian (and protodeconstructive) fashion, it reproaches baroque politics for transgressing transcendental boundaries between spheres of cognition and value. Version two, introduced in the context of Benjamin's critique of fascism, rethinks the first model on the basis of a materialist theory of history and experience (chapters 2–6). Reckoning with modes of sense perception that are peculiarly modern and technologically mediated, this second variant relies on the assumption that the conceptual apparatus of aesthetic theory and autonomous art are no longer adequate challenges to the cultural politics of fascism. A peculiar intervention in the dialectics of cultural modernization, aestheticization now emerges as an ideological practice that makes instrumental use of industrial culture in order to simulate experiences of community and seduce the masses into spectacles of charismatic renewal. Aesthetic politics engenders auratic effects with the means of mechanical reproduction; it engineers primal sentiments with modern machines. The third and final version, which I reconstruct against the backdrop of Benjamin's unfinished *Arcades Project*, as well as recent research on the National Socialist period, defines fascist aestheticization as the transformation of Great Politics and warfare into a viable consumer item (chapter 7). Nazi aesthetic politics, I argue, refurbishes political action into a market factor, a highly desired commodity consumed not simply in public rallies, but also in seemingly unpolitical niches of private, American-style diversion.

Fascism, in Benjamin's understanding, interrupts the dialectics between aesthetic and popular modernism, between avant-garde art and modern industrial culture. It employs the instruments of twentieth-century culture, yet only in order to foil the democratic power of the popular and eliminate whatever is potentially subversive about the avant-garde. Political aestheticization, according to versions two and three, is the logical result of this double suspension. But, as we shall see, to speak of aesthetic politics does not simply mean to address a shrewd stylization of political action – a seductive organization of public signs, meanings, and iconographies. Instead, what aesthetic politics does is to colonize the structures of modern experience, to engage popular sentiments, and to discipline sense perception with the ambition of integrating society and mobilizing the masses for future warfare. The fascist spectacle massages minds and emotions in such a way that modern postauratic perception loses its progressive thrust and succumbs to the signifiers of vitalistic power. Fascist aesthetics, in the concept's original meaning, is anaesthetic – it assaults perception, neutralizes the senses, and denies the private body as an autonomous site of corporeal pleasure.[3] Mechanical reproduction, Benjamin's benchmark of cultural modernity, serves in fascism the attempt to sanctify resolute and charismatic leadership as a self-sufficient force, an auratic presence. Fascist aestheticization organizes individual and collective experience so as to entertain structures of domination that taboo their actual effects.[4] It causes individuals to identify with that which forces them into submission and conformity and, ultimately, fosters their destruction. It is not the excess of aesthetics – independent sensory experience – but the lack of it that makes fascism totalitarian and defines what Benjamin calls the aestheticization of politics.[5]

Benjamin's aestheticization thesis, then, shifts our attention away from the public choreography of political action toward what we must understand as a subtle domestication of peculiarly modern structures of seeing, perception, and experience. The organization of auratic sensations in a postauratic culture is at the core of aesthetic politics. A seemingly unrelated passage from DeLillo's *White Noise* comes much closer to this definition than the novel's above-quoted reference to Leni Riefenstahl's mass ornaments and Albert Speer's light domes. In this passage, we follow Hitler scholar Gladney and his friend Murray to a midwestern tourist attraction known as the most-photographed barn in America, a pastoral scene produced for the circuits of commodity consumption and the cameras of a myriad of visitors. Taking a photograph of this barn becomes a religious experience. It amplifies rather than destroys the barn's unique presence in time and space. An expert in questions of American popular culture, Murray asks what the barn was like before it was photographed: "What did it look like, how was it different from other barns, how was it similar to other barns? We can't answer these questions because we've read the signs, seen the people snapping the pictures. We can't get outside the aura. We're part of the aura. We're here, we're now."[6] Aura here emerges as an effect of mechanical reproducibility. It is manufactured by people taking pictures of other people taking pictures, and thus, it is the result of the postauratic desire to take home the event in the form of a photographic copy. Yet although it is a human fabrication, the barn's synthetic aura holds the spectator in check. A mere simulation, it nevertheless engenders submissive and highly conformist spectator positions. Not what is shown but how the viewer sees it; not the barn itself but how society succeeds in closing down alternative ways of looking at its objects of desire; not the presence of cameras and massive crowds but how industrial culture in this particular instance renders its own work invisible and seeks to reenchant the world – all this makes DeLillo's barn into a spectacle that in Benjamin's understanding deserves the name aesthetic politics indeed.

But is it useful, or even appropriate, to call such peculiar aesthetic pleasures "fascist," as Benjamin seems to suggest, whether we understand the term "fascist aesthetics" in the conceptually strong sense as a *fascist* way of looking at pleasurable objects, or in the weaker one as a way of looking at pleasurable objects under the condition of fascism? Doesn't any exclusive analysis of fascism as the aestheticization of politics obscure the historical uniqueness of the National Socialist period and belittle the Holocaust, which was clearly hidden from view and thus never given any aestheticizing gloss? Doesn't the primary focus on cultural politics and structures of perception level all distinctions that matter for a critical understanding of the past, of social modernization, and of historical progress? If fascism is aesthetic politics, is all aesthetic politics fascist? We are clearly not in the position to answer these questions yet, and we should build up our case much more carefully before attempting to draw any final conclusions. *Walter Benjamin and the Aesthetics of Power*, by first examining Benjamin's theory of aesthetic politics (part 1), and then by rethinking its legacy against the backdrop of recent historical research and the spectacular dimension of postmodern culture (part 2), seeks to build up this case. It hopes to offer some answers and conclusions and stimulate the reader to propose many more.

More than sixty years after its conception, Benjamin's aestheticization thesis remains a puzzle, a challenge, and a provocation. No rigorous encounter with it will, and for that matter should, avoid the opening of multiple cans of worms – theoretical, political, and historical. What I want to do in the remainder of this introduction is to address a number of issues that require preliminary clarification when approaching Benjamin's writing on fascism today. The following discussion of the current status of Nazi historiography, the relation of fascism to modernity, and the contemporary evaluation of the avant-garde will demonstrate why we should recognize Benjamin's aestheticization thesis in the first place as a matter of our own ongoing concerns.

Recent historical discussion of the National Socialist period is characterized by a curious, surprisingly peaceful coexistence of generic theories of and historicizing approaches to interwar fascism. Popular among leftist scholars of the 1960s and 1970s, "fascism" as a generic label for various dictatorships of the 1920s to 1940s had become a taboo concept by 1980, "a code word associated with a crude Marxism that seemed to assail universities and debase political discourse in general."[7] The generic concept of fascism was originally intended to expose the inherent relationship between the Third Reich and the dynamic of capital in the twentieth century. In the polarized academic and cultural atmosphere around 1970, this approach sought to examine the kind of economic, political, and social hierarchies that were shared by interwar Germany, Italy, and Spain. The decline of "fascism" during the 1980s coincided with various and often incompatible attempts to historicize the National Socialist past – either to situate the Holocaust in the context of European history and deny its uniqueness, to emphasize neglected continuities rather than radical ruptures between Weimar, Nazi, and postwar Germany, or to shift attention away from the general mechanisms of Nazi leadership and domination to the local structures of ordinary life. Generic concepts of fascism have resurfaced during the 1990s, now no longer occupying the grounds of Marxist theory. In many instances, this resurgence of generic "fascism" can be seen as a direct response to the ways in which 1980s historicization tended – intentionally or not – to explain away Nazi terror and to dissolve the singularity of the Holocaust. Historicizing approaches to Nazi Germany today, on the other hand, to a large extent have left behind what made them an object of outrage in the so-called 1986 *Historikerstreit*. The claim that Nazi Germany, while appealing to archaic desires and premodern structures of integration, helped modernize certain areas of German society has thus become standard among historiographers of the 1990s.

It is useful briefly to review in further detail the present status of both paradigms – the generic and the historicizing approach – so as to see how Benjamin's analysis of fascism as the aestheticization of politics may still fit into the picture and how it may contribute to contemporary discussions. Generic theories of fascism during the 1960s and 1970s understood Nazism, as Tim Mason has pointed out, not only as a cumulative moment of organized capitalism in modern Europe but *"also* as a repository of possible lessons, warnings, and injunctions about economic and political developments in the near future; the Third Reich was 'relevant.'"[8] Though often based on reductive and monocausal models of historical development, the generic concept of "fascism" called for a differentiated recognition of the past as a means to understand and negotiate the present. Wrestled away from their Marxist origin, post–Cold War theories of generic fascism clearly share the comparative aspirations of previous approaches. But the concept of "fascism" now no longer seems to serve as a political code word, as part of a unified political project. Instead, it works as a heuristic device that sorts through the messiness and heterogeneity of past phenomena. As a quasi-Weberian ideal type, "fascism"today helps categorize necessarily diverse historical formations under homogenous and theoretically purified terms. Roger Griffin, for instance, has defined the nature of fascism *tout court* as a "political ideology whose mythic core in its various permutations is a palingenetic form of populist ultranationalism."[9] Fascist ideology propagated a phoenixlike rebirth of nation, spirit, and culture; it relied on cross-class populist appeals of highly nationalist agendas during the interwar years. Similarly, Stanley G. Payne has suggested a complex typological grid including numerous references to the ideological goals, the peculiar negations and enemies, and the style and organization of interwar fascisms. Yet in contrast to Griffin, Payne intends not to "establish a rigidly reified category but a wide-spectrum description that can identify a variety of differing allegedly fascist movements while still setting them apart as a group from other kinds of revolutionary or nationalist movements."[10] And finally, in a conceptual exercise akin to Wittgenstein's notion of a game, Umberto Eco has specified fascism as a *"fuzzy* totalitarianism, a collage of different philosophical and political ideas, a beehive of contradictions."[11] Though constituting a unique form of thinking, feeling, and desiring, fascism in Eco's view is characterized by structured confusion. What in fact makes fascism fascist is its discombobulation of all-purpose ideologies, to make an eclectic mishmash of machismo, cult of tradition and heroism, glorification of struggle, irrational vitalism, fear of difference, and populist xenophobia.

However different in scope and character, theories of generic fascism today utilize the concept of "fascism" as a telescope that enables historians to focus on and sift through the various and heterogenous images of past realities. Concepts of generic fascism allow us to view Nazism not as a mere historical accident, an extraterrestrial event rupturing the normal course of national history. Rather, they make it possible to draw synchronic comparisons between various twentieth-century totalitarianisms, and thus may help better understand what is different – and singular – about the Nazi state in the European context. At the same time, however, in their treatment of fascism as a discrete synchronic phenomenon, theories of generic fascism also tend to obscure the peculiar diachronic settings in which twentieth-century fascisms emerged, succeeded, and disappeared. Preoccupied with questions of classification and periodization, these theories bracket historical developments in self-contained concepts and, in so doing, deemphasize the need to recognize critically the legacy of the past in the present.

Post-*Historikerstreit* efforts at historicization suggest manifold antidotes to the diachronic blind spots of generic approaches to fascism. Historicizing the past in this context means placing the Nazi regime in the continuities of modern German history. It implies tracing how the National Socialist era related to earlier periods, Weimar in particular, and how it has preshaped the paths of the Federal Republic after the war. Seeing Nazi Germany as a peculiar intervention in the course of German modernization, projects of historicization revise traditional notions of Nazism as a coherent leap back into barbarism. They attempt to reveal what happened behind the spectacular veneers of Nazi politics and ideology, hoping not only to uncover the local disparities between everyday beliefs and practices but also to expose the patterns of normalcy that connect the various Germanies of the twentieth century. In an influential anthology, Michael Prinz and Rainer Zitelmann have presented a series of contributions all of which feature the ways in which economic thought, social policy, urban planning, school education, Americanism, historiography, and even psychiatry during the Nazi period helped accelerate the overarching process of German modernization.[12] In like manner, recent literary scholarship has moved away from traditional taxonomies of Nazi literature in order to emphasize the continuities – the cross-temporal and cross-spatial dialogues of literary texts during the Nazi era. Weary of discriminating literary productions according to the seasoned triad of ideological conformism, inner emigration, and exile, some scholars in fact no longer hesitate calling into question whether we can or should treat the years 1933 to 1945 as a separate period in the first place.[13] And last but not least, film historians, too, increasingly draw our attention to the pre- and afterlife of Nazi visual culture. Far from simply producing austere propaganda spectacles, Nazi cinema is seen as part of a modern "distraction factory" developing its idioms in close exchange with Hollywood. Nazi entertainment films, it has been argued, aspired to bring Hollywood home and, in so doing, took part in an ongoing transformation and globalization of narrative forms, generic conventions, acting styles, and forms of spectatorial address.[14]

By focusing on the modernizing functions of Nazi society or the relative normality of life under Nazi rule, historicizing approaches intend not to trivialize the darkest chapter of German history, but to reveal the barbaric possibilities inherent in ordinariness and the process of modernization. Yet in many cases, as Dan Diner has recently demonstrated, this kind of historicization strangely joins hands with the attempt to anthropologize or universalize the Holocaust, that is, to demonstrate the omnipresent possibilities of atrocious crimes against humanity.[15] To be sure, historicization has been instrumental in demonstrating crucial discrepancies between Nazi ideology and everyday practice. In many instances it has helped revise the image of Nazi Germany as a completely coordinated society solely driven by the ideological imperatives of the Nazi movement. In a way that is similar to that of generic views of Nazism, historicization refutes the worn notion of a German *Sonderweg* culminating in the Holocaust. But in its preoccupation with what Germany during the 1930s and 1940s shared on the one hand with nonfascist regimes and, on the other, with Weimar and the Federal Republic, historicization often results in a certain blindness toward the peculiar – and singular – position of Nazi society in the course of Western modernization. It is therefore hardly surprising that some advocates of historicization accuse modernity itself, not fascism, as the actual nemesis of twentieth-century German history. Situating the Nazi period in the continuities of social, economic, and cultural modernization, historicization in this peculiar understanding can cause the synchronic and diachronic uniqueness of fascist terror and fascist modernism curiously to recede from the picture.

Though arguing from opposite ends of the spectrum, both the generic and the historicizing view of the Nazi period and the Holocaust thus may potentially produce similar blind spots. Both perspectives result in a precarious loss of memory and historical substance as they erase the curious aura of iconic symbolization that endows historical concepts and experiences with meaning. "Historical constructions of past realities are always much more than just an objectified mirroring of bygone events, for a response to pressing ethical questions is part and parcel of history writing."[16] Driven to its respective extreme, neither the comparative nor the close-range empiricist approach can yield satisfying answers to the ethical and most central questions of Nazi scholarships: What lessons can we learn? How can or should present generations relate to the Nazi past and its legacy? How can we critically recognize the Nazi past as an ineradicable element of any future formulation of German identity? The astounding popularity in Germany of Daniel Goldhagen's recent book *Hitler's Willing Executioners* indicates that a broader German populace continuously expects its historians to provide pertinent answers to such questions and, hence, correct the critical shortcomings of contemporary scholarship.[17] But the book's popular triumph at the same time also testifies to how postmodern media culture today manages to succeed in transforming the German past and the singularity of Nazi terror into a highly viable commodity item. Curiously fusing generic and historicizing approaches to Nazi Germany, Goldhagen claims to make the Third Reich – in Mason's words – relevant again. His book combines generic definitions of Nazi Germany with a historicizing perspective that emphasizes how anti-Semitism long before Hitler had structured the ordinary lives of all Germans. Yet by interpreting 1945 as a fundamental turning point in German political and everyday history, *Hitler's Willing Executioners* makes even the most ghastly aspects of the German past available as safe objects of consumption. As he promises a path out of the diverted landscape of recent Nazi scholarship, Goldhagen actually helps transform the Nazi era into an exotic phenomenon. First fiercely panned by academics and then victoriously marketed to popular audiences, the book empowered particularly a younger public to revel in new and fashionable idioms of German self-hatred. Assured by Goldhagen that the present and past have no relationship to one another, German readers could recognize the Nazi period as a repository of absolute evil, but also of absolute distance. Traveling back to the past in this way turned out to be not much different from traveling to a remote island, a theme park of grisly wonders. Goldhagen's willing German executioners and Spielberg's Jurassic monsters end up as creatures of the same age.

Benjamin clearly never provided a sustained analysis of fascism. We therefore ought to be careful not to render entirely coherent what is scattered across his overall work of the 1930s. It remains, for instance, relatively unclear whether Benjamin would have denied other types of political aestheticization, aside from the fascist spectacle, as possible. But Benjamin's aestheticization thesis, as revisited from today's perspective, nevertheless offers a much more unsettling way of reconciling the generic and historicizing inclinations of contemporary research. Not only does it allow us simultaneously to contest and bridge the gap between the two dominant paradigms without denying the singularity of fascism or its continuous relevance. It also provides critical tools that may help brace historical and theoretical inquiries against the kind of commodification that typified the case of Goldhagen. At first, Benjamin's remarks on fascism appear to imply a generic definition of the subject. Benjamin seems to explain fascism unequivocally as the introduction of aesthetics to politics. He implies the existence of a generically fascist art. He even proposes that there is an intrinsically fascist way of looking at things – an innately fascist type of visuality. Among Benjamin's interpreters, this penchant for generic abstraction has led to many irritations. On the one hand, the universalizing equation of fascism and political aestheticization has been seen as all too narrow to conceptualize crucial differences between, for instance, Hitler's Germany and Mussolini's Italy. Although written well before Nazism showed its full hand, Benjamin's comments have been criticized for completely eluding the role of racism and anti-Semitism in his theoretical definition of fascism. On the other hand, Benjamin's argument, while ignoring aesthetic politics under Stalin, has been seen to present too sweeping a generalization in order to distinguish adequately between different versions of aesthetic politics in the twentieth century. If we consider every spectacle as potentially or even necessarily fascist, don't we lose sight of significant distinctions that matter for the evaluation of competing political agendas today?

Upon closer consideration, however, it should become clear that Benjamin attempted to interlace his generic definition of fascism with a highly original and continuously provocative project of historicization. Benjamin, much more of a historicist than he himself was willing to admit, historicizes generic fascism along two interrelated vectors. First, he argues that fascism concludes an apocalyptic process of modernization and disenchantment that from its very inception has failed to develop its own inherent possibilities. Fascism ferociously finalizes what capitalist modernity ever since the middle of the nineteenth century has done all along. It mobilizes technological and economic rationalization against the normative substance of political modernity, against post-Enlightenment values of political justice, equality, freedom, and democracy. What Benjamin understands as fascist aestheticization serves the attempt to naturalize this uneven and fundamentally unfinished modernization of society. Dedicated to the vitalist dream of Great Politics, the fascist spectacle markets the truncated gestalt of modernity as an object of highest pleasure, of a desire desiring the end of desire. Second, in conceptualizing fascist aestheticization primarily as a politically effective orchestration of sense perception rather than merely as the stage-managing of politics, Benjamin situates his critique of fascism in the context of a materialist history of individual and collective experience. History, for Benjamin, is neither the history of thought nor the history of politically leaders but the history of experience, a history that foregrounds the contingent ways in which we appropriate cultural material within the fabrics of everyday life in order to construct identities and take position in time and space.[18] According to this understanding, fascism reckons with the fact that industrial culture has fundamentally changed the ways in which people look at what surrounds them. Aesthetic politics redefines not merely the canon of beautiful objects but also how we see them from the vistas of industrialized everyday life. The fascist spectacle organizes modern experience so as to deploy sensory perception for the purpose of political coordination and total mobilization. Although fascism relies on people's feelings and sentiments, it strives – as Simonetta Falasca-Zamponi has put it in her recent analysis of Musssolini's Italy – "to neutralize the senses, to knock them out."[19]

Benjamin's creative fusion of generic and historicizing perspectives urges us to understand the modernity of everyday life and popular culture under fascist rule without letting the most dreadful aspects of fascism disappear from the picture. Though placing fascism in the continuities of modern history and capitalist modernization, Benjamin clearly does not ask us to question the historical uniqueness of Nazi Germany or Italian fascism. In his view, fascism constitutes a historically specific and singular regime of political representation and experience in which vitalist conceptions of power and warfare become perverse objects of desire and commodity consumption. Thus, Benjamin succeeds in keeping in check the potential weaknesses of the generic and the historizicing view of fascism, respectively. Unlike the generic theorist of fascism, Benjamin does not bracket historical periods as self-containing entities; nor does he sacrifice questions of historical specificity on the altar of heuristic overgeneralizations. In contrast to many emphatic historicists, on the other hand, Benjamin asks us to operate with a differentiated notion of modernity and explore how fascism set up a framework in which the ordinariness of modern experience and culture could serve modern and antimodern purposes alike.

The cornerstone of the aestheticization thesis – Benjamin's theory of historical experience and sense perception – alerts us not to draw any quick conclusions about the universality of aesthetic politics in modernity. Although proclaiming a charismatic interruption of history, the fascist spectacle in Benjamin's view is itself a historical phenomenon, and – as I argue in chapter 8 – neither pre- nor postfascist societies entail structures of experience identical with those that enabled fascist aestheticization to assume its ultimately catastrophic role. Benjamin's critique of fascist modernism therefore does not result in a wholesale rejection of the modern as a regime of totalitarian reason and disenchantment necessarily culminating in fascism (or Stalinism). Dismayed by the vicissitudes of modernity, Benjamin nonetheless insists on alternative paths of social modernization. What he calls the politicization of art – the "communist" response to fascist aestheticization – seeks to align peculiarly modern structures of experience with post-Enlightenment visions of justice, autonomy, and rational collective will-formation. However persuasive in its actual form, Benjamin's juxtaposition of aestheticized politics and politicized art hopes to define criteria of difference that distinguish between the normative possibilities and the factual course of nineteenth- and twentieth-century modernization. In so doing, Benjamin offers powerful antidotes to the most recent philosophical theories about fascism, modernism, and the avant-garde, theories that thrive on the leveling of all distinctions that matter for a cogent analysis of modern culture and politics. It is to these theories, in particular the neo-Heideggerian revision of fascism (Philippe Lacoue-Labarthe) and the avant-garde (Boris Groys), that I turn in the next two sections so as to better understand Benjamin's continuous and critical relevance to contemporary criticism.

Throughout the past decade, some of the most challenging claims about the role of Nazi culture have surfaced in the debates around Martin Heidegger's complicity with National Socialism. In particular, French philosopher Philippe Lacoue-Labarthe has taken a prominent stance in these controversies, advancing a number of propositions about the "unseverable link between art and politics" in the metaphysical tradition of the West.[20] Ensnared in an Aristotelian concept of *techne*, Western metaphysics, according to Lacoue-Labarthe, describes the history of an illusion: the self-production of the subject through work, through calculated activity, through the autopoesis of subjectivity and the state. Modern politics still draws heavily on this belief, this confusion of human action with aesthetic creativity. In spite of the functional differentiation of modern society, Lacoue-Labarthe contends, modernity continuously envisions political practices in terms of aesthetic paradigms of action inherited from the Western metaphysical tradition. Through art, we self-consciously regenerate myths to strengthen this metaphysical desire for autopoesis, myths we may use to locate our place in history and fancy total control over its course.

Fascism, for Lacoue-Labarthe, represents nothing less than the culmination of two thousand years of Western metaphysics of presence – the last incarnation of "humanism."[21] Lacoue-Labarthe believes that Nazism – far from escaping the West, far from celebrating its decline – embodies Western metaphysics in its most consequential form. Accordingly, National Socialism not only promised national and racial self-formation along the lines of the ancient metaphysics of *techne*, but also pursued a total politicization of life to allow "the people to accede to its own language and thereby to situate itself as such in History."[22] Lacoue-Labarthe says that this appeal to a boundless control over the making of history is the operative fiction of modern politics; he calls it modernity's "national-aestheticism."[23] Under its hallmark, political action appears as a transposition of artistic practices, of the aesthetics of genius, into the public realm. Motivated by its megalomania to make history, national-aestheticism reduces the people to an amorphous mass of clay to be formed in the mold of the nation-state. It pervades all spheres of social life so as to bewitch the masses with a spectacle of total presence and self-formation. It pretends to conclude what has propelled the history of the West in its restless search for "the *truth* of the political" all along.[24] Fascism, in the eyes of Lacoue-Labarthe, is metaphysics presenting itself as what it always desired to be: art.

In his Manichean attack on Western metaphysics, Lacoue-Labarthe levels all differences between competing political projects of the twentieth century. Whether they are leftist visions of emancipation or rightist prospects of renewed state authority, all fall victim to the aesthetic appeal of *techne*. Lacoue-Labarthe's totalizing gesture is revealed most clearly when he discusses Brecht's and Benjamin's responses to the fascist aestheticization of politics, their call for a politicization of art: "In its syntax (overturning), this response is Marxist in type. Nonetheless, it is very strangely consonant with that other watchword, 'politicized science', which the NSDAP students had used not long before against Rector Heidegger. Now it is true that 'politicization' is the starting point of 'totalitarian logic', from which absolutely no one seems to have been immune during this period."[25] Simply another chapter within the history of the Western metaphysics of presence, Brecht's and Benjamin's critiques of Nazism turn out to be just as totalitarian and national-aestheticist as fascism itself. What Brecht and Benjamin failed to realize is that only Heidegger's post-turn *Gelassenheit* and modesty could have offered a point of resistance to the totalitarianism of aesthetic politics. "Modesty is the recognition of a limit. . . . This limit is the limit of philosophy: not a limit fixed by eternal boundaries or assigned to it, nor one imported from elsewhere, but the limit against which philosophy has itself run up, the limit it has encountered within itself."[26] Modesty prevents art and philosophy from spilling over into the realm of the political. It sets limits to metaphysical speculation and thus to the possibility of aesthetic politics. It redeems the credibility of philosophy at the cost of denouncing political action.

It is not without irony that in his very criticism of terrorist aesthetics and metaphysics, Lacoue-Labarthe's account itself draws a totalizing picture of the relation between art and politics and thus tends to obscure rather than elucidate the politics of culture in Nazi society. Lacoue-Labarthe finds fault not with politics, but rather with art and Western metaphysics. As a result, he presents too broad a definition of what aesthetic politics might entail. Accusing cultural resources per se responsible for political atrocities, Lacoue-Labarthe's attack on Western metaphysics will hardly enable us to do adequate justice to the specificity of, say, the aesthetics of feudal representation, the poetic masking of industrial progress during the nineteenth century, the fascist aestheticization of modern warfare, or the spectacles of media societies in the late twentieth century. According to Lacoue-Labarthe, such transgressions constitute an excess of the aesthetic that is representative for the logocentric history of the West in general. Thus, as Robert Holub has argued, he "vitiate[s] most of the distinctions that really matter for politics"and precludes necessary inquiries into the actual mechanisms of power that instigate the political deployment of art in the first place.[27] To the extent that he fails to embed his critique of aesthetic politics in any larger social theory, to the extent that he argues against terrorist aesthetics and metaphysics from the vantage point of aesthetic theory and metaphysics itself, he renders art and *techne* the primary agents within the twentieth-century marriage of aesthetics and politics and thus – implicitly – reinforces what political elites tried to proclaim all along.

Benjamin clearly shares Lacoue-Labarthe's misgivings about the masking of political action by means of the aesthetic myth of autopoesis. As I argue in particular in chapter 3, the aestheticization thesis hopes to debunk the ways in which fascism superimposes nineteenth-century notions of artistic creativity and genius expressivity onto the political. It denounces any attempt to present the realm of political action as a self-containing and self-producing entity. Yet at the same time, Benjamin – unlike Lacoue-Labarthe – is at pains to infuse his remarks about aesthetic politics with greater historical specificity, not least of all in the hopes of qualifying competing political projects in the twentieth century. Although his findings may not always be convincing, thanks to their own air of theoretical overgeneralization, Benjamin allows us to see what is all too totalizing in Lacoue-Labarthe's attack on Western metaphysics. In contrast to this neo-Heideggerian philosopher, Benjamin discusses the issue of aesthetic politics within a critical framework theorizing the course of Western modernization. Not a general excess of Western aesthetics or metaphysics but certain predicaments built into the process of capitalist modernization effect, in Benjamin's view, the introduction of aesthetics to politics. Instead of constituting the ultimate triumph of Western thought, as Lacoue-Labarthe would have it, the fascist cult of political creativity indicates a murderous collapse of capitalist modernity, since – prioritizing technological and economic over political rationalization – it failed to live up to its own possibilities. In sharp distinction to Lacoue-Labarthe, Benjamin's own notion of national-aestheticism thus brings into focus the refusal of modernity to complete what it promised at the outset. Aesthetic politics à la Nazism is possible neither before nor after the caesura of fascism.

Critically historicizing the emergence of aesthetic politics in twentieth-century modernity, Benjamin insists that both concepts, "the political" and "the aesthetic," are historical products. Whereas Lacoue-Labarthe seems to presume a timeless identity of their meaning, Benjamin considers these concepts as peculiar offsprings of modernity. To speak of aesthetic politics, for Benjamin, becomes possible only once modern society has sufficiently differentiated the realms of art and politics in the first place. Benjamin thus refuses to hypostatize the realms and boundaries of art and politics. He refuses to resort to transcendental principles in order to distinguish these realms once and for all from one another. The most challenging aspect of Benjamin's aestheticization thesis in fact is that the institutionalization of new technologies of reproduction has redefined the location of art in society, has leveled former distinctions between bourgeois high art and popular culture and entertainment. The question is not so much whether relative or partial autonomy is no longer possible, or whether aesthetic autonomy may persist in some form in the future. Rather, what is at stake for Benjamin is to think through the historicity of aesthetic autonomy itself and to expose how fascism employs postautonomous means in order to generate illusions of wholeness, integrity, and autonomy. If Lacoue-Labarthe suggests that we cannot speak about fascism without speaking about art, Benjamin – much more radical, in fact – reminds us that we must also and foremost speak about mass culture and the popular. Fascism recycles vestiges of autonomous art through the circuits of a state-controlled culture industry. Seen through Benjamin's eyes, Lacoue-Labarthe, like many other critics, once again brackets the prominent and politically effective role of the popular in Nazi Germany, its ubiquity in cinemas, radio programs, dance halls, and advertisements.[28] Whereas Lacoue-Labarthe, in sum, relies on an unhistorical and undialectical concept of art and aesthetic autonomy, Benjamin's aestheticization thesis faces the fact that twentieth-century culture is largely political and that twentieth-century politics is often defined via cultural material. To aestheticize politics does not mean to collapse the natural autonomy of art and wickedly mingle aesthetic and political principles. It instead means to infuse mechanical reproduction with the aura of high art, to enlist postautonomous industrial culture in the service of creating the image of charismatic leadership and unified political action. Fascist aestheticization, in Benjamin's view, seems to act like a parasite on the avant-garde and its attempt to dismantle former boundaries between high and low. It turns the avant-garde against itself in order to refute its call for political change.

Benjamin's sympathy for the historical avant-garde and its various blind spots are now well marked. In his "Surrealism" essay of 1929, Benjamin endorsed the Parisian avant-garde and its attempt to transcend the autonomous phase of bourgeois art such that "all revolutionary tension becomes bodily collective innervation, and all the bodily innervations of the collective become revolutionary discharge" (REF 192; GS 1:310). French surrealism, in Benjamin's view, breaks away from the program of aesthetic autonomy, and it is this militant renunciation of romantic notions of artistic practice that allows surrealist artists to place the power of their imagination in the service of political transformations – to become a true avant-gardist. Five years later, in "The Author as Producer," Benjamin radicalized this vision of the avant-garde project, now calling for a functional transformation of all aesthetic practices into public properties. In this essay, Benjamin celebrates the Soviet author Sergei Tretiakov, an "operative" writer who bases literary qualification no longer on specialized but rather on polytechnical training, and thus makes his talents available as communal assets. A postaesthetic artist, Tretiakov's mission when going to the "Communist Lighthouse"commune is "not to report but to struggle; not to play the spectator but to intervene actively" (REF 223; GS 2:686). Like his surrealist colleagues, Tretiakov puts art in the service of the revolution and thereby denounces the former separation of art from everyday life, the nineteenth-century paradigm of aesthetic autonomy. In addition, however, Tretiakov's avant-gardism also seeks to redefine the concept of art in analogy to dominant Western understandings prior to the nineteenth century, understandings that referred to art as a skill next to the skills of a craftsman, a housepainter, or a shoemaker.[29] Challenging aestheticism and nineteenth-century notions of aesthetic autonomy, avant-gardist art according to this model embraces certain forms of dexterity in order to strengthen the unity of a particular culture and community.

Neither Benjamin's particular endorsement of surrealism and functional transformation, nor the historical avant-garde in general, receives the kind of favorable treatment today they earned during the 1960s or 1970s. It has been rightly pointed out, for example, that Parisian surrealism, contrary to its own program and to Benjamin's emphatic assumption, clearly remained within the bounds of autonomous art. In spite of the attack on turn-of-the-century aestheticism, surrealism reveled in fragmentary works of art that remained works of art nevertheless. As Richard Wolin has argued, surrealism consciously divested itself "of the beautiful illusion, the aura of reconciliation, projected by art for art's sake, while refusing to overstep the boundaries of aesthetic autonomy, beyond which art degenerates to the status of merely a thing among things."[30] More importantly, however, it has become a commonplace in postmodern criticism to put the historical avant-garde on the stand, suspecting that its attack on bourgeois art prepared the ground for totalitarian terror. According to this argument, in revoking nineteenth-century boundaries between art and life, the avant-garde helped infuse the everyday with aesthetic values and, in so doing, opened the door for both Hitler's theatrical politics and Stalin's choreography of power.[31] Liquefying the domains of autonomous art, the role of the avant-garde is thus seen not – like Benjamin – as an antidote, but as a crucial stepping-stone to the aestheticization of politics à la fascism or Stalinism.

Boris Groys's *The Total Art of Stalinism* aptly exemplifies the extent of present revisions of the historical avant-garde.[32] Groys understands Stalinism as an attempt to replace social chaos with the harmonious image of a homogenous society organized according to one unitary artistic perspective. Stalinism aspired to control and redesign all aspects of private and public life – the economic, the social, the political, and the cultural – from the viewpoint of absolute leadership. It imagined the political ruler as a kind of artist who overcomes the inherent resistance of his amorphous material, makes it malleable, and shapes it into stable, ideal forms. In this way, Stalinism fulfilled what Groys presents as the dreams of the avant-garde; namely, to penetrate life with aesthetic values and reorganize the everyday in monolithic artistic shapes. Presenting socialism as the supreme measure of beauty, Stalin directly continued the utopia of the avant-garde to overcome the museums and weave art into the fabrics of life. Both the avant-garde and Stalin in fact hoped to resurrect by artistic and technological means the wholeness of God; both hoped to assume the position of a demiurge who creates reality from scratch and thus conquers the vicissitudes of time and space. Like Stalin, "the avant-garde artist believed that his knowledge of and especially participation in the murder of God gave him a demiurgic, magical power over the world, and he was convinced that by thus crossing the boundaries of the world he could discover the laws that govern cosmic and social forces. He would then regenerate himself and the world by mastering these laws like an engineer, halting its decline through artistic techniques that would impart to it a form that was eternal and ideal or at least appropriate to any given moment in history."[33]

What makes the avant-garde essentially, not just potentially, Stalinist is the utopian belief in the making of history. Stalinism, in Groys's formalized understanding, is an articulation of human hubris. It results from the hope not simply to muddle one's way through, but to actively shape the architectures of individual and collective existence. Benjamin's critique of fascist aestheticization clearly echoes some of these concerns. The aestheticization of politics, in his view, occludes the bureaucratic complexity of modern politics and exchanges it for the image of unified, controlled, and masculine leadership – for the image of the ruler as a law-giving God. At the same time, however, in his hope to find alternatives to fascist aestheticization, Benjamin embraces concepts of social engineering that reflect his commitment to radical political change. The demiurgic aspects of the avant-garde, for Benjamin, seek to emancipate humanity from the false gods of aesthetic politics and charismatic authority; they empower the human collective to intervene in a history that is theirs and yet hardly ever appears as the product of their own making. For post–Cold War critics such as Groys, this belief in the makeablity of history clearly represents yet another chapter in the history of political terror. Groys's texts implicitly ask us, "How Stalinist is Benjamin's avant-gardism, his antidote to fascist aestheticization?"

The key text on the position of the avant-garde, all recent revisions notwithstanding, remains Peter Bürger's *Theory of the Avant-Garde* (1974), not least of all because some of Bürger's theoretical and historical observations are deeply influenced by Benjamin's own thought.[34] It is with Bürger that we therefore must begin in order to find a meaningful answer to Groys's question. Bürger's position is well-known now, and there is no need to reiterate his point at great length here. He argues that our conceptual understanding of the avant-garde is directly linked to the institutional development of art. According to his premise, the avant-garde not only attacked the styles, forms, and canons of bourgeois art but sought to undo the entire institution of art so as to reintegrate the aesthetic into everyday life. This undoing was possible only after bourgeois art had reached its full autonomy and differentiation in turn-of-the-century aestheticism.

The blind spots of Bürger's account are not difficult to see, and they darken many of the text's merits. They pertain to both the theoretical and the historical trajectory of his analysis. First of all, in comprehending the diversity of early-twentieth-century avant-gardism as a single dominant paradigm, Bürger implies that one universal theory will suffice to theorize the avant-garde and its critique of bourgeois art.[35] This understanding of the avant-garde as a paradigm leads Bürger, contrary to his own neo-Marxist intentions, to suggest that we can explain the emergence of the avant-garde – in a Weberian mode – exclusively in terms of the evolution of art itself, i.e. in terms that omit any reference to the social, political, and economic changes around 1900 that redefined the position of art in society in the first place.[36] Bürger resorts to some kind of intrinsic criticism claiming that non-aesthetic developments had no impact on the formation and subsequent critique of bourgeois art as an autonomous value sphere. Secondly, in endorsing a Kuhnian model of paradigm shift, Bürger overlooks the extent to which certain avant-gardisms hoped to unravel the very epistemes that allow Bürger to think about historical phenomena in terms of paradigmatic simultaneity and sequentiality. While occluding the contemporaneity and significance of other non-avant-gardistic practices in early twentieth-century culture, Bürger ignores the fact that many avant-gardists aspired to mark a shift in the overall framework that makes notions such as art, time, and history thinkable to begin with.[37]

Groys, although he clearly opposes Bürger's endorsement of the historical avant-garde, ironically shares some of the pitfalls of *Theory of the Avant-Garde*. On the one hand, Groys, like Bürger, treats the avant-garde like a paradigm, and thus obscures the historical framework to which avant-gardist practices responded in the first place. In his hostility to the avant-gardist claim that aesthetic innovations could be linked to political changes, Groys ends up being more Weberian than Max Weber himself.[38] As he insists in the wake of Weber on the autonomization of separate value spheres in modernity, Groys hypostatizes the logic of the aesthetic sphere as the sole mover of the historical development of art. In doing so, he underestimates the fact that twentieth-century attacks on bourgeois art ensued not simply from inner- or anti-aesthetic impulses, but from the contention that bourgeois culture had not lived up to its own program of autonomization. Bourgeois capitalism, resulting in the emergence of modern consumer society and commodified mass culture, eroded nineteenth-century visions of autonomous art from "outside" much more forcefully than any dadaist, surrealist, or futurist project was ever able to do from "within." The twentieth-century crisis of aesthetic autonomy, as Groys claims, was not a result of avant-garde activities; by way of contrast, it was the avant-garde that responded to forms of economic and political domination that produced increasingly spurious notions of autonomous art and, thereby, paved the way for the aestheticization of politics.

On the other hand, Groys's brisk critique of the avant-garde – like Bür-ger – implicitly follows some of the crucial misunderstandings that mark the center of many avant-gardisms themselves. Denouncing possible links between aesthetic revolt and political transformation as essentially totalitar-ian, Groys simply takes it for granted that cultural resources in the first half of the twentieth century were able to reorganize modern politics as a new totality. The shortcomings of this assumption become particularly clear when seen against the backdrop of the German, not the Russian, context. Throughout the nineteenth century, the category of "culture" was consti-tuted in Germany as an antitechnological realm of the spirit and the soul, an autonomous sphere compensating for or even contradicting the thrust of social and technological modernization. A repository of antimodern sen-timents, the category of culture thus failed to integrate the manifold aspects of the modern lifeworld; it failed to provide symbolic meanings in order to interpret the full spectrum of modern society.[39] Numerous avant-gardists, by contrast, hoped to restore a more comprehensive notion of culture by means of a one-sided explosion of aesthetic resources. Opening the bound-aries of autonomous art, they sought to connect aesthetic meanings to the entire bandwidth of the modern experience. But such a one-sided opening hardly sufficed in order to reinvent social totality; it in fact replaced one kind of one-sidedness with another: "If, without any regard for the intrin-sic meaning of the cultural sphere, one were to break open the vessels of aesthetic appearance, the contents would have to melt away – there could be no liberating effect from desublimated sense and destructured form."[40] In its most radical formulation, the avant-garde envisioned art to be a thing among other things. It thereby canceled what had made art into a possible catalyst of negation and critique in the first place; namely, aesthetic auton-omization, transcendence, and appearance. What Groys polemically re-bukes as the avant-garde's integrated totalitarianism, its Stalinism, in actual fact represented nothing other than a new particularism, a one-sided prior-itization of aesthetic over other tracks of social modernization.

Benjamin is clearly not innocent when it comes to sweeping generaliza-tions and conceptual shortcuts. Similar to the avant-garde (and Groys, for that matter), Benjamin at distinct points in his intellectual career enter-tained hopes to restore social totality by breaking the vessels of au-tonomous art from within. At the same time, however, his aestheticization thesis urges us – unlike Groys – to carry debates about aesthetic politics be-yond the conceptual force field of autonomous, political, and avant-garde

art. What is at stake for Benjamin is to link the emergence of political aestheticization to the advent and course of modern industrial culture. Aesthetic politics resulted not from the peculiar attack of the avant-garde on
aesthetic autonomy, but from the peculiar trajectory of capitalist modernization – that is to say, the expanding commercialization of art since the
middle of the nineteenth century on the one hand, and the concomitant introduction of cultural elements and aesthetic resources to the spheres of
economic and political legitimation on the other. Long before the arrival of
the avant-garde, some of the crucial components of aesthetic politics had already surfaced and taken effect in the figure of the poet roaming through
the marketplace, in the display of commodities in nineteenth-century department stores, in the exhibitionist tendencies of post-1871 architecture,
and in the spectacular self-representations of monarchical authority during
the Wilhelminian era.

What Benjamin defines as aesthetic politics, then, does not address the
role of bourgeois art in twentieth-century society but, on the contrary, renders problematic the way in which political dictates drape modern mass culture as art and thus transform the popular into a tool of domination and
manipulation. Benjamin's avant-garde alternative, on the other hand – that
which he calls, confusingly, the politicization of art – designates nothing
other than forms of mass cultural practice that take themselves seriously
and, therefore, reject the tactics of disavowal inherent to aesthetic politics.
Modern industrial culture, Benjamin implies, undoes the very categories
according to which Groys and others today continuously evaluate the validity of certain aesthetic and political agendas. For Benjamin, the twentieth
century signifies a historical moment at which cultural production emerges
as largely integrated into economic production and the political. This integration, on the one hand, makes possible the aestheticization of politics à la
fascism, but it also, and as importantly, opens up the possibility of a cultural
politics that may progressively intervene in the course of economic and political development. Opposing fascism, Benjamin's avant-gardism hopes to
channel the potentially democratizing force of industrial culture, not into
spectacles of ideological incorporation but into principally open and heteroglossic scenes of emancipation. To follow Groys's suggestion and historicize this endorsement of the modern popular – Benjamin's popular
modernism – as an essentially Stalinist project not only at once belittles the
atrocities of Stalinism and misses the complexity of Benjamin's program; it
also silences the many ways in which Benjamin's work could still inform a

critical analysis of our own age, an age marked by the ever more global incorporation of culture, economy, and politics.

The following volume will repeatedly employ the famous myth about the Gorgon Medusa as an allegory for Benjamin's concept of aesthetic politics. Similar to Medusa, who transformed sentient bodies into stone, fascism in Benjamin's perspective incapacitates sentience and agency: it petrifies individual and collective bodies in time and space. A peculiar modern technology of power, aesthetic politics maps the relationship between representation, collective action, and history as a self-producing one, as a phantasmagoria. It naturalizes political action and the semantic inventory of the state and thus strips away the possibility of engaging effectively in the production and circulation of symbolic representations; it thus strips away the resources to make and mark history. Fascist power according to Benjamin turns to aesthetic pleasures because it seeks to secure a peculiarly repressive system of representation and symbolic integration. Wickedly intervening in the dialectics of modern culture, fascist aestheticization makes existing institutions of domination taboo, makes culture into nature, and thus curtails hopes for alternative architectures of life.

Given the expansive reception of the Frankfurt School in American academic institutions during the last three decades, one might wonder about the overall location of the concept of aesthetic politics within the broader topography of classical critical theory. Like Benjamin, the works of Theodor W. Adorno, Max Horkheimer, and Herbert Marcuse during the 1930s and early 1940s were deeply implicated in theorizing what Andreas Huyssen has called the great divide between modernism and mass culture.[41] Yet, in sharp contrast to Benjamin's later work, classical critical theory understood aesthetic modernism as the primary site of resistance to the reified structures of modern science and society, while it largely refused to consider the spaces and practices of everyday life, in a rather phenomenological perspective, as a possible location of meaningful action, opposition, or even emancipation. In the Anglo-American context, Adorno's intricate reflections on art and modernism have recently experienced an impressive revival. In particular, Adorno's last and perhaps most difficult work, *Aesthetic Theory*, has finally received the kind of attention it so clearly deserves.[42] In recent debates about mass or popular culture in postmodern society, on the other hand, Adorno's reading of culture in the age of organized capitalism has "received less than favorable treatment."[43] Though often miscontrued as a mere expression of cultural elitism, Adorno's privileging of high modernism and autonomous art is no longer seen as a viable model to understand the overall dynamic of culture in the late twentieth century, not simply because scholars have lost faith in Adorno's equation of modernism and emancipation, but also because postmodern culture itself has blurred the gap between high- and low-cultural forms. If modernism was constituted "through a conscious strategy of exclusion, an anxiety of contamination by its other: an increasingly consuming and engulfing mass culture,"[44] then postmodern art and culture has indubitably leveled the great divide between the enigmatic and the exoteric, between idiosyncratic modernism and popular entertainment.

Commodified mass culture today surely does not produce the same subversive forces Adorno unearthed in the modernist works of Schoenberg or George. When heroizing the popular as a site of carnivalistic insurrection, contemporary cultural studies often tend to falsely, and romantically, equate the construction of identities, differences, and forms of agency through mass culture with successful acts of resistance or emancipation.[45] On the other hand, however, the comprehensive canonization of modernist and avant-garde art through modern classics editions, university syllabi, newspaper feuilletons, or TV commercials makes any attempt to define modernism as a perennial site of noncommodified subversion into a rather nostalgic endeavor. Seen from today's vantage point, Adorno's early work overestimated the emancipatory potential of modernist art, while it all too swiftly denied mass culture and everyday practice of having any critical potential. Although early critical theory has sharpened our perception for the inscriptions of power and coercion in modern cultural manifestations, its dichotomization of symbolic activities – however dialectical in nature – poses serious problems when we try to map the scenes of postmodern culture as well as to detect its – no doubt precarious – critical potentials. After the end of the great divide between modernism and mass culture, what is at stake for critical theory is not so much to locate subversive meanings in enigmatic texts alone, but on the one hand to explore points of agency and resistance in the commodified domains of both mass culture *and* art, and on the other hand to account for the complex bearing of this new aesthetic culture on the forms of political legitimation. "The relevant legacy of classical critical theory is therefore neither in the aesthetics of hermetic modernism nor in a postauratic popular culture but in the recognition of the aesthetic dimension as a medium of domination, the 'aestheticization of politics.'"[46]

Walter Benjamin – Adorno and Horkheimer's elder – throughout the

1930s dedicated most of his energy to the task of working through the emergence and role of aesthetic politics in modernity. Given the historical circumstances of Benjamin's intellectual career, it would be naive not to expect critical shortcomings in both his theoretical and historical perspective. Its striking originality notwithstanding, Benjamin's thought is clearly a product of its time, a time of ideological polarizations and rash commitments, a time in which the scandal of fascism penetrated to the core of every authentic theoretical effort. By reconstructing the aestheticization thesis first within the context of Benjamin's own work (part 1) and then against the backdrop of our own contemporary inquiries and debates (part 2), the following pages will suggest a number of ways to overcome Benjamin's shortcuts and dilemmas. In each moment of this effort, *Walter Benjamin and the Aesthetics of Power* is guided by the assumption that Benjamin's aestheticization thesis is still of great concern to us, not only because there is much work to be done in thinking through the spectacular elements of fascism and postmodern consumer society alike, but also because Benjamin's notion of aesthetic politics might indeed turn out, today and in the future, to be one of the most enduring legacies of German critical theory.

ONE

BENJAMIN AND THE FASCIST SPECTACLE

INTRODUCTION TO PART I

Max Weber has suggested that we may best define and understand the modern state in terms of its monopoly over the legitimate use of force within a specific territory, whereby this force is either directed outward to protect given political institutions against foreign aggressors or inward to stabilize the prevalent order of social action.[1] From the late eighteenth to the early twentieth century, numerous German intellectuals – from Schiller to Nietzsche, from Novalis to Wagner, from Burckhardt to Borchardt – sought to draw on art in the hopes of overhauling or defending this monopoly.[2] In the face of ever more accelerating processes of social differentiation, bureaucratization, and commodification, a multitude of artists, philosophers, and ideologues turned to aesthetic resources in order to counterbalance experiences of social fragmentation and redefine the contours of communal or national identity. They invoked poetic energies to warrant the legitimate use of power or envision alternative organizations of the body politic. Aesthetic experience was seen as a means to reduce social complexity and institutional abstraction, as a formula to overcome the loss of sacred, uncontested meaning, to heal putative pathologies of capitalist modernization, and to reinstate stable networks of social interaction.

Its broad and charismatic appeal notwithstanding, this call for an aesthetic state did not remain unchallenged, to be sure. Arguing from a plethora of ideological perspectives from within or without the realm of art, numerous nineteenth- and early-twentieth-century critics and artists in fact attempted to stabilize the borders between art and politics, whether they aspired to defend the political space from an intrusion of the aesthetic or to protect art from prostituting itself in the alleged gutters of power. In *Faust II,* Goethe contested the fusion of politics with art, only to embrace the autonomy of the aesthetic as the last remaining site of historical experience vis-à-vis what Goethe considered the increasingly senseless orders of modern life.[3] Karl Marx, in the famous introductory pages of *The Eighteenth Brumaire* (1852), critiqued the relocation of dramatic categories into the realm of historical action as a form of delusion, a transformation of revolutionary upheaval into entertaining farce, a "world historical conjuring of the spirits."[4] In his satire *Det nya riket* (The new empire), published in 1882, the Swedish dramatist August Strindberg – deeply rooted in the German intellectual tradition – ridiculed the aesthetic appeal of modern political institutions as "days of illusion" ("Illusionernas dagar" – the wording of a chapter heading) as mere humbug.[5] And Thomas Mann, in his 1917 *Betrachtungen eines Unpolitischen* (Reflections of an unpolitical man), debunked what he called "aestheticist politics" in the attempt to protect nationalist politics from the inherent decadence of art.[6]

Martin Jay has recently reminded us that any meaningful critique of aesthetic politics – whether directed at the nineteenth-century idea of the aesthetic state or at the spectacular elements of Nazi politics – must define its criteria of difference; that is, that which it understands as the specificity of competing arenas of expression, action, or judgment in modernity. "Any discussion of the aestheticization of politics must begin by identifying the normative notion of the aesthetic it presupposes. For unless we specify what is meant by this notoriously ambiguous term, it is impossible to understand why its extension to the realm of the political is seen as problematic."[7] In his preliminary venture to clear the ground for less-ambiguous debates about the aestheticization of politics, Jay identifies a number of different aesthetic incursions upon the political, all of which rely on distinct definitions of the peculiarly modern specificity of the aesthetic sphere. Three of these models strike me as most interesting for our purposes here. The first model, understood as an *epistemological* or *judgmental fallacy*, confuses aesthetic judgments with moral or political judgments. Aesthetic politics, according to this model, induces us to evaluate political facts and actions according to genuinely aesthetic categories, to transcendental principles of form, beauty, or sublimity. Closely related to this first model, the second transgression – a *pragmatic fallacy* – produces illegitimate equations of political action and artistic practices. It presents the political leader as a God-like genius who generates the very kind of rules, norms, and principles according to which his actions ought to be evaluated. The third confusion of art and politics, finally, may be called a *representational* fallacy. Under the spell of this third fallacy, images rather than language, visual distractions rather than rational arguments, operate as the main catalyst of political legitimation and social integration.

Jay's taxonomy is extremely welcome and helpful. His call for normative self-reflection urges any critic of aesthetic politics today to define the specificity of the very spheres whose boundaries – according to the critic – should be kept separate. And yet, in the case of Benjamin's critique of fascism – the mature version of his aestheticization thesis – Jay's principles of classification meet some odd resistance. Benjamin, as we shall see in the following pages, considers the aestheticization of politics as both at once a fallacious strategy of transgression and as a false and ideological insistence on political autonomy and differentiation under the condition of modern industrial culture. Aesthetic politics extends the concerns of art-for-art's-sake to the realm of the political. In analogy to the way in which turn-of-the-century art sought to cut all ties between aesthetic expressions and the socioeconomic, aesthetic politics marshals the inventory of postautonomous mass culture in order to propagate the absolute self-referentiality of the political and to recast power as an auratic presence, a self-sufficient spectacle. Although all three fallacies referred to above play a significant role in Benjamin's discussion, he gives each a curious and challenging turn. First, Benjamin understands aestheticization not as an exchange of aesthetic for political judgments, but rather as the attempt to drive the political beyond all facts, norms, and values. Aesthetic politics fulfills the dreams of interwar decisionism, the attack on procedural politics in the name of existential self-assertion, authenticity, intensity, and pure resolution. Second, fascist aestheticization does not simply collapse distinct spheres of action back into some kind of premodern, originary totality. Instead, it subscribes to its own vision of autonomization, to the emancipation of political action from the putatively emasculating impact of moral, economic, social, or cultural dictates, from the peculiar emergence of multiple power centers in a bureaucratic society. And third, it is not the profusion of images in modernity per se that engenders aesthetic politics but rather the unique attempt to graft the visual registers of autonomous bourgeois art, of auratic art, onto postautonomous mass culture. Aesthetic politics in fascism gives modern industrial culture the appearance of folk and high art alike; it presents modern mass culture as a self-sustaining articulation of collective identity.

According to Benjamin's understanding, aesthetic politics therefore may aim at a dedifferentiation of modern politics and its procedural and institutional complexity. But in contrast to many of his nineteenth-century predecessors, Benjamin does not believe that political aestheticization necessarily aspires to undo the differentiation of separate value spheres in modernity altogether. Aesthetic politics in fact wants to keep apart what under the rule of organized capitalism and modern industrial culture can no longer command absolutely separate status: bureaucratic administration from political leadership; economic imperatives from statal power. Aestheticization glorifies pure expressions of power so as to purge politics from any reference to the logic of modern administrative institutions and the dynamic of capital. Recasting state and nation as existential spaces of muscular and manly control, of self-realization, aesthetic politics positions the people in a passive role at the mercy of some superhuman force. It defines politics as destiny, not as a site at which we actively and continuously negotiate the traditions, institutions, values, and procedures that should govern the body politic.

It has often been pointed out that Benjamin's aestheticization thesis shares many insights with what is unquestionably the most influential postwar text on the nexus of power and art in National Socialism, Susan Sontag's "Fascinating Fascism" (1974). Sontag writes:

Fascist aesthetics . . . flow from (and justify) a preoccupation with situations of control, submissive behavior, an extravagant effort: they exalt two seemingly opposite states, egomania and servitude. The relations of domination and enslavement take the form of a characteristic pageantry: the massing of groups of people; the turning of people into things; the multiplication of things and grouping of people/things around an all-powerful, hypnotic leader figure or force. The fascist dramaturgy centers on the orgiastic transaction between mighty forces and their puppets. Its choreography alternates between ceaseless motion and a congealed, static, "virile"posing. Fascist art glorifies surrender, it exalts mindlessness, it glamorizes death.[8]

Like Benjamin, Sontag is careful enough not to describe the profusion of aesthetic materials under fascism merely as a perverse approach to art, as a giant art exhibition organized for degenerate audiences. Aesthetic politics is political through and through. It provides imaginary solutions to real contradictions and creates formal patterns of assent and submission in the very structures of cultural exchange. Unlike Benjamin, however, Sontag ends up reducing the question of fascist aesthetics to a question of style, iconography, and representation, to a chapter in the development of modern art that bears no relationship to broader social transformations. Her critique of fascist aesthetics relies on the implicit assumption that art fares much better if it remains autonomous, not involved in politics. She thus completely eludes what is perhaps the most challenging aspect of Benjamin's intervention; namely, the contention that fascist aestheticization – in its pursuit of autonomous politics – simultaneously avows and disavows the emergence of modern industrial culture; that industrial culture has changed the very parameters according to which nineteenth- and early-twentieth-century critics have pondered over the politics of art. Unlike Sontag, Benjamin wants to open our eyes to the fact that fascist aesthetics is postaesthetic, that we need to think it through within the context of a post-Kantian theory of industrial culture, not one tracing the transcendental specificity of modern art.

The chapters of part I reconstruct this Benjaminian theory of aesthetic politics and fascist mass culture. In my reconstruction, I attempt to, literally, sort through the materials at hand, identify their discrete components, supplement them with what might make individual lines of argumentation stronger, and thus recompose these components in a more systematic fashion. Surely less sensational than its deconstructive sibling, the reconstructive effort is nevertheless a highly critical exercise. It is inextricably tied to today's debates about the past and the present, and it is fueled by the assumption that often only brutal acts of de- and recontextualization may actualize the past for our own present debates. Like a car mechanic, the advocate of reconstruction is dedicated to the idea of making an old engine run again, an engine that for some reason has lost momentum but may still promise a powerful performance.

Part I understands aesthetic politics as a shrewd technology of social homogenization, and this is true even of the first chapter, which discusses Benjamin's initial and metaphysical version of the aestheticization thesis. Accordingly, aestheticization precariously attempts to reconcile what seems to have broken into pieces in modernity. It undertakes a restoration of emotional authenticity and unalienated experience, and in so doing it hopes to counteract the disintegration of modern society into a minefield of social, economic, and political conflicts. In contrast to part 2, in which I read the spectacle as a site of fragmentation and atomization, part I reconstructs the fascist spectacle thus as a tool of mythic unification and uncompromising coordination. The figures of Medusa and Perseus – chosen here to allegorize respectively the reifying operations of aesthetic politics and Benjamin's critical project – point, of course, not only toward a discourse on power and myth, but also to one on gender and desire. As I will argue at several points throughout part I, Benjamin's aestheticization thesis construes aesthetic politics as a precarious feminization of the modern masses vis-à-vis the manly spectacle of power and leadership, a feminization that undermines the masculine powers of proper judgment, moral reflexivity, and expressive authenticity. Although hailed in recent years as a heroic advocate of otherness, marginality, and nonidentity, Benjamin bases his account of fascist aestheticization on a strikingly problematic notion of gender identity, grafting his own male anxieties onto the critique of fascist culture and visuality. As I will indicate in the final chapter of part 1, Benjamin's encoding of the effects of aesthetic politics as feminine correlates intimately with the visual preoccupation of his philosophical style – what critics have frequently labeled as his metaphorical materialism. While Benjamin pictures himself as a heroic Perseus, attempting to slay the horrible third Gorgon, he tends to get caught in the pictorial ambivalences of his own physiognomical program.

I

BAROQUE DRAMA AND THE QUEST
FOR AUTONOMOUS POLITICS

Benjamin's artwork essay intends to unravel how fascist politics mobilizes
the masses and channels desire into the mold of political spectacles. Benjamin's critique of fascism does not focus on the content, the ideological
substance of fascist politics. It largely ignores the role of racism, anti-
Semitism, or social-Darwinism, abstaining from analyzing their polarizing
and unifying functions. Instead, what is at stake in Benjamin's remarks of
the 1930s about politics rendered aesthetic is a particular deformation of
political communication and its effects on the production of mass loyalty.
To the extent that aesthetic politics "sees its salvation in giving the masses
not their right, but instead a chance to express themselves" (ILL 241; GS
1:506), it valorizes form over content and silences the masses. Relying on
modern technologies of mass communication, the fascist theatricalization
of the state solicits public spaces that enable a cathartic release from everyday constraints. Although fascism employs the hardware of modernity, it
proliferates archaic software. Only in so doing can it promise to undo the
putatively feminizing effects of the modern differentiation of power and
value; only thus can it succeed in unifying the body politic. Benjamin's
commentaries on aesthetic politics debunk decadent modes of aesthetic address and exchange that do not unfold what he considers the emancipatory
potential of technologically advanced mass media. According to Benjamin,
it is precisely this truncation of symmetrical forms of intersubjectivity, this
petrification of charismatic energies in the cast of well-organized, well-
surveyed, and mechanically reproduced mass ornaments, that empowers
fascism to warrant political authority.

On the other hand, Benjamin also contends that an alternative alliance of
the most advanced hardware and software in postauratic communication
may potentially yield revolutionary effects. In the very form and structure
of modern cinematic address and exchange, he detects a blueprint for com-

munities that differ radically from fascist mass politics. Fascism implements modern communication technologies to cast a mythic spell over the masses. Visual communication in modern cinema, on the other hand, at least in theory, allows for the formation of critical, sober audiences that appropriate modern technology for the purposes of their (self-)representation, objective information, and enhanced reflection. Just as Brecht sought to transform the modern radio into a site of unconstrained exchange between listener and sender,[1] Benjamin construes the microcosm cinema as a social space in which we can enact new forms of political integration and collective reason. Benjamin praises the new technology of film, not because its imagery presents the audience with silencing spectacles, but, on the contrary, because formal qualities of cinematographic representation, montage and constructivism, destroy illusion and pave the way to language. In his rather idiosyncratic account, filmic address and cinematic spectatorship thus simultaneously inherit and revolutionize the social function of premodern storytelling. Cinematic montage modernizes the epic breath of narration, while critical audiences in movie theaters modernize the crowd of listeners gathered around storytellers. In sum, Benjamin criticizes fascism and its aesthetic self-fashioning within a theory that not only negates autonomous forms of aesthetic production and reception, but also emphatically calls for a convergence of aesthetics and politics. Taking position as a determined avant-gardist, Benjamin no longer aims to preserve the autonomy of the aesthetic, and he instead seeks to break away from the sequestering of art in a separated social value sphere.

Though unique in its merging of various and often conflicting lines of argumentation, this examination of aesthetic power in the artwork essay is not without predecessors in Benjamin's earlier work. As I will illustrate in what follows, Benjamin's book on the *Trauerspiel* already inquires into the nexus of power, legality, and representation, the nexus of political sovereignty and visuality, and thus anticipates some of the central elements of the aestheticization thesis in the artwork essay. Emerging from the tension-ridden atmosphere of the early Weimar Republic, Benjamin's treatise on baroque theater and some related essays delineate a subtle critique of the political dimension of art and the aesthetic dimension of modern power. In a metaphysical rather than materialistic fashion, these works try to come to terms with political strategies of legitimation that hinge upon the charisma and stage management of monarchical authority. Surely, in contrast to the model of the artwork essay, the *Trauerspiel* book bases its argument on a quasi-Kantian isolation of the aesthetic sphere as it defines the specificity of art against the transcendental categories of myth, morality, and the expressionless. In what appears from today's perspective as a protodeconstructive enterprise, Benjamin hopes to find in art itself what could prevent possible transgressions; that is, an intrusion of the aesthetic upon things political. As a result, the argument not only remains distant to Benjamin's later avant-gardism – his parallel endorsement of aesthetic innovation and political change – it also falls short of what in later chapters I will discuss as the artwork essay's most viable theoretical figure; namely, the grounding of Benjamin's critical agenda in a materialistic theory of individual and collective experience, one that will map the ways in which historically contingent organizations of sense perception change our attitudes toward beauty and pleasure. Yet Benjamin's peculiar examination of baroque power, and – as I argue – his subtle critique of Carl Schmitt's political existentialism, deserves our attention nevertheless. It reappears, as we will see later, in various guises in the formulation of the aestheticization thesis during the 1930s. Furthermore, in contradistinction to those who continuously emphasize Benjamin's apolitical posture prior to his discovery of Marxism around 1925, it also identifies already the early Benjamin as a critic very well aware of and concerned with the political dimension of the aesthetic, the aesthetic moment in modern politics.

Unlike other influential twentieth-century critics such as Theodor W. Adorno or Georg Lukács, Benjamin never produced a separate treatise theorizing the specificity of the aesthetic, its constitutive forces, its modalities of experience, or its standards of judgment. True to what Hans Heinz Holz called "prismatic thinking,"[2] Benjamin in particular during the 1920s primarily investigated the distinctive laws of the aesthetic within the context of broader interpretative works or commentaries.[3] In his seminal essay on "Goethe's *Elective Affinities*" (1922/23), for instance, Benjamin defines the aesthetic by juxtaposing the categories of work and author, aesthetic product and act of production, character morality and the ethics of the whole artifact. Polemically attacking both Wilhelm Dilthey's neoromantic hermeneutics and Friedrich Gundolf's aesthetics of genius, Benjamin challenges not only sentimental monumentalizations of the author but any confusion of work and life. Neither Dilthey, reading the life of the author as a work, nor Gundolf, rendering the work an expression of the artist's life, do justice to the implicit logic of the artwork. Work and life, Benjamin contends on the contrary, are incommensurable; neither one can be reduced to or deduced from the other. In contrast to neoromantic fusions of religion, ethics, and aesthetics through the concepts of sentiment and aesthetic form, Benjamin grounds aesthetic autonomy in the emancipation of the work from its process of production, literary criticism from biography. By accentuating the abyss between life and work, Benjamin implies that what constitutes the aesthetic is precisely that which always already transcends the signature of the author. Benjamin, in other words, predicates the specificity of the aesthetic upon the absence of the authors in their own work. In contrast to other modes of production, the creator of an artistic artifact engenders that which contains its meaning entirely in and of itself. Objects of aesthetic import efface all traces of their coming into being. True artworks begin whenever artists succeed in writing themselves out of their own texts.

What remains if the creator takes refuge from the creation, if the literary critic is able to cut through the false links between work and biography? Nothing more and nothing less than the category of semblance *(Schein)*. Artworks may be called art only if it is obvious that they are a substitution for nature, if they represent semblance through and through. Situated in the aesthetic tradition of German idealism, of Kant and especially Hegel, Benjamin interprets the literary artwork as a privileged site in which the semblance of truth takes place. Yet whereas theoretical knowledge "creates a regulative form of reasoning, truth resists the order of possession, observation, and mastery of the object and inconspicuously resides in moments of discontinuity."[4] According to Benjamin, the semblance of truth is neither a linguistic fact nor an absolute presence but, rather, the form of self-representation. Truth, as one of Benjamin's critics writes, "blocks all attempts at closure."[5] Therefore, critics have to destroy the artwork's semblance if they desire access to its inner truth content. Criticism entails the art of mortifying the work and its mythic totality, its appeal to beauty, in order to unearth the kernel of truth that is hidden underneath the work's material content. In a fragment related to the early Goethe essay, Benjamin defines the constitutive function of semblance for the artwork as follows:

In every work and every genre of art, the beautiful semblance is present; everything beautiful in art can be ascribed to the realm of beautiful semblance. . . . There are different degrees of beautiful semblance, a scale that is determined not by the greater or lesser degree of beauty but by the extent to which a thing has more or less the character of semblance. The law governing this scale is not just fundamental for the theory of beautiful semblance, but essential for metaphysics in general. It asserts that in an artifact of beautiful semblance, the semblance is all the greater the more alive it seems. This makes it possible to define the nature and limits of art, as well as to establish a hierarchy of its modes from the point of view of semblance. (SW 1:224; GS 1:832)[6]

Benjamin's doctrine of semblance recalls Nietzsche's *The Birth of Tragedy*, in particular the construction of Apollonian art as the "beautiful illusion of the dream worlds."[7] Yet although Benjamin himself indicates such resemblances, he at the same time is at pains to contain the role of semblance, to curtail Nietzsche's infinite regression from appearance to appearance of appearance, and, thus, to halt the philosophical transformation of the world into a merely aesthetic phenomenon. In contrast to Nietzsche, Benjamin insists on a grounding and self-limitation of art and its will to semblance.[8] In his treatise on the German *Trauerspiel*, Benjamin in fact calls Nietzsche's hypostatization of aesthetic semblance the "abyss of aestheticism" (OTD 103; GS 1:281). Refuting Nietzsche's idea that "it is only as an *aesthetic phenomenon* that existence and world are eternally justified," Benjamin criticizes Nietzsche for his annihilation of both theoretical and practical reason, truth and morality.[9] For Benjamin, the abyss of aestheticism embodies a lack of reason and a lack of foundation. "Where art so firmly occupies the centre of existence," Benjamin contends, "as to make man one of its manifestations instead of recognizing him above all as its basis *[Grund]*, to see man's existence as the eternal subject of its own creations instead of recognizing him as its own creator, then all sane reflection is at an end" (OTD 103; GS 1:281–82). Instead of falling into the abyss of aestheticism, art ought to relate to the grounds of human existence, of being. Instead of denying moral autonomy and involving its spectator in totalizing spectacles of semblance, art should recognize the moral existence as both its other and its limitation.

In spite of his attack on Nietzsche's aestheticism, the early Benjamin "makes no plea for art to discharge a moral duty."[10] If art, if writing and reading, entails an ethics, it is by no means contained in an artwork's statements about the nature of good and evil. Rather, what is ethical about aesthetic artifacts lies solely in their limitation of the range of art. Following Benjamin, art constitutes itself by means of its very separation from the spheres of politics and morality, through difference rather than totalization. Accordingly, true art needs to define itself constantly against the other at its edges. To create aesthetic artifacts means to recognize and reenact the initial act of demarcation, of suspension, of interruption, but also to respect what is beyond these boundaries as a semantic reference point, as creativity's memory bank, and as a horizon of possible *sujets*. In radical opposition to the later Benjamin, who will become highly suspicious about any attempt to declare art (or politics, for that matter) as utterly autonomous and demarcated from the social, Benjamin in the 1920s endorses the very act of respecting limits and the refusal to overstep boundaries as the defining mark of art and its ethical dimension. In a sense, the early Benjamin believes that the social legitimacy of art emerges from a kind of orchestra pit, a sunken, invisible border space between aesthetic performance and spectatorship, semblance and sober judgment. In contrast to the abyss of aestheticism, the no-man's-land of the orchestra pit ruptures the realm of semblance. It halts the trembling of the artwork and allows us to see its inner life as a petrified one; that is to say, it enables us to see it as an artwork in the first place.

With his early theory of ancient tragedy, Nietzsche hoped to present an alternative to the cultural crisis of modern life and the problems of legitimation in nineteenth-century politics.[11] In his book on the German *Trauerspiel*, Benjamin, by contrast, delivers a theory of modernity, a modern age that fails to live up to the possibilities it has made available and, therefore, not only confronts but generates cultural and political predicaments. As the heroes of baroque drama fall short of the secularized concept of politics they originally bring into play, the *Trauerspiel* in Benjamin's reading bears testimony to political imbalances at the origin of modernity that precipitate a pathogenesis of the modern age, an early version of aesthetic politics.

With the seventeenth-century *Trauerspiel*, dramatic art emancipates itself from the subject of timeless myth and enters the realm of history in order to become a scene of historical time and progress. In contrast to the heroes of ancient tragedy, baroque protagonists are endowed with historical agency, whether they realize it or not. Whereas Greek tragedy staged the human encounter with divine forces, the hero's surrender to fate, or the sudden recurrence of a prehistoric past and mythical law, the *Trauerspiel* involves its players in historical narratives in the center of which we find the test of political virtues, of diplomatic skills, of techniques of domination, of realpolitik.

Benjamin believes that the heroes of ancient tragedy, in a sense, are always already dead. Engulfed by prehistoric laws, tragic heroes appear sentenced even before they enter the stage, and it is this absence of genuine mortality that fails to provide them with the power to make history and fully escape the mythical order. Every performance reiterates their mythical trial only to silence them as they attempt to escape their inescapable sacrifice, the agonal. Quoting his own short study on "Fate and Character" (1919),[12] Benjamin contends:

[I]n tragedy pagan man realizes that he is better than his god, but this realization strikes him dumb, and it remains unarticulated. Without declaring itself, it secretly endeavours to gather strength. . . . There is here no question whatever of a restitution of the "moral order of the universe," but it is the attempt of the moral man, still dumb, still inarticulate – as such he bears the name of hero – to raise himself up amid the agitation of that painful world. The paradox of the birth of the genius in moral speechlessness, moral infantility, constitutes the sublime element in tragedy. (OTD 109–10; GS 1:288–89)[13]

It is in an act of speechlessness, however, that Benjamin observes the end of tragedy and the advent of a new kind of dramatic art, the martyr play. With Socrates' calculated silence, the agonal, mute sacrifice becomes meaningless. In contrast to the numb "derailing of speech" (OTD 117; GS 1:296) in ancient tragedy, Socrates' speechlessness is conscious and, thus, lays the tracks for a new moral world order, for forms of individual agency and historical consciousness that are predicated upon the emancipation of human speech from the powers of myth. Sentenced to death, the martyr Socrates remains silent to open the path for dialogue and thus to subvert the mute sublimity of mythical predetermination. Instead of death the martyr drama will emphasize suffering; instead of sacrifice it calls for pedagogy; instead of circular time it produces linear, historical time; instead of moral silence it articulates the decline of myth, demonic fate, and the struggle for moral autonomy.

The words of post-Socratian morality, however, are by no means a given. Just as the *Arcades Project* will uncover the mythic subtexts of nineteenth-century capitalism, Benjamin's early work provides us with principally ambivalent narrations of progress. In his essay on Goethe's *Elective Affinities*, for instance, Benjamin argues that morality's discourse can collapse into mythic silence again; Ottilie's final resignation reverses the historical consciousness born out of Socrates's silence and the musical lament of the martyr play. An allegory for the beautiful semblance, for symbolic and metaphorical totality, Ottilie has to die so that allegory – the critical armature of modern art – may live.[14] Whereas the inner parable of Goethe's novel supplies the novel's characters as well as the novel's readers with strategies to escape mythical guilt and captivity, Ottilie's self-imposed silence speaks for her renewed subordination to nature and, as Bernd Witte maintains, to her "ideological reproduction of myth."[15] Far from endowing her with saintly stature, Ottilie's departure from speech embodies her final complicity with the amorality of mythical domination.

In a similar, even broader vein, Benjamin's *Trauerspiel* book argues that baroque drama, although historically based in post-tragic idioms of morality, subterraneously reproduces the complicity of tragedy with myth. Focusing on realpolitik rather than divine authority, the *Trauerspiel* shows political rulers who subscribe to a new model of political sovereignty that aspires to remove religious, moral, or aesthetic concerns from the mechanics of domination. Ironically, however, in trying to live up to this new autonomy of the political, *Trauerspiel* rulers turn domination into an electrifying drama while effacing the foundations for individual autonomy and agency. Incapable of matching the demands of modern sovereignty, *Trauerspiel* monarchs naturalize their leadership through engrossing aesthetic spectacles. They collapse history back into nature, render the speeches of morality silent again, and in so doing revive mythic residues in a disenchanted, differentiated society.

It is well-known that Carl Schmitt's political thought had a profound impact on Benjamin's conceptualization of absolute monarchy in the *Trauerspiel* book.[16] In fact, Schmitt's construction of sovereignty, his account of the secularization of theology in modern political thought, as well as his anchoring of political legitimacy in the formal criterion of existential decisiveness during periods of exception are all essential to Benjamin's understanding of the modern state and his analysis of power in baroque drama.[17]

Schmitt's political thought during the 1920s is part and parcel of the notorious crisis mentality that proliferated among German intellectuals after the end of World War I and the breakdown of the Wilhelminian Reich. Responding to the allegedly feminizing weakness of liberal rationalism and the increasing bureaucratic routinization of everyday life, Schmitt, like many of his contemporaries, hoped not only for a total transformation of all existing values, but rather for their expulsion from public life altogether. Resonating in many different ways in the works of Martin Heidegger, Ernst Jünger, and Oswald Spengler, the Weimar quest for new decisiveness envisioned as a cure to the present crisis a Nietzschean self-assertion of the will to power and the grounding of political legitimacy in the existential criterion of resoluteness rather than practical, goal-reflecting reason.

In his study of Heidegger's political ontology, Pierre Bourdieu calls the relocation of Nietzschean conceptions of ethics into the political realm "ethicopolitical."[18] Schmitt's political philosophy is ethicopolitical through and through, not only because it wants to base sovereignty on the state of exception – that is, outside the realm of political normalcy – but also because it elevates resoluteness to the central measure of authority. Schmitt defines "sovereign," in the famous first sentence of his *Political Theology* (1922), as "he who decides on the exception."[19] Valorizing counterrevolutionary thinkers such as Louis de Bonald, Joseph de Maistre, and Juan Donoso-Cortés, Schmitt discovers alternatives to modern parliamentarism in voluntary acts of pure decision and pseudodemocratic acclamation that are enacted beyond the arenas of social conventions and legal norms, beyond rational discussion and public exchange.[20] In fact, Schmitt considers nineteenth-century liberalism to be antipolitical. With its principle of rational debate and its desire for a separation of public and private spheres, liberalist thought failed to recognize the uncompromising essence of the political – namely, struggle.

Central for any understanding of Benjamin's account of baroque politics, Schmitt's elaboration on modern sovereignty claims that all significant conceptions in modern political thinking represent secularized theological concepts. The category of exception, as the Archimedean fulcrum of Schmitt's doctrine, transfers to the theory of the state the functions theology attributed to the miracle. Accordingly, the state of exception provides energies that transcend the weary, disoriented realm of everyday life. It discontinues the endless terrors of repetition and routine:

The exception can be more important to it [the philosophy of concrete life] than the rule, not because of a romantic irony for the paradox, but because the seriousness of an insight goes deeper than the clear generalizations inferred from what ordinarily repeats itself. The exception is more interesting than the rule. The rule proves nothing; the exception proves everything: it confirms not only the rule but also its existence, which derives only from the exception. In the exception, the power of real life breaks through the crust of a mechanism that has become torpid by repetition.[21]

Where the peril is greatest, during the state of exception, the saving powers increase. Schmitt's claim about the structural analogy of miracle and exception, of otherworldly revelation and discontinuous inauguration of new laws, here clearly discloses the Nietzschean underpinnings of his conceptualization of modern politics: redemption from profane repetition is possible only to the degree that the will to power triumphs. True to Hobbes's verdict that *autoritas, non veritas facit legem*, Schmitt consequently claims that the basis of any legitimate system of juridical norms and political institutions lies in the discontinuous moment of a pure decision, a self-assertion of the will, a resolute, superhuman leap into what is beyond traditional norms, codes, and values. Challenged through states of emergency, resolute leaders simultaneously assume the role of "judge, dictator, sovereign, and pope."[22]

Schmitt's praise of voluntaristic determination is supposed to counter the deficiencies of twentieth-century parliamentarism and also the occasionalistic pleasure principle that governed romantic approaches to politics. In his study on *Political Romanticism* (1919), Schmitt faulted conservatives and counterrevolutionaries such as Adam Müller and Friedrich Schlegel for their subjectivism; far from shaping the world through resolute actions, political romanticism transforms the body politic into an occasion, a stimulus for aesthetic experiences, and therefore forfeits its own ideological aspirations.[23] Ironically, however, although Schmitt discredits romantic subjectivism and, by contrast, aims at a radical self-referentiality of politics and authority, his decisionism clearly bears the signature of aesthetic residues itself.[24] Schmitt's notion of political identity, grounded in the ability to distinguish between friend and foe, fundamentally relies on the spectacular enactment of leadership in the public realm, on the total visibility of power. Schmitt explores the visual field as a field to display and naturalize hierarchy. Rather than understanding the theatrical aspects of politics as a means to negotiate the norms that underlie the present order and to attest to a however precarious sense of public accountability, Schmitt wants to organize vision in order to induce wonder and admiration toward power. Schmitt's stages of power, to use Yaron Ezrahi's important distinction between nonattestive and attestive modes of political visibility, employ the aesthetics of sight "not to establish factual reality as a potential check on the claims of political authority but rather to uphold epistemologically and adorn aesthetically as well as to celebrate its powers to defy the limits imposed by any extragovernmental social or public norms like 'common sense' reality."[25] If politics and struggle become destiny, they require constant dramatization and symbolization to address and mesmerize the viewing masses.[26] For Schmitt, the aesthetic in turn is therefore "always political because politics is inescapable."[27] Though propagating the autonomy of the political, Schmitt freely traverses the boundaries between art and life, politics and aesthetics, in order to functionalize aesthetic expressions and modes of sense perceptions for the construction of total sovereignty.

Far from achieving its self-proclaimed aim, then, Schmitt's decisionism hinges on the very kind of aesthetic experiences it originally sought to remove from the political arena. It invokes a peculiarly modern, secularized, autonomous logic of political action only to subjugate the aesthetic to the demands of domination, indeed even to conflate political action with principles of aesthetic experience and sense perception. It is this hidden nexus of aesthetic sensibility and political thought in Schmitt, the "aestheticizing oscillations" of Schmitt's theory of modern power, that Benjamin's *Trauerspiel* book uncovers in its very own way.[28] According to Benjamin, baroque drama on the one hand testifies to the origin of modern secularized conceptions of power and realpolitik; on the other hand, however, it directs our attention to seventeenth-century constellations in which this new concept of pure, autonomous politics breaks down, consumed by the very forces it originally unleashed. In Benjamin's reading, political rulers in baroque drama in order to counterbalance the decisionistic impoverishment of practical reason activate spectacular modes of self-representation; they functionalize aesthetic forms and sanctify authority publicly in order to restore political authority and induce mythic wonder toward the modern language of power. Rather than to use the visual field as a space to attest, account, explain, or demonstrate political agendas, baroque monarchs employ the sense of sight and the theatrical aspects of political representation in order to consecrate expressions of power as auratic presences and aesthetic attractions. Even though Schmitt's decisionism is key to any understanding of Benjamin's early politics indeed, the *Trauerspiel* book implies that Schmitt in his valorization of modern secularized power does not differentiate rigorously enough between the realm of art and the one of politics.[29] Schmitt's political existentialism foils the ethical self-limitation of art and thus drives modern life into the abyss of aestheticism.

Informed by Schmitt, Benjamin locates the emergence of decisionistic concepts of sovereignty in the seventeenth century, inaugurated by the Counter Reformation yet decisively shaped through the Protestant insistence on innerworldly salvation. The baroque concept of sovereignty, Benjamin writes, "emerges from a discussion of the state of emergency, and makes it the most important function of the prince to avert it. The ruler is designated from the outset as the holder of dictatorial power if war, revolt, or other catastrophes should lead to a state of emergency" (OTD 65; GS 1:246–47). With the new doctrine of sovereignty, seventeenth-century monarchs respond to a hundred years of religious warfare and suffering as well as material and moral ruin. Accordingly, absolute monarchy originates from the existential void of the sixteenth and early seventeenth century, and its explicit function is to exclude the possibility that history once more collapses into chaos. Not utopian visions but functionalist imperatives govern the political agenda of the baroque. As a consequence, absolute monarchy gives birth to a secularized economy of power. To the extent that it endows its monarchs with dictatorial powers, the seventeenth century ceases to render the state an allegory of God, a training ground to qualify for heaven. Rather, in the wake of the new concept of sovereignty, the baroque intends to conceive of the political as a nonmetaphysical space in which individual and collective projects are regulated through the gadgets of absolute authority. Machiavellian technicians of power much more than representatives of God, baroque monarchs justify their rule in constant reference to the abyss that looms at the edges of the fragile order of the day.

Benjamin's baroque *Trauerspiel* illustrates this new conception of power in an instructive fashion. It shows that kings are by no means exempted from the mourning that characterizes the baroque, the kind of sadness and sorrow produced by the loss of the world's metaphysical unity and semantic plentitude. *Trauerspiel* sovereigns derive their original authority from the process of secularization, but, as creatures among other creatures, they at the same time cannot escape the logic of this "empty world" (OTD 139; GS 1:317) and, hence, eventually fall prey to melancholy and depression. "The prince, who is responsible for making the decision to proclaim the state of emergency, reveals, at the first opportunity, that he is almost incapable of making a decision" (OTD 71; GS 1:250). Baroque secularization thus simultaneously generates and undermines the possibility of decisionistic enactments of sovereign power. It is through pomp and ornament that baroque rulers seek to paper over this crucial "antithesis between the power of the ruler and his capacity to rule" (OTD 70; GS 1:250). Baroque monarchs adorn their fragile power by means of an excess of visible representation; they convert their own suffering into a public site of attraction, a stage of well-choreographed self-stylizations. Unable to maintain the kind of resolution that would justify their authority, baroque rulers instead showcase absolute power as an engrossing melodrama so as to arouse empathy and identification. They relocate aesthetic material to the political order with the intention to redress their court as a celebratory theater of human fate and in so doing to render natural what in truth is a product of historical contingencies.

If Schmitt defined the foundation of autonomous politics in the formal will to decide over the exception, Benjamin's monarchs forfeit resolution because, for them, the decisionistic formalization of politics turns out to be too narrow an approach to the complexity of rulership. Instead, they generate visual codes that glorify rulership and transform the court into what Benjamin calls a "Schauplatz" (OTD 92; GS 1:271), an exhibition site and an escapist simulation of grandiose power. Contrary to their own aspirations, baroque politicians thus institutionalize public spectacles and excessive theatricality in order to attain authority; they fail to sustain an autonomous logic of political action. At the origin of modernity, we therefore observe with Benjamin a fallacious attempt to distinguish between the aesthetic and the political. Staging the paths of a peculiar dialectic of political functionalism and social differentiation, the *Trauerspiel* reveals that the peculiar secularization and autonomization of politics in the seventeenth century ends up corrupting the grounding of art in gestures of self-limitation and separation. Just like the phantasmagorias of modernization in nineteenth-century Paris, the theatricality of power during the baroque constitutes "an acute disorientation not only of the sense but in particular of the rational faculty."[30] What provokes this catastrophic origin of modernity and its dire conflation of aesthetics and politics is not an excess but a dearth of reason: the strangling of practical reason through instrumental rationality, decisionistic power politics, and its appeal to aesthetic display. In contrast to Schmitt, Benjamin sees the baroque seeing the new doctrine of sovereignty as a force that triggers a pathogenesis of modern politics. Whereas Schmitt hails the decisionistic will to power that unites Machiavelli and Hobbes, Bonald and de Maistre, Donoso-Cortés and – finally – Hitler, Benjamin uncovers the inner contradictions of ethicopolitical authority when he portrays the seventeenth-century invention of secularized politics as a misdirected start into the modern age. Benjamin's *Trauerspiel* study detects in the birth of *this* modernity a true "nightside of history."[31]

Benjamin's early critique of the aestheticization of politics is fueled by an impulse to define distinct spheres of cognition, value, and signification. In contrast to the later version, in which the critique of the spectacle will be developed in the context of a materialistic theory of sense perception and historical experience, the early work identifies aesthetic transgressions against the backdrop of Benjamin's highly speculative metaphysics of truth, morality, and myth. The *Trauerspiel* book defines political aestheticization mostly as a confusion of different registers of representation. It develops the concept in terms of a moral and epistemological fallacy, not – like the artwork essay – as a technology of power reckoning with and realigning a historically specific organization of the senses and of desire. As a consequence, the early Benjamin can find in the realm of art itself what may unveil the deceptive nexus of art and power: allegory. Allegory offers a corrective to the fallacies and terror of aesthetic symbolism. In contradistinction to the symbolic spectacle of baroque rulership and its task to naturalize modern power, allegory probes and bespeaks the very modes of artistic signification, the impossibility of containing unchangeable meaning in a single work of art. It provides self-reflective forms of aesthetic representation that in their transitory nature remind us of the untimely and forgotten, of the imperfection and brokenness of the sense world. In contrast to the falsifying transfiguration of symbolic politics, the allegorical gaze undermines any cult of beauty, figurative transcendence, and affective self-representation. Extinguishing aesthetic semblance, allegory allows us to contemplate the boundaries between the human and the inhuman and thus serves as antidote to myth.[32] It keeps art from allying itself with what is not art, from overstepping the proper boundaries of the aesthetic.

It is not difficult to see that Benjamin's early critique of aesthetic transgression, as well as his valorization of allegory, prefigure what, in the work of Paul de Man, has been carried out as a highly demanding offensive on "aesthetic ideologies."[33] Instead of focusing on the aesthetic excesses of the baroque spectacle, however, de Man will bring into view the political hubris of modern aesthetic theories and practices that attempt not only to transcend the very nature of language by appealing to the power of metaphor and symbol, but also to invest historical reality, human finitude, with transcendental value. Aesthetic ideology – according to de Man – perceiving political action transfigured through the power of figural thought, ignores the constraints placed upon human knowledge by time, chance, and mortality and, therefore, illegitimately merges epistemology, practical reason, and aesthetic impulses into one. Allowing for an intrusion of the aesthetic upon issues beyond the genuine scope of art, aesthetic ideology prepares the ground for political terror, which – following de Man – emerges whenever absolute principles are applied to the unpredictable sphere of historical time, whenever individuals under the impact of their poetic faculty push their aesthetic sensibility to the extreme and identify through organic metaphors act and interpretation. Aesthetic ideology, in its excessive search for autopoesis, for an aesthetic identity of moment and eternity, particular and general, not only transcends temporality and finitude as the conditions of human life, but also the kind of distinctions that empower human knowledge and judgment in the first place.

Similar to Benjamin's critique of baroque power, de Man rings the alarm whenever artists overstep their field of competence and cloud the faculties of pure and practical reasoning, "to the detriment of clear thinking about issues of epistemology, ethics, and politics."[34] Like the Benjamin of the 1920s, de Man is suspicious about any gesture that provokes the limits of knowledge, about moves that superimpose aesthetic notions, the bewitching elements built into metaphorical language, on other modes of judgment, representation, and reasoning. De Man's quasi-Kantian impetus, however, does not stop him from casting a critical glance at Kant's philosophy itself, trying to uncover illegitimate alliances between aesthetic judgments and epistemological considerations, between art and ethics in Kant and his romantic successsors. In "Phenomenality and Materiality in Kant," de Man argues, for example, that Kant's aesthetics, though often hailed for its conceptual installation of aesthetic autonomy, is not so autonomous after all. Putatively establishing a causal link between the first and the second critique, between "critical philosophy and ideology," Kant's *Critique of Judgement* cannot fully conceal that it is instrumental for both the coherence of the system in general and the inner stability of the domains of theoretical and practical reason in particular.[35]

If Benjamin traces the politics of aesthetic transgression in the baroque spectacle of sovereignty, de Man – more than half a century after Benjamin – zooms in mostly on the hidden political agendas of Kant's romantic students Schiller and Kleist. In his essay "Aesthetic Formalization: Kleist's *Über das Marionettentheater,*" de Man polemicizes against reading Schiller's notion of aesthetic education as a training ground for unhampered modes of communicative exchange. Rather, what de Man observes in Schiller is a colonizing gesture by means of which Schiller inscribes aesthetic principles in the forms of theoretical and practical reasoning. Stripping practical reason of its autonomy, Schiller transforms the aesthetic into a hegemonic system of formalization that lends legitimacy to political terror: if mankind, de Man contends, is human only by virtue of art and form, aesthetic considerations will seize dictatorial authority.

The "state"that is here being advocated is not just a state of mind or of soul, but a principle of political value and authority that has its own claims on the shape and the limits of our freedom. It would lose all interest if this were not the case. For it is as a political force that the aesthetic still concerns us as one of the most powerful ideological drives to act upon the reality of history. But what is then called, in conscious reference to Kant and to the questionable version that is found in Schiller, the *aesthetic*, is not a separate category but a principle of articulation between various known faculties, activities, and modes of cognition. What gives the aesthetic its power and hence its practical, political impact, is its intimate link with knowledge, the epistemological implications that are always in play when the aesthetic appears over the horizon of discourse.[36]

De Man's Benjaminian critique of aesthetic ideologies exposes any attempt to unlock the closure of the aesthetic form as it may support the totalizing ends of political domination and homogenization. As a consequence, de Man reads Kleist's celebrated essay on the *Marionettentheater* not – as many other critics – as a utopian blueprint that continues Kant's and Schiller's aesthetic program and promotes a restoration of communal sense through grace and aesthetic form; rather, de Man depicts the dance of Kleist's marionettes as a lethal model of political formalization, a dystopian anticipation of fascist drill, violence, and aesthetic mobilization: pushing the aesthetic over its limits, Kleist's image of the dance represents an "ultimate trap, as unavoidable as it is deadly."[37]

According to de Man, fascism is art that has fallen into its own trap. To thwart such terror of aesthetic formalization, literary criticism after Auschwitz must install warning signs at the edges of art's own abyss. It must teach art how to turn against itself and repress its desire to colonize what is not art. When Benjamin, a decade after the conception of the *Trauerspiel* book, directs his critical gaze at the political aesthetics of fascism, he will clearly depart from what in today's perspective appears to be his protodeconstructivist predilections. His philosophical and methodological turn away from a metaphysical model of cognitive, ethical, and aesthetic autonomy toward a materialistic theory of historical experience is highly instructive. It proactively accentuates crucial shortcomings of de Man's attack on aesthetic ideologies. Fascism's aesthetics causes Benjamin to historicize Kant – to map the politics of art no longer in transcendental terms that locate the social responsibility of art solely in its strategies of self-limitation and self-correction. Fascism, for Benjamin, becomes a test case to theorize the historical contingencies of what different eras consider as beautiful and pleasurable in the first place. Retrospectively, the speculative framework of the earlier version of political aestheticization will prove being all too inflexible and totalizing in order to distinguish between the historical specificity of the aesthetics of baroque representation, the poetic masking of industrial progress during the nineteenth century, or the fascist aestheticization of modern warfare. Fascism, Benjamin argues in the artwork essay, makes use of a comprehensive redefinition of the sphere of the aesthetic ever since the middle of the nineteenth century. To critique the role of art in fascism against the background of a transcendental concept of aesthetic experience would therefore miss the most diabolical aspects of fascist aestheticization, and thus vitiate most of the distinctions that really matter for politics. At the same time, it would cancel out the legitimacy of any alternative use of aesthetic material, suggesting an apathetic withdrawal of art into a self-chosen inner exile.

The fundamental transitions in his intellectual career notwithstanding, Benjamin's critique of fascism as an aestheticization of politics recycles some of the motifs and tropes of the *Trauerspiel* book. Like the account of the baroque spectacle, the critique of fascism centers around the visibility of power, the staging of seemingly pure political action and strong leadership, and the politics of simulated experiences and domesticated affects. And similar to the earlier study, though not always persuasively, the later aestheticization thesis is at pains to distinguish between different varieties of visible politics and thus to overcome a long tradition of understanding the visibility of power per se as a sign of evil politics and deceptive mystification. A footnote to the artwork essay, often strangely forgotten in the discussion of Benjamin, throws into sharp relief what links and separates the critique of the seventeenth- and of the twentieth-century spectacle:

The present crisis of the bourgeois democracies comprises a crisis of the conditions which determine the public presentation of the rulers. Democracies exhibit a member of government directly and personally before the nation's representatives. Parliament is his public. Since the innovations of camera and recording equipment make it possible for the orator to become audible and visible to an unlimited number of persons, the presentation of the man of politics before camera and recording equipment becomes paramount. Parliaments, as much as theaters, are deserted. Radio and film not only affect the function of the professional actor but likewise the function of those who also exhibit themselves before this mechanical equipment, those who govern. Though their task may be different, the change affects equally the actor and the ruler. The trend is toward establishing controllable and transferable skills under certain social conditions. This results in a new selection, a selection before the equipment from which the star and the dictator emerge victorious. (ILL 247; GS I:491–92)

Similar to the *Trauerspiel* book, the artwork essay will associate dominant paradigms of aesthetic signification with the modalities of political representation. The modern media dictator, in analogy to the baroque tyrant, explores aesthetic technologies of representation in order to surround himself with charisma; he makes use of the visual field to appeal to the masses' auratic desires, their peculiarly modern hunger for diversion and distraction. In contrast to the baroque ruler, however, whose symbolic self-stylization turned history into myth, the twentieth-century dictator is at the forefront of technological and cultural transformations. Selected and successful because of his media appeal, the twentieth-century despot undoes not only the procedural mechanism of bourgeois democracies but also the putatively outmoded theatricality and the attestive visual codes of the bourgeois public sphere. The fact that Benjamin can think of the relation of fascism to bourgeois democracy as analogous to the relation between film and nineteenth-century theater,[38] yet at the same time emphatically can endorse film as an agent of progressive social change and a different kind of political visibility, indicates the extent to which his thoughts about the location of art in society have changed since the *Trauerspiel* book. Reckoning with the ambivalent potential of film either to fabricate or destroy fascism's charisma, Benjamin presupposes that a transcendental concept of aesthetic autonomy no longer will do to map the politics of art and culture in the twentieth century. The artwork essay will therefore develop its concept of aestheticization in a theoretical framework that radically differs from the argument of the baroque study. Not only will this essay suggest that we need to think of the concept of art in dialectical terms and historicize the notion of aesthetic autonomy; it will also develop its central analytical armature within a complex theory of individual and collective experience that – however successfully – seeks to emphasize the peculiar ways in which people make use of the symbolic materials of culture in historically contingent public spheres and under shifting regimes of sense perception and pleasure. It is to this much more challenging and politically volatile concept of aestheticization that I will turn my attention in the next chapters.

2

CARNIVAL, INDUSTRIAL CULTURE, AND THE POLITICS OF AUTHENTICITY

A good ten years after his first encounter with the question of aesthetic politics, Benjamin in his critique of fascism will realign his critical apparatus both politically and methodologically. The *Trauerspiel* study defined the baroque spectacle as a cunning manipulation of the aesthetic for the sake of political legitimation. Baroque leaders, according to Benjamin's reading, domesticated the aesthetic in order to secure their own position. They relied on public spectacles so as to master in a self-contradictory fashion the arrival of new concepts of secularized power and political autonomy. The rise of European fascism during the 1920s and 1930s urges Benjamin to rethink this conceptual armature, though many elements of his earlier thought – as we shall see – continuously inform his critical approach. In its most extreme formulation, Benjamin's work now understands the very grounding of political action in concepts of autonomous power and resolute leadership as an ideological instance of aesthetic politics. Rather than merely blurring the lines between the spheres of the political and the aesthetic, fascist aestheticization moves beyond any systematic encoding of action in a shared repertoire of values or norms, moral principles or aesthetic beliefs. It marshals the tools of postautonomous art and image making in the hope of removing former standards of valorization and legitimation and of glorifying expressions of power as auratic presences. In analogy to turn-of-the-century art-for-art's-sake, which reveled in radical formulations of aesthetic autonomy, fascism conceives of the political as a self-enclosed system of existential relevance. Fascist aestheticization defies normative discourses and critical evaluation; it presents the preconceptual articulation of vitalistic power and masculine resolution as the exclusive media of political action and integration.

It is tempting when approaching the spectacular dimension of fascism first to review the competing ways in which eighteenth- and nineteenth-century aesthetic theory and practice have defined the boundaries and social tasks of art. Particularly in the heated atmosphere of the early 1970s, many critics have taken recourse to the aesthetic heritage of Kant, Schiller, and Wagner in order to understand the peculiar calibration of art and politics in National Socialism. Ever since, it has become a commonplace to read the orchestration of politics during the Nazi period as a direct heir to the legacies of German idealism, classicism, or romanticism. The Nazis, according to this logic, either politicized classicism's preoccupation with symmetry, harmony, and order, or they relocated the Wagnerian conception of a total work of art from the Bayreuth Festival house to the marching grounds at Nuremberg. Such reasoning is surely welcome as it calls into question the historical vacuum in which many postwar historians have often situated the rise and success of fascism during the 1920s and 1930s. It seems questionable, though, whether such strategies of historicization really help to make sense of the mass appeal of the fascist spectacle as well as Benjamin's critique thereof. First, in a precariously idealistic fashion, this mode of inquiry ends up elevating aesthetic reflection and artistic expression to be the primary agents of historical development and political change. Second and more importantly, it overlooks the most striking irony of Benjamin's argument; namely, his claim that twentieth-century mechanical reproduction has irreversibly shifted the very territory on which eighteenth- and nineteenth-century aesthetic theory and practice articulated their principles and agendas. Although Schiller or Wagner may have linked aesthetic concepts to certain political projects, their aesthetic thought and sensibility still relied on a categorical separation of high and low culture. Early-twentieth-century theory, by way of contrast, must reckon with fundamentally different preconditions, the most important of which is the progressive leveling of former distinctions between autonomous high art, on the one hand, and popular culture or postbourgeois mass entertainment on the other. Fascism, in Benjamin's eyes, proposes a scandalous response to the dialectics of modern culture. As it exploits and in some respects even accelerates the demise of bourgeois art and aesthetics, the fascist spectacle erases both the historical and the conceptual landscapes of Kant's, Schiller's, and Wagner's world. An ardent critic of bourgeois liberalism and society himself, Benjamin in response cannot simply return to eighteenth- and nineteenth-century paradigms and present aesthetic autonomy as an antidote to the fascist spectacle. Instead, he must wrestle modern culture away from the iron grip of fascism – beat fascism at its own game. If art no longer can enjoy the kind of status it assumed in the nineteenth century, then aesthetic theory, similarly, must realign its modes of inquiry; it must refashion itself as a politically entrenched theory of mass culture, of modern industrial culture.

It is useful here to contrast Benjamin's peculiar approach to the dialectics of modern mass culture with the critical analysis of cultural modernization in the seminal account by Max Horkheimer and Theodor W. Adorno of the twentieth-century culture industry. In Horkheimer and Adorno's view, the movement from nineteenth-century liberal to twentieth-century organized capitalism triggers the collapse of former divisions between aesthetic refinement and popular culture into the "ruthless unity" of what they – with their eyes on the Hollywood studio system of the 1930s and 1940s – called the culture industry.[1] Symptomatic for a postliberal mass society in which all aspects of cultural production and consumption are controlled by the dynamic of capital, the culture industry appeals to a Fordist logic of standardization so as to provide everyone with something. It forges into a false unity what no longer can add up to a whole. "Light art has been the shadow of autonomous art. It is the social bad conscience of serious art. The truth which the latter necessarily lacked because of its social premises gives the other the semblance of legitimacy. The division itself is the truth: it does at least express the negativity of the culture which the different spheres constitute. Least of all can the antithesis be reconciled by absorbing light into serious art, or vice versa."[2] But that is precisely, they conclude, what the culture industry attempts and simulates. In its spectacles of pseudoindividualization, Fordist mass culture glosses over existing cultural and political fault lines. It transposes into an object of ritualized consumption what Horkheimer and Adorno comprehend as the utopian residue of aesthetic experience, and in so doing it nullifies the subversive potential of cultural expressions. Manipulating the masses, the culture industry promises to reconcile the antinomies of modern culture within an imaginary and organic whole, a false but ruthless unity that ensures guaranteed satisfaction and absolute conformity.

Adorno and Horkheimer understood the American culture industry as a not-so-distant relative of Nazi Germany; both formations enlisted culture in the service of mass deception. And yet, by presenting the transition from liberal to organized capitalism as the primary cause of cultural transformation, Horkheimer and Adorno at the same time insisted on crucial distinctions between America's and Germany's paths into the twentieth century. Prefascist Europe, they argued, to some degree escaped the trend toward the commodification and monopoly of culture; it was spared from the logic of the culture industry. In Germany in particular, state interventions during the nineteenth century created conditions under which cultural activities remained largely exempt from market forces. "The German educational system, universities, theaters with artistic standards, great orchestras, and museums enjoyed protection. The political powers, state and municipalities, which had inherited such institutions from absolutism, had left them with a measure of the freedom from the forces of power which dominates the market, just as princes and feudal lords had done up to the nineteenth century."[3]

In Horkheimer and Adorno's view of nineteenth-century German culture, state protection warranted the relative autonomy of artistic expression and reception and, in a certain sense, postponed the rise of modern industrial culture. This interpretation of the role of the state belies overwhelming historical evidence, yet in so doing it allows us to see some empirical and methodological shortcomings of Horkheimer and Adorno's critical vision. As Peter Uwe Hohendahl has shown in minute detail, Horkheimer and Adorno deny mass cultural elements in Germany and idealize nineteenth-century state protection because they completely elude the possible impact of political and bureaucratic institutions on the course of modern industrial culture.[4] As they directly correlate the dynamic of private capital with the politics of culture, they overlook the extent to which the social and political elites during the Wilhelminian era were able to utilize not only the scenes of autonomous art but also the newly emerging arenas of mass culture in order to freeze social conflict and deflect possible unrest. While it would be imprudent indeed to argue that the interests of nineteenth-century political elites would categorically differ from the interests of capital, Horkheimer and Adorno divest themselves from all conceptual means to distinguish adequately between the economic and the political aspects of any cultural manipulation from above. Transfixed by Hollywood circa 1940, Horkheimer and Adorno's model thus remains blind to what is historically and nationally contingent about industrial mass culture. "The relationship of the culture industry to the state is almost lost sight of in this analysis. Since *Dialectic of Enlightenment* is primarily concerned with mass culture in the United States, the description stresses the manipulation of the masses by the privately owned film and radio industries. This model would obviously not have applied to Germany under national socialism. To understand the origins of mass culture in Germany, one must examine more closely the importance of the state."[5]

At variance with Horkheimer and Adorno's assumption, the case of Germany even prior to the National Socialist period urges us to think of modern mass culture not solely as a response to economic imperatives and the laws of the market. Rather, following Hohendahl's lead, we have to take into consideration that from their very inception various formations of industrial culture – unlike the American model – were shot through with variegated political or administrative agendas. Although we should clearly be very careful not to isolate the political from the economic, on the other hand we ought not to fall into the kind of determinism that views political measures as sole effects of economic dictates. Moreover, as the Wilhelminian example indicates, we can no longer ignore the fact that certain class- or group-specific cultural practices were able to survive the breakthrough of organized, postliberal capitalism; that is, that industrial culture was more heterogenous and pluralistic than Horkheimer and Adorno believed. Horkheimer and Adorno's seminal model may still be intriguing. Its sensibility for scenarios of coercion and manipulation remains unsurpassed. But given both its historical and theoretical shortcomings, the culture-industry thesis clearly needs correction. It neither allows us to understand mass culture as a political tool administering the masses' emotions from above, providing instrumental spaces for cathartic expression, and aligning diversion with political projects; nor has it much to offer to explore alternative versions of industrial culture, to map the popular as a however precarious site of struggle, symbolic negotiation, and cultural empowerment, or to see modern mass culture as a laboratory of what Miriam Hansen calls popular modernism: non-avant-gardistic mass formations of primarily the interwar period usually subsumed under the rubrics of Americanism or Fordism; heterogeneous and often competing public spheres that not only responded "to a new culture of leisure, distraction, and consumption" but also "absorbed a number of artistic innovations into a modern vernacular of its own."[6]

Not without its own flaws and overgeneralizations, Benjamin's second version of the aestheticization thesis – as I argue in this and the following chapters – allows us to correct and amend some of the theoretical and historical blind spots of Horkheimer and Adorno's culture-industry model. An exercise in postaesthetic theory as it were, Benjamin's critique of fascism inquires into the political dimensions of twentieth-century mass culture. Unlike Horkheimer and Adorno, Benjamin scrutinizes the ways in which mass-mediated diversion may either serve as a vehicle of political coordination and subordination or as a catalyst of collective empowerment and autonomous agency. Fascism, in Benjamin's view, employs and shapes mass cultural practice for its own political ends. Relying on a state-controlled culture industry, fascism employs postautonomous art and distraction for its populist projects of national rejuvenation and total mobilization. What Benjamin – strangely ignoring the Stalinist variants of aestheticized politics – calls "communism," on the other hand, symbolizes an emancipatory version of industrial culture. It renders the popular a politically relevant site at which people can appropriate the symbolic materials of mass culture in order to negotiate intersubjective meanings, articulate them into their everyday life, and thus actively partake of the construction of individual and collective identities. Although Benjamin's noncritical attitude toward the USSR and Stalin's aestheticization makes his analysis incomplete at best, the precarious label for this alternative use of mass culture, "communism," should not keep us from exploring the conceptual substance of Benjamin's alternative to aestheticized politics.

Fascism, in Benjamin's reading, exchanges procedural politics for symbolic mass spectacles. It removes normative claims from the political sphere and celebrates the iconography of resolute leadership as an autonomous manifestation of the will to power. In order to do so, the fascist state recycles selected elements of nineteenth-century aesthetic culture within the horizon of a postaesthetic century. Like Hollywood in Horkheimer and Adorno's analysis, fascism forges into a ruthless and violent unity what no longer can add up to a whole; it hopes to provide something for everyone so as to ensure that no one may escape. What distinguishes Benjamin's aestheticization thesis from Horkheimer and Adorno's model, however, is that Benjamin thinks fascism is right to recognize the mass cultural bases of twentieth-century politics, yet wrong to annihilate the democratizing potentials of industrial culture. This radically unorthodox stance, as scandalous at it may appear to us, was clearly a product of Benjamin's own times – times in which no authentic theoretical effort could avoid addressing the scandal of fascism. As Jürgen Habermas has summarized, "The victory of the Fascist movement in Italy and the National Socialist takeover of power in the German Reich were – long before Auschwitz – phenomena from which issued waves not only of irritation but also of fascinated excitement. There was no theory of contemporaneity not affected to its core by the penetrating force of fascism."[7]

Irritating and fascinating alike, fascism for contemporary intellectuals such as Walter Benjamin thus posed both a political and a theoretical challenge. It called for a radical revaluation not only of previous ideological positions but also of former methodological and epistemological tools. Although the aestheticization thesis – as we shall see – echoes many insights of Benjamin's earlier "metaphysical" phase, it at the same time urges us to reconsider Benjamin's thought prior to the triumphs of National Socialism during the 1930s. It is understandable, then, that Benjamin's critical engagement with fascism can only appear to us as a highly intricate endeavor, a walk on a theoretical and political tightrope. As I will argue in this and the following chapters, the revised aestheticization thesis in fact critiques the precarious role of fascist mass culture on three interconnected planes: as a calculated simulation of carnivalistic fraternization and communal redemption (chapter 2); as a transformation of the political space into a playground of aesthetic geniuses, a cultic site of expressive renewal (chapter 3); and, finally, as a spectacle of visual seduction that addresses peculiarly modern desires for scopic pleasure and bereaves the individual of autonomous agency (chapter 4). On all three planes, Benjamin is at pains to describe how National Socialism and Italian fascism curtail the utopian power of the popular. Recycling selected traditions of eighteenth- and nineteenth-century aesthetics on the grounds of an industrial mass culture, fascism revels in existentialist appeals to heroic leadership and Great Politics so as to suture the individual into a simulation of a homogenous community. It is to Benjamin's analysis of fascist mass culture as a regressive form of carnivalistic excess and Dionysian frenzy, as a spectacle of expressive energies and charismatic desires, and as a postautonomous reinscription of the aesthetics of the beautiful and the sublime that I turn my attention in this chapter.

Whatever Germans considered "golden" about the 1920s corresponded with contemporary aspirations to emancipate art from bourgeois highbrow culture and liberal rationalism. Whether it was the expressionist call for a new humanity, the dadaist attack on reason, the surrealist expedition into the subconscious, or the futurist intoxication with speed and technology – the works of aesthetic modernism responded in so many ways to the rise of charismatic hopes in the immediate postwar era and thereby sought to connect art to new postbourgeois audiences.[8] Furthermore, the popularity of film and cabaret, of spectator sport and dancing, of American mass culture and the pleasures of commodity consumption – these for many contemporaries evidenced a revolutionary surge of the popular dimension, a leveling of former distinctions between the domains of high and low culture. Whether aesthetic modernists searched for antidotes to the foreign outlook of social modernity and its bureaucratic institutions, or whether the sudden breakthrough of mass cultural elements enabled a multiplicity of new pleasures and diversions, it was this abrupt hegemony of the cultural sector that has fueled, despite all economic hardships and political polarizations, myths about the golden twenties through today.

But this cultural protest against the traditional spheres of the aesthetic did not merely seek to open art to mass consumption. Rather, by offering novel aesthetic experiences through new technological means of representation, Weimar culture also sought to represent these new masses in its very artifacts. Thus, the masses' messianic hopes, their threat to bourgeois notions of subjectivity, their taming in outmoded social constructions, and their revolutionary power became objects of aesthetic experience and consumption themselves. Released on 18 September 1919, Ernst Lubitsch's film *Madame Dubarry (Passion)* allowed for one of the first of such self-encounters of the masses. Ironically, however, Lubitsch's portrayal of the masses depicted the French Revolution solely as a function of individual emotions and, hence, dehistoricized modern politics. In addition, and in spite of its creative depiction of urban crowds through mobile cameras, Lubitsch's cinematic pageant also tended to decompose the masses visually and "to exhibit as its nucleus 'one single figure' who, after the crowd's dissolution, was left alone in the void. Thus the individual appeared as a forlorn creature in a world threatened by mass domination."[9] Clearly reflecting the tension-ridden atmosphere of the immediate postwar period, Lubitsch captured impressive mass scenes only to present collective power as a lethal threat.[10]

In contrast to *Madame Dubarry*'s sentimental redemption of bourgeois individuality, Fritz Lang's *Nibelungen* viewed the masses from beyond the watchtowers of nineteenth-century individualism. If Lubitsch's historical piece spoke for the hesitation to embrace democratic principles already at the beginning of the Weimar Republic, Lang's epos, released in 1924, prefigured coming fatal attractions: the transformation of the masses into a human ornament. At Gunther's court in Burgundy, the ordering of architectural space and the abundance of geometrical forms serve as direct expressions of authority and legitimize the monopoly of power in the hands of the nobility. When Gunther and his men return from Iceland, soldiers appear cast into symmetrical patterns, into a public aesthetics of subordination. Submerged up to their chests in the Rhine, Gunther's subjects support a gangway for their leaders, while other vassals, neatly lined up on a hill, salute the arrivals with Wagnerian pomposity.[11]

During the 1930s, Lang's stylized rendition of the masses left the movie theaters and invaded the political space. "In Nuremberg," Siegfried Kracauer writes about the political aesthetics of National Socialism, "the ornamental pattern of *Nibelungen* appeared on a gigantic scale: an ocean of flags and people artistically arranged."[12] But Nazi aesthetics sought not merely to impress the masses. In tandem with the ruthless coordination of public and private life, Nazi aesthetics was meant to replace the complexity of modern democratic institutions, of legal mechanism, of administrative apparatuses and norm-generating mechanisms. Exchanging political discourse for both crude violence *and* the beautiful appearance of vitalistic strength, the Nazi state pursued a new vision of political life and action. Both direct force *and* ornamental designs in a domesticated public sphere, both open violence *and* the aesthetic appearance of charismatic leaders, in particular Hitler, were to restore what society discarded in terms of rationality and institutional differentiation. By means of impressive mass spectacles, politics was supposed to lose its bureaucratic face and reemerge as a harbinger of religious revelation and community building. "The *personification* of politics suggested the triumph over the structural and anonymous aspects of politics in modern societies, that is law, regulated procedures, bureaucracy, etc. In any case, this personification promised authenticity, emotionality and symbolic representation and thus a compensation for the depressive and disorienting alienation in industrial, mass-oriented life."[13] Anti-Semitism in turn provided a vent to release the powers of repression that were instigated by these politics of displacement. Fascism engaged in anti-Semitism as an atrocious strategy of othering, of branding the Jew as ugly, to justify the politics of mass annihilation, but also to strengthen the always precarious unity and racial identity of the community of the folk against the decentering powers of capitalist modernization. The putative pleasures of fascist aestheticization were not all-inclusive: they addressed some, yet excluded others.[14]

Supplanting the intricate structures of modern political decision making, the fascist spectacle unleashed a general upheaval of cultural forces against political modernity. This upheaval, however, did not neglect the technological possibilities inherent in the modern world. The Nazi state did not simply halt the institutional and technological modernization of the Weimar Republic. Instead, it embraced an alternative, a parallel branch of modernization, that which Jeffrey Herf and others call "reactionary modernism."[15] Synchronizing national traditions with selected products of modern economy, technology, and mass culture, the Nazi movement attempted to channel both broad resistance against modern society and an abundance of palingenetic hopes into all-inclusive social structures. In order to do so, fascism maintained a national industrial culture disguised in the cloak of folk art; it venerated advanced technology and instrumental reason via premodern principles such as the spirit, folk, and race.[16] Relying on modern machines, Nazi mass culture "endeavored to discipline distraction, to instrumentalize sights and sounds in the hopes of engineering and orchestrating emotion."[17]

It is only in the last three decades that postwar historians and literary critics, political scientists and art historians have begun to inquire seriously into this nexus of art, politics, and mass culture in National Socialism,[18] the synchronicity of "lure and force, seduction and crime."[19] This late arrival of rigorous investigations into the aesthetic moment of fascism may be surprising, given the fact that outstanding Weimar intellectuals had examined the symbolic economy of the Nazi movement as early as during the 1920s and their exile years in the 1930s; they debunked its fascination and unveiled the violence of its quest for all-encompassing beauty. In his famous 1927 essay on Tiller girls and the mechanization of the body, Kracauer inquired into the aesthetic homogenization of urban masses.[20] Ernst Bloch, by contrast, in his *Heritage of Our Times* (1924–35), brought into view what he called the fascist "inventories of revolutionary appearance."[21] Accordingly, National Socialism reappropriated unifying symbols from the workers' movement, not only to spellbind the masses but also to feign redemption from the instabilities of capitalist modernization. With his notion of affirmative culture, Herbert Marcuse finally pointed in 1935 to the preparatory function of bourgeois art and its cult of beauty for the augmentation of political terror.[22] Promising happiness in the exclusive realm of art alone, Marcuse argued, nineteenth-century bourgeois aesthetics paves the way for mass subordination in twentieth-century politics, for drill, self-annihilation, and poetic ideologies of heroic individuality.

Although Kracauer, Bloch, and Marcuse helped open the eyes of their contemporaries, it was in Walter Benjamin's writings that the debate about the fascist nexus of art and politics found its most influential formulation. In contrast to Kracauer, whose analysis of the mass ornament at crucial points resorted to metaphysical vocabularies, Benjamin sought to base his account on a materialistic theory of modern art, society, and sense perception. In contrast to Bloch, Benjamin did not merely investigate the use and misuse of political symbols and thus see aesthetic politics as only a surplus decor of everyday violence. Rather, he chose to theorize historical developments that promulgate the collapse of art and politics in the first place, developments that yield the fatal metamorphosis of society into appearance through and through. And in addition to Marcuse's critique of German nineteenth-century culture, Benjamin finally revealed the complicity of political spectacles with the advent of twentieth-century mass culture and certain tendencies in postwar avant-garde art, in particular the futurist fascination with accelerated speed and the sublimity of modern machines.

Given the feverish reception of Benjamin and his analysis of fascist aesthetics after 1970, the quantitative dearth of original material may be surprising. Benjamin never developed a systematic theory of National Socialism or Italian fascism. True to his prismatic mode of thinking, he refused theoretical abstractions that would sacrifice the particular on the altar of methodology and systematization. For Benjamin, methods were excursi, and excursi became method. He followed paths of reflection that enabled a discontinuous, often surprising unfolding of a "wealth of sense and meaning."[23] As a consequence, even Benjamin's political critique of fascism took the form of fragments and essaistic sketches, primarily located in three texts, all of which amount to no more than thirty printed pages in the *Gesammelte Schriften*.

At the core of Benjamin's physiognomy of fascism is the legendary epilogue of his essay "The Work of Art in the Age of Mechanical Reproduction" (ILL 217–52; GS 1:470–508). Benjamin drafted the essay in fall 1935 in Paris. He hoped to publish it in the Moscow exile journal *Das Wort*, a project that failed due to the opposition of one of the journal's editors, Bertolt Brecht. It was only after some major editorial changes that Benjamin finally succeeded, in 1936, in publishing this article in Adorno and Horkheimer's *Zeitschrift für Sozialforschung*.[24] Benjamin's review of Ernst Jünger's compilation *Krieg und Krieger* (War and warrior), published in *Die Gesellschaft* in 1930 under the title "Theorien des Faschismus" (TGF), constitutes the second pillar of the aestheticization thesis. Whereas the artwork essay is primarily dedicated to the interplay of modern mass culture and the politics of representation, this earlier text discusses the beautification and mythologization of warfare in postwar Germany. In the third text relevant to his diagnosis of fascism, the so-called "Pariser Brief" (GS 3:482–95), published in *Das Wort* in 1936, Benjamin finally examines certain features of fascist art proper. Although this third text may be understood as a journalistic reformulation of the more theoretical artwork essay, it nonetheless yields interesting insights into what was considered beautiful, an object of aesthetic pleasure, under fascist domination.[25]

It is interesting to note that in all of these three texts, Benjamin only briefly discusses what he considers the genesis and socioeconomic roots of fascist terror, as he clearly does not intend to formulate an original diagnosis of the historical forces that elevated Hitler or Mussolini to power.[26] Although Benjamin alludes to Marxist terminology and refers to Rosa Luxemburg's crisis model of imperialism, his explanations remain general and do not commit themselves to any single orthodoxy. The category of technology occupies a central position in his model. Benjamin writes in the "Paris letter": "The development of productive forces, which determine the role of the proletariat and of technology, results in a crisis that seems to call for a socialization of the means of production. By and large, then, this crisis is a function of technology. He who thinks he solves it inadequately, violently, by preserving privileges, is interested in masking the functional nature of technology as far as possible" (GS 3:490). According to Benjamin, technological progress has prompted a critical condition that can be mastered only in two fundamentally different directions. The one is to understand the functional character of technology and appropriate it for the sake of an equal distribution of wealth. Although German society, in terms of its economical structure, appeared mature enough to Benjamin to make technology an organ for collective interests, its structures of consciousness inhibited such a transformation. Although the productive forces offered sufficient material to satisfy the needs of the masses, the property structures denied any just utilization of modern technology.

In order to solve this imbalance of productivity and property, technological progress and social stratification, Germany chose the second possible route, one that Benjamin considers an unnatural release of energies since it enables the continuation of existing hierarchies: war. "If the natural utilization of productive forces," he writes in the epilogue of the artwork essay, "is impeded by the property system, the increase in technical devices, in speed, and in the sources of energy will press for an unnatural utilization, and this is found in war. The destructiveness of war furnishes proof that society has not been mature enough to incorporate technology as its organ" (ILL 242; GS 1:507). Hoping to stabilize the explosive situation and to provide simultaneously dynamic and regressive outlets, the fascist ideology of war renders technology a force that follows its own autonomous logic and will. Fascism endorses technological progress, not to inaugurate social equality, but to preserve the privileges of a class society. Fascism transposes technology into myth and destiny rather than presenting it as a tool of collective emancipation.

Fascism, then, projects premodern modes of thinking and perception on the vectors of modern technological rationality. It uncouples machines and means of production from rational legitimation. Displacing discourse, fascism cloaks technology in aesthetic imagery and hopes to persuade the masses from the vitalistic power of modern machines. Instead of empowering the human collective, fascism channels charismatic hopes for political renewal and redemption into public spectacles that merely simulate the experience of equality and community, public niches that coexist with the architectures of a class society. In the first sentences of the epilogue of the artwork essay, Benjamin summarizes his argument as follows: "The growing proletarianization of modern man and the increasing formation of masses are two aspects of the same process. Fascism attempts to organize the newly created proletarian masses without affecting the property structure which the masses strive to eliminate. Fascism sees its salvation in giving the masses not their right, but instead a chance to express themselves" (ILL 241; GS 1:506). Fascism satisfies hopes for emancipation symbolically. Appealing to the masses' call for new communities and powerful collective experiences, fascism installs popular playgrounds in which the impoverished masses can partake of "integrative symbolic actions."[27] Not justice and equality but mass exhilaration and symbolic appeasement; not a reorganization of the social order but affective identification and catharsis – these mark the fascist response to the crisis of modern technology.

Following Benjamin, then, fascism engenders mass cultural scenarios from above so as to distract from real contradictions and solicit a false sense of community. The fascist spectacle does justice to emotional demands but not to reason, to sentiments rather than to reflection, to aesthetics rather than ethics. Representation, visibility, and visuality in fascism become repressive. Nazi mass aesthetics drowns its recipient in a flood of images. Its modes of aesthetic address resemble military commands, depriving the individual of "independent thinking and leaving him neither time nor space for his own associations and dreams."[28] The fascist spectacle appeals to powerful emotions and desires, but at the same time it intends to overwhelm the participant, to control the entire bandwidth of perception and response, and to negate the individual body as a site of desire and sensual pleasure. Although the masses experience their public ornamentalization as a restoration of emotional authenticity and mass solidarity, the spectacle reinstates factual inequality and helps coordinate all aspects of private and public life: "The masses have a right to change property relations; Fascism seeks to give them an expression while preserving property. The logical result of Fascism is the introduction of aesthetics into political life. The violation of the masses, whom Fascism, with its *Führer* cult, forces to their knees, has its counterpart in the violence of an apparatus which is pressed into the production of ritual values" (ILL 241; GS 1:506).

A catalyst of ritual values, the fascist spectacle solicits a charismatic interruption of ordinary routines and practices. It opens a cultural space in which the disenfranchised modernite may reexperience society as an organic and structured totality, a space void of the boundaries and functional differentiations that typify the modern condition. Similar to a religious holiday, the spectacle temporarily reconnects public and private meanings, infusing everyday life with new spirit and vigor. It entertains the participant with a view of society in which culture knows no separation between everyday practice and art and, thereby, it pretends to allow access to prehistoric strata of experience. An effect of modern machines and advanced technologies of representation, the spectacle appeals to the utopia of a pastoral society, to the vision of a preindustrial culture in which the instrumental, the moral, and the expressive appear as seamlessly integrated.

When traveling to Naples more than a decade before the composition of the artwork essay, Benjamin believed he was witnessing in reality what the fascist spectacle according to his later account merely simulates: a preindustrial organization of urban space and culture in which the organizing demarcations of capitalist modernity, the boundaries between work and leisure, between public and private space, were not yet operative. It is useful, therefore, to backtrack for a moment to this earlier experience in order to better understand the skewed power of the latter. The Naples of Benjamin's 1924 travelogue emerges as an undifferentiated society, and it is precisely because of its lack of institutional separation that the city is able to elevate individual life to a moment of a higher, albeit fundamentally open, aesthetic configuration. Despite there being ubiquitous signs of poverty, Benjamin expresses his sympathy for the spontaneity, the public sense of enjoyment, the performative skills that prevail in the streets of Naples:

> [N]othing is concluded. Porosity results not only from the indolence of the southern artisan, but also, above all, from the passion for improvisation, which demands that space and opportunity be at any price preserved. Buildings are used as a popular stage. They are all divided into innumerable, simultaneously animated theaters. Balcony, courtyard, window, gateway, staircase, roof are at the same time stage and boxes. Even the most wretched pauper is sovereign in the dim, dual awareness of participating, in all his destitution, in one of the pictures of Neapoli-

tan street life that will never return, and of enjoying in all his poverty the leisure to follow the great panorama. (REF 166–67; GS 4:310)

Naples's architectural porosity and openness – the absence of the northern demarcations of life and the lack of differentiated political institutions – correspond intimately to the city's theatrical passions. To the degree that the streets emerge as a theater, everyday life unfolds a quasi-natural spectacle of emotions and gestures, of expressive authenticity and spontaneity. Naples's street art, however, is far from following a one-dimensional, monological dramaturgy. On the contrary, Naples's social *tableaux vivants* are principally open and unrepeatable. Aware of its transitory nature, the Neapolitan theater of everyday life is bound to a specific here and now and, therefore, vanishes in the very moment of its enactment. As it is part and parcel of the fleeting textures of enjoyment and performativity, urban poverty loses its *scandalon*, the kind of shock it transmits in societies that deny its existence. In a society to which bourgeois utopias of suburban homeownership are fundamentally foreign, homeless people are those that hide in confined spaces and withdraw from populating the only true home there is, the street.

To Benjamin's clearly romanticizing eye, Naples represents an urban landscape of preindustrial exteriorization. Whereas northern modernity hides, confines, or erases emotionality and communality in the cages of bourgeois intimacy, Naples conflates personal and communal life and thus preserves meaningful and aesthetically significant structures of interaction. In fact, in the absence of bureaucratic institutions and northern demarcations between private and public spaces, Benjamin detects a unique source of anarchic freedom, one that is akin to the subversion of authority enacted in carnival. Integrating art and everyday practice into a homogenous unity, Naples engages architecture in a playful game of cross-references, surprising correspondences, dialogical exchanges, and displacements: "Just as the living room reappears on the street, with chairs, hearth, and altar, so, only much more loudly, the street migrates into the living room" (REF 171; GS 4:314). But this freedom of architectural form and urban life also echoes in the modes and conventions of discourse. According to Benjamin, Italians own a good sense for interrupting dialogues at unexpected moments, not to undercut communication's content and afterlife but, on the contrary, to permit its unfinished hereafter in the first place. As Benjamin writes in a fragment of 1929, suddenly discontinued dialogues follow us like small dogs, whereas the (German) attempt to bring discussion to a final conclusion often leaves us with empty hands: "Discussion as a rhetorical school that does not oblige to anything.[29] The Italian enters into its practices as a return to his true Roman home, the German enters discussion like a warm Gothic room" (GS 6:199).

There is no doubt that the ornamental spaces of the fascist spectacle in Benjamin's later analysis are Gothic indeed. Their affective warmth radiates terror and violence. Unlike Naples's street art, the fascist spectacle suppresses discussion altogether. Far from liberating the senses, the spectacular coordination of private and public spaces in fascism controls the individual's imagination and drowns reason in a vast flood of mechanically reproduced representations that are meant to contain their entire meaning in themselves and, therefore, can do without any explanatory word, productive imagination, or critical reading skill. Massively producing "ritual values" (ILL 241; GS 1:506), fascism undoes the complex structures of modern politics not as a result of too much but rather too little fantasy. The "big parades and monster rallies" (ILL 251; GS 1:506), understood as a utilization of modern mass culture for the sake of propaganda and domesticated entertainment, testify to the fact that fascist leaders hope to discipline affects and regulate their subjects' private imagination. Nazi aesthetics drags utopian desires into a univocal field of representation in the hopes of manipulating emotions and utilizing diverse fears and anxieties. Just as does Naples's urban society, the fascist spectacle exteriorizes life, erasing nineteenth-century boundaries between public and private, personal and collective. In contrast to premodern Naples, however, fascism simulates the preindustrial experience of communal totality by means of advanced tools of mass communication. Whereas Benjamin believed that in Naples the absence of boundaries between interior and exterior spaces, between the aesthetic and everyday life, permitted a kind of anarchic freedom, the Nazi attack on political modernity results in architectures of domination and subordination. It transforms the body into a functional puppet on the public stage, while promising to remake German culture and the nation's body politic. Naples, for Benjamin, subscribes to a public aesthetic of openness and discontinuity, whereas the fascist political artwork grounds in an aesthetic of closure. Naples's porosity neither transfigures nor effaces the omnipresent embodiments of poverty and misery; fascists, on the other hand, organize the masses aesthetically and relocate the categories of identification and catharsis into the public sphere, to entertain their audience and render paucity invisible, but also to suggest equality and the reemergence of new communal harmony, indeed the elevation of *Gemeinschaft* to the level of *Gesellschaft*.

Following Benjamin, then, to introduce aesthetics to politics à la fascism means to invert Marx's famous eleventh thesis on Feuerbach: fascist spectacles aim not at a change of reality, but at one of its perception. Alluding to a premodern identity of public and private, person and community, fascism aspires to mask the disenchanted outlook of administrative apparatuses and regulated modes of behavior in the modern bureaucratic world. The fascist spectacle appeals to populist desires for spontaneity, emotionality, and authenticity, yet only to push "cultural despair"[30] and self-alienation to such a degree that humankind "can experience its own destruction as an aesthetic pleasure of the first order" (ILL 242; GS 1:508). Selecting imagery from nineteenth- and early-twentieth-century inventories of proletarian and bourgeois self-representation, the Third Reich and Mussolini's Italy transform the political arena into a stage on which mythological references blend with the signifiers of modern technology and thus offer symbols that yield broad affective syntheses.

To the intellectual and no doubt romantically inclined tourist Benjamin, Naples's porosity promised a heteroglossic alternative to the ossified and monological structures of bourgeois interiority. Regarding the fascist aestheticization of politics, on the other hand, Benjamin observes a lethal annihilation of the structuring boundaries of modern capitalism, one that however does not touch the principal dynamic of capital. Political spectacles are therefore not simply a mask of violence, but its necessary complement. "All efforts to render politics aesthetic culminate in one thing: war. War and war only can set a goal for mass movements on the largest scale while respecting the traditional property systems" (ILL 241; GS 1:506). War and violence constitute the flipside of the fascist spectacle. Though operating with other means, only imperial warfare can finally uphold the kind of repression that fascism seeks to apply to the modern masses. Understood as the other side of mass killing and violence, the fascist spectacle prettifies domination and assists individuals to adapt themselves to the cause of total mobilization, but at the same time it induces the kind of horror we feel when facing terrifying death masks amid the gaiety of carnival. It is to the carnivalistic proper that we therefore must turn our attention in the next section.

In his celebrated book on Dostoevsky's poetics, Mikhail Bakhtin argues that carnivalistic activities temporarily reverse existing social codes, bonds, and hierarchies. A site of preindustrial popular culture, carnival delimits a niche within the continuum of domination – a niche in which surprising shifts pierce the quotidian order of signification and in which discontinuous displacements and renewals take place. Following Bakhtin's argument, carnival constitutes a ritual festivity that, for a brief moment, interrupts the vectors of history, space, and power. Accordingly, the foremost carnivalistic action consists of the mock crowning and subsequent decrowning of a carnival king, indicative of carnival's *"joyful relativity* of all structure and order, of all authority and all (hierarchical) position."[31] Whenever carnival neutralizes prevalent structures of subordination and allows for a spectacular suspension of the reality principle, Dionysian excess rather than immediate devices of power figure as decisive catalysts for social integration.

Benjamin's diagnosis of fascism understands the fascist spectacle as a perverse appropriation of carnivalistic elements for the sake of the actual preservation of authority. Whereas many critics have embraced Bakhtin's notion of carnival as a popular expression of anarchistic freedom and cultural subversion, Benjamin's account of fascism indicates a more precarious nature of carnivalistic moments in politics. Bakhtin's joyful masquerades, in Benjamin's model, become effective tools of pseudo-emancipation that help increase authoritarian rule. A spatial and temporal niche interrupting the quotidian order, the fascist spectacle emerges as a privileged site for the execution and stabilization of power. Manifesting itself in the big rallies and through symbolic references to national and socialist traditions, the fascist masquerade allegedly neutralizes the existing hierarchy, only to reinscribe its very foundations in the body politic. In well-choreographed public liturgies, individuals experience a joyful relativity of position and partake in delusive images of equality, yet fail to realize that in so doing they are pressed even harder into the patterns of actual subordination and coordination. The fascist spectacle, in other words, utilizes the subversive moment of the popular dimension; it transposes carnival's power of transitory displacement, reversal, and cathartic outlet into a project of synchronization and national renewal. If Bakhtin observed in carnival's annihilation of regular social time and space a source of anarchistic freedom, fascism colonizes the other-timeliness of carnival and subjects it to the continuum of suppression. Instead of yielding brief instances of playful emancipation, fascism turns carnival's subversive power against itself.

Benjamin's familiarity with theories of carnival leads us back to the first decade of the twentieth century. It was not Bakthin's writings, however, but those of Benjamin's friend Florens Christian Rang that provided Benjamin with insights into the social alchemy of carnival. Rang's theory about the agonal origin of Greek tragedy figures as a cornerstone of Benjamin's book on the German *Trauerspiel*;[32] aspects of Rang's *Historical Psychology of Carnival* (1909) seem to reverberate in Benjamin's critique of fascism and its carnivalistic separation of expression and political interest. Similar to Bakhtin, Rang understands the intoxicating effects of carnival as a force of radical negation. As a spatiotemporal niche, carnival permits a Dionysian interruption of normalcy and routinization, a rejuvenating leap into a messianic realm of total presence. Rang describes carnival as "an aspect of the history of religion, the laughter of carnival as the first blasphemy. The frenzy broke out in temporal cycles; the mockery of humanity manifested itself as carnival. As an intoxicated and Babylonian laughter, carnival masked and inverted the world in leap-processions. Through the hole in the calendar of chaos broke the triumphal procession of the drama of exceptionality."[33] Drawing from Nietzsche's *Birth of Tragedy*, Rang highlights the categories of discontinuity and messianic inversion of time as the primal features of carnival. Carnivalistic masquerades decenter fossilized forms of subjectivity and social hierarchy. Not progress but cyclical renewal, not evolution but Dionysian excess, mark the center of Rang's religio-historical construction of carnival.

According to Benjamin's aestheticization thesis, the fascist spectacle organizes and contains the Dionysian energy of carnival in Apollonian ornaments of mass representation. Fascist mass culture domesticates the extraordinariness of carnival and raises its joyful state of exception to a tool of national integration and social individuation. Thus, the fascist spectacle not only levels the messianic content inherent in the Western tradition of carnival, but also transposes carnival's popular mockery of civilization into open terror. Enacted in organized mass parades, the fascist carnivalization of the state is no longer blasphemous, but simply a mask of and a corollary to everyday violence. It petrifies the carnivalistic leap into pure presence and erases carnival's power of temporal and spatial transcendence. To the extent that fascism, through pseudosocialist masquerades, compensates for political rights with mass presentations of expressive action, Dionysian spectacles of rejuvenation serve nothing other than the reproduction of the always same.

In spite of close intellectual ties between Benjamin and Rang, one must be careful when citing Rang's psychology of carnival in order to better understand Benjamin's attacks on the political masquerade of fascism. Whereas Rang's account is grounded in a unique coalition of theology and Nietzschean *Lebensphilosophie*, Benjamin instead takes issue with the twentieth-

century politicization of Nietzsche and his rebellion against Western morality and rationality. It is in particular the vitalistic category of expression that
serves Benjamin to identify the intimate complicity between the fascist
spectacle and ideologies of expressive action as articulated in the wake of
Nietzsche's exploration of the will to power. Although Benjamin never carried his plan through, he intended to write an additional note to his artwork essay on the principle of expression and its reactionary function.[34]
Accordingly, fascism, through its political symbolism, not only aims at
emotive syntheses of the masses, but provides the masses with cultic arenas
of expressive action and immediacy in order to reward submissiveness. Fascism, as Ansgar Hillach has superbly pointed out, politicizes Oswald Spengler's and Ludwig Klages's physiognomical protest against the allegedly
meaningless routines of modern life, thereby translating Nietzsche's philosophy of will, power, and form into political formulas.[35]

Yet, although Benjamin directs his critique at reactionary politicizations
and popularizations of Nietzsche's *Lebensphilosophie*, the aestheticization
thesis at the same time revives a mode of cultural criticism that Nietzsche
himself exercised in his *The Case of Wagner* half a century before. As in Benjamin's analysis of fascism, the category of expression plays a central role in
Nietzsche's polemic against his former idol Wagner. Nietzsche ridicules
Wagner's musical style because, as Nietzsche maintains, it privileges the
theatrical expression of dramatic content over the integrity of the musical
composition. According to Nietzsche, Wagner's musical dramas sacrifice
compositional development for the sake of gestures of persuasion and authority: "Wagner was *not* a musician by instinct. He showed this by aban-
doning all lawfulness and, more precisely, all style in music in order to turn
it into what he required, theatrical rhetoric, a means of expression, of un-
derscoring gestures, of suggestion, of the psychologically picturesque."[36]
Wagner's art is one of calculated seduction. His musical dramas convert "art
into histrionics."[37] A musical magician, Wagner knows only too well how
to address, agitate, and utilize his listener's "overexcited sensibility" and
"weary nerves."[38] Assaulting the listener's perception with an excessive
choreography of sights and sounds, Wagner hopes to obliterate the individual body as a site of desire and autonomous experience. Wagner for
Nietzsche therefore not only rouses powerful affects but at the same time
wants to control all possible effects. "As advocate of the effect," Adorno
would continue Nietzsche's critique half a century later, "the conductor is
the advocate of the public in the work. As the striker of blows, however, the
composer-conductor gives the claims of the public a terrorist emphasis.

Democratic considerateness towards the listener is transformed into connivance with the powers of discipline: in the name of the listener, anyone whose feelings accord with any yardstick other than the beat of the music is silenced."[39] Wagner's compositional imperatives are meant to beat audiences into delightful submission, to engineer the listener's response in the text itself and thereby to erase alternative ways of reception. Wagner's rhetoric of expression, according to both Nietzsche and Adorno, prioritizes the theatrical over the dramatic.[40] His music dramas rely on a closed system of ideas and representations that resolves problems of theme and plot according to predetermined principles while removing essential contradictions by the element of consecration and spectacle. Driven by the desire to orchestrate effects and invoke subordination through expression, Wagner eschews the presentation of conflicts that are irresolvable even if a drama's plot may suggest certain forms of closure.

Similar to Nietzsche's (and Adorno's) attack on Wagner, Benjamin's critique of fascism hopes to throw into relief what is both histrionic and theatrical about the political obsession with expression. Like Nietzsche, Benjamin tries to unveil the complicity between the pathos of expressive action and a political aesthetic of assent and subordination. Accordingly, what culminates in the fascist displacement of political discourse with expressive action reflects the basic hypothesis of ideologies of expressions, claiming that anything particular constitutes a mere symbol of some higher essence or organism. Vitalistic traditions of physiognomy render historical events and cultural institutions expressions of general metaphysical powers; they present diffuse irrational forces as the driving powers of history. In the name of social rejuvenation, the vitalist ideology of expression obliterates difference and autonomy as it invokes the hegemony of the national will: "To conceive of an appearance as symbol means to identify in it the productive life as an unlimited center of power, one which possesses its autonomous metaphysical wisdom; to subject oneself to it as a symbol means to sacrifice one's individuality and concrete will for the sake of a general that proceeds (unrecognized) through history, one to which man may concede with faith alone in order to gain through it the deeper meaning of one's self."[41] The vitalist metaphysics of expression considers human particulars as transitory reflections of some irrational essence. It claims that the meaning of identity and subjectivity transcend the confinements of individuation: only a self-negating leap into the vitalistic deep-grammar of "life" and "soul" may lead toward redemption and self-realization. As a consequence, within the political realm, meaningful activity emerges as a direct function of annihilating any liberal claim for autonomous subjectivity and merging with "other, parallel symbols to a cosmos of political totality."[42]

In his review of Jünger's compilation *Krieg und Krieger*, Benjamin examines how fascist discourse during the 1920s appropriates such vitalist ideologies of expression in order to glorify World War I. Benjamin attacks Jünger and his fellow ideologues of war, not only because they retrospectively strive to justify World War I, thereby undermining the democratic foundations of Weimar Germany. Rather, what is at stake for Benjamin is the attempt to elevate technological warfare to a manifestation of true Germanness. Jünger and his followers render war a display room in which elementary forces emanate from the German will to power. War is destiny. It empowers the soldier to exercise masculine resolution, to reconnect to the eternal wellspring of the German soul. Benjamin, on the other hand, wants to remind his readers of the cynicism inherent in such patterns of legitimation, in particular after the advent of the modern *Materialschlacht*. Accordingly, the technological modernization of warfare in the twentieth century belies any attempt to conceive of war in terms of soldierly virtues. Fascist ideologies of war, in order to counteract the erosion of individual heroism, transpose battle technology into a mythical force, present it "as the highest revelation of existence" (TGF 121; GS 3:239). They describe war theaters as focal sites of modern aesthetic experience and thus deny that war represents a field of social action and human control – however alienated and perverted.

In that Jünger et al. picture the distinctively modern character of World War I as a symbol for the mythic German soul, Benjamin finds, they disavow that humans could ever become masters of their own history and utilize technology for productive common targets rather than destructive ones. "And the point is this: War – the 'eternal' war that they talk about so much here, as well as the most recent one – is said to be the highest manifestation of the German nation. It should be clear that behind their 'eternal' war lies the idea of cultic war, just as behind the most recent war lies that of technological war, and it should also be clear that these authors have had little success in perceiving these relationships" (TGF 122; GS 3:241–42). As they reconstruct battle activities as transient representations of incomprehensible essences, Jünger et al. imbue warfare's modernity with cultic meaning. Accordingly, soldiers march into the warfare of technology and material not simply to gain a victory for their country, but to save their souls, to discover their true identity, and to express their self-annihilating commitment to the national spirit. Fascist authors depict war as a Dionysian festivity of redemption, one that erases the boundaries of bourgeois subjectivity and the social demarcations of liberal rationalism. They celebrate the speed and machinery of modern warfare as a source of aesthetic intoxication preparing for a "wedding with cosmic forces" (GS 4:147), as Benjamin contended in his 1928 *One-Way Street*.

Similar to the carnivalization of the state in the fascist spectacle of the 1930s, then, fascist apologias for World War I compensate for political discourse and rational collective action with calculated constructions of emotional immediacy and expressive action. Modern battle technology emerges as a laboratory for national and racial revival, a phoenixlike rise of a postbourgeois German collective. In particular, Jünger's writings present war as a cosmic spectacle in which individual feelings of alienation consume themselves on a massive scale, in electrifying storms produced by the intoxication with the speed and presumed beauty of battle machines. War revokes traditional boundaries of subjectivity and identity by overwhelming the subject with a plethora of stimuli. A technological sublime par excellence, war reconfigures the feminized bourgeois subject and emplaces him in the transhistorical soil of the German soul. Much more than simply an exposition of national chauvinism, warfare thus rises to a field of existential self-realization and salvation, a mass escape not from but into modern technology and terror, into a popular cult of beauty and violence. This sublimity of war should urge us further to think through the ways in which the fascist spectacle recycles traditions of the beautiful and the sublime on the basis of a fully developed industrial mass culture.

During the eighteenth century, the emerging discipline of aesthetics attributed feelings of terror not to the category of the beautiful but rather to the concept of sublime art. Edmund Burke in his *Philosophy Enquiry into the Origin of Our Ideas of the Sublime and Beautiful* (1757–59) argued for the superiority of sublime sentiments over aesthetic pleasure derived from beautiful appearances. Coupled with subjects such as power, solitude, vast extension, or infinity, sublimity allows for greater sensational intensity than the tame pleasures of beauty, which originate from features such as symmetry, delicacy, smoothness, elegance, and closure. According to Burke, sublime horror constitutes a peculiar psychological balance, a state of the soul in which the individual foresees possible pain and danger and thereby transforms them into objects of intense pleasure. Defined as a condition of fundamental ambiguity, the sublime rests on anticipated danger rather than actual danger. It results from the astonishing insight that pain and danger "are simply terrible, but at certain distances, and with certain modifications, they may be, and they are delightful."[43]

In his *Critique of Judgement*, Immanuel Kant investigated in further detail how and what kind of distance and modification arouse feelings of sublime horror. According to Kant's transcendental rather than psychological definition, sublimity is stimulated in front of objects that reveal to us the limits of our imagination, the restrictions of our inner screens of representation. In contrast to Burke, Kant locates the origin of sublimity not in the object itself, but rather in the individual's sentiment and cognitive apparatus. Whenever we consciously affirm and willfully defy the limitations of our perception and cognition, sublime feelings may be the result. In the context of the late-eighteenth-century cult of sublimity, Kant, however, tried to reserve sublime feelings exclusively for our experience with nature and to expel it from the realm of autonomous art. Highly aware of the proximity of sublime excess and pompous affectation, Kant's aesthetic seemed to anticipate Napoleon's famous remark that it is only one step from the sublime to the ridiculous. Contrary to Burke, Kant, therefore, situated the sublime merely in the antechamber of true art and our disinterested pleasure of beautiful appearance.

If Benjamin diagnoses fascism as politics rendered aesthetic and analyzes the simultaneity of aesthetic form and open violence, beautiful appearance and direct terror, one can hardly avoid questioning the relation between the fascist aesthetics and the traditions of the sublime and the beautiful. Does mass culture in fascism, as seen through the eyes of Benjamin, rearticulate eighteenth-century notions of sublimity? Do Nazi mass rallies challenge the limits of the imagination and thereby transpose feelings of horror into sources of pleasure? Or does the fascist spectacle relocate the bourgeois category of the beautiful appearance to the arena of modern culture so as to superimpose abstract patterns and control on the amorphous forms of modern life, and thus to reduce modern complexity by means of mass geometry?

These questions are no doubt as much theoretical as they are practical ones, and therefore they require thorough historical analyses for them to be answered sufficiently. The formation of proletarianized masses in big rallies, for example, clearly reinvokes the classical aesthetics of symmetry and balance, and hence depicts a politicization of the beautiful appearance. On the other hand, the aestheticization and eroticization of violence – most obviously pursued in Nazi Germany with regard to the elite cadre of state control, the SS – seem to echo Burke's principle of sublimity. Rooted in a calculated "aesthetic of exceptionality,"[44] the cultic representation of the SS implied a transformation of horror and fear into an aesthetic fascination. At first sight, the issue seems to be even further complicated given the theoretical reformulation of the category of sublimity in twentieth-century aesthetic discourse, in particular in the writings of Adorno and François Lyotard. Wolfgang Welsch, in his collection *Ästhetisches Denken*, argues that Adorno's unfinished *Aesthetic Theory* sought to revise Kant's sublime precisely because Kant initially had restricted its scope to human experiences with nature.[45] Accordingly, Adorno rethinks Kant's sublime not merely because it opposes bombastic hypostatizations of the human spirit, but because it implicitly hints at a possible reconciliation between humanity and its suppressed inner and outer nature. In contrast to the totalizing thrust of the beautiful, sublime art interrupts the false totality of art. Sublimity derives from principles such as discontinuity, rupture, and surprise, and reminds us of the limitation of representation and instrumental rationality. In Adorno's late aesthetic theory, sublime art recalls in the recipient the forgotten nature in humanity, the lost human in nature, and therefore it transcends domination, administrative control, and reification. Whereas the beautiful appearance erases plurality for the sake of totalizing syntheses, sublimity preserves the utopian promise of uncensored difference, otherness, and mimetic spontaneity. What is at the core of Adorno's modernist version of the sublime, in other words, is not terror and distance, but rather a future redemption from instrumental reason. Adorno's sublime encodes the desire for a harmonious interplay of humanity and nature, resulting from the recognition of our own boundaries through art.

Whether or not Welsch's reconstruction does full justice to Adorno's *Aesthetic Theory*, the revaluation of the sublime can be essential to our understanding of Benjamin's critique of fascism and its simultaneous practices of seduction and terror. For what Benjamin emphasizes with regard to the fascist spectacle is precisely that to which Adorno's modernist construction of sublime art is opposed. According to Benjamin, the fascist spectacle propagates a totalization of appearance and thus tries to erase all difference, to remake the modern state into an expression of unified and resolute action, and to integrate the masses into a symbolic synthesis. In addition, fascist mass aesthetics also debases the semantic wealth of nature: projecting its reactionary modernism on the features of the modern world, fascism dreams the megalomaniac dream of unlimited reality control and technological domination over nature.

In order to prolong the experience of war into the civilian life of Weimar

Germany, theories of fascism, in an exemplary fashion, subject the category of nature to the imperatives of modern warfare and thus strip nature of its transcending power; that is, its utopian appeal to reconciliation. In these visions of a landscape of total mobilization, the notorious poetic German fascination with nature celebrates an unprecedented, albeit totally perverted reoccurrence:

The pioneers of peace, those sensuous settlers, were evacuated from these landscapes, and as far as anyone could see over the edge of the trench, the surroundings become a problem, every wire entanglement an antimony, every barb a definition, every explosion a synthesis; and by day the sky was the cosmic interior of the steel helmet and at night the moral law above. Etching the landscape with flaming banners and trenches technology wanted to create the heroic features of German Idealism. It went astray. What it considered heroic were the features of Hippocrates, the features of death. Deeply imbued with its own depravity, technology gave shape to the apocalyptic face of nature and reduced nature to silence – even though this technology had the power to give nature its voice. (TGF 126; GS 3:247)

In the aestheticizng view of modern warfare, and under the hallmark of fascism's mythologizing use of technology, nature loses its otherness, its force to generate images out of which humanity may create powerful utopias. Fascist ideologies of war render technology as an aesthetic myth that effaces all boundaries and correspondences between the realm of nature and social life. Contrary to Adorno's construction of the sublime, then, Jünger's art of war declares the boundlessness of the will to power and the human systems of representation. Not the discontinuous, decentering promise of sublimity, but references to the synthesizing force of the beautiful appearance – piped through the tubes of a nationalistic mass culture – are primarily at work in the fascist attack on political modernity, according to Benjamin. Instead of reconciling humanity with the forgotten forces of nature, and instead of preserving the utopian dream of such a reconciliation, fascist theories of war silence nature through aesthetic myths of technological omnipotence. Although the landscapes of total mobilization might suggest some sort of intimacy and reciprocity between technology and nature, humanity and the other at its fringes, they in fact only testify to the utter erosion of nature under the false totality of fascism's aesthetic excess.

For Benjamin, as for Adorno, legitimate modernist art cannot be anything but an art of discontinuity, rupture, and self-limitation. Whether referring to the aesthetic modernism of Charles Baudelaire, Franz Kafka, and Bertolt Brecht, the functionalistic appropriation of art in the Soviet Union during the 1920s, or any progressive utilization of the new medium, film, Benjamin valorizes modern aesthetic practices whenever they succeed in subverting traditional claims to continuity, totality, and closure. Allegorical fragmentation and instability rather than metaphorical harmony establish the modes of address and aesthetic exchange that Benjamin believes emancipatory according to his leftist political agenda. The fascist aestheticization of politics, on the other hand, relies on a bewitching hypostatization of appearance and the beautiful, one that eliminates social tensions, polyphony, and difference in bogus imagery of equality and coherence. Reformulating eighteenth- and nineteenth-century aesthetic concepts within the terrain of industrial culture, the fascist spectacle corrupts nature and utopian wish-energies and, thereby, also obliterates the foundations of sober judgment and moral autonomy. Fascism renders the beautiful appearance and social masquerade a practical expression of the will to power and, thus, drives society into the "abyss of aestheticism" (OTD 103; GS 1:281).

It has become commonplace to speak of this reckless will to beauty and beautification as a grand exercise in kitsch. Fascism is bad style, so the argument goes. It quotes the language of high art out of context, driven by an uncompromising will to art, an eclectic, intrinsically styleless, and hence hyperbolic *Kunstwollen*. Benjamin's aestheticization thesis urges us to think of this argument in more complex terms and not to sever the question of kitsch from the dialectics of modern culture. Kitsch, the artwork essay and some of Benjamin's earlier studies suggest, wants to trigger high-cultural effects by means of a mass-cultural apparatus, and therefore it remains badly understood if simply theorized in the concepts of aesthetic theory or the history of artistic styles.[46] Kitsch signifies a false reconciliation between bourgeois aesthetics and postautonomous art, between high and popular culture. It masquerades industrial mass culture as folk art and endows it with the cultural capital of aesthetic refinement. A forced fabrication of authenticity and spontaneity, the fascist spectacle therefore is kitsch not because of its stylistic overdetermination but because it gives modern culture the appearance of a vibrant and unified aesthetic folk culture. Circulating standardized and prefabricated meanings, the fascist spectacle enlists kitsch so as to enforce emotional identification and assure political conformity. Nazi kitsch, by tapping the masses'legitimate dreams of a better life, serves the purpose of political and cultural homogenization. It simultaneously evokes and channels the charismatic hopes of the masses into organized displays of expressive action, spectacles that merely feign movement and participation, that merely simulate utopia. What looks like a sublime Wagnerian total work of art and seems to reconstruct emotional spontaneity, in truth only produces a ruthless unity of high and low on the basis of industrial culture, numbing whatever comes close to any authentic sentiment.

And yet, in spite of all its kitsch, the fascist spectacle is deeply entrenched in an existentialist attack on mediocracy and everydayness – on all forms of regulated political normalcy. It continues the Weimar revolt against liberal democracy as an inauthentic rule of bourgeois reason and modesty, and – like Weimar's political existentialism[47] – it is characterized by a dazzling fascination with boundary situations. It is the exception of the spectacle rather than the norm that decides over the value of political institutions and interventions. Spectacular existentialism conceives of the political as a clearing at which the action of great and resolved individuals is expressed. Situated beyond norms and principles, beyond good and evil, the spectacle is meant to delimit the quintessential locus of intensive life. It offers the ultimate space where authenticity comes into being and explodes the allegedly banal routines of modern parliamentarism and bureaucratic politics.

Fascism reinscribes the elitist vocabulary of Weimar's political existentialism in the domesticated scenes of the popular. Like Weimar intellectuals of the extreme Right, fascism collapses morality and legality, intention and action, into a ruthless unity. To aestheticize politics, to allow for popular expressions but no rights, does not simply mean to reduce political legitimation to a matter of form, beauty, and gesture. Instead, fascist aestheticization severs political action from any moral signifier; it sanctifies Great Politics and expressive participation as a value in and of itself. Declarations of formal commitment and belonging, of resolution, therefore displace public debates over norms and contents. "We are not," Alfred Baeumler argued, "contemplative human beings who become guilty through activity and struggle, but we are active, action-oriented human beings, and we become guilty only insofar as we neglect our essence through neutrality and tolerance."[48] Moving the political beyond the liberal-rational codes of legality and morality, the fascist spectacle recasts Baeumler's existential will to action and struggle as a category of popular identification. The spectacle is the site at which the postbourgeois subject can commit himself to the course of the movement and thus experiences absolution from any moral guilt.

In pursuing the autonomy of the political, fascism's spectacular existentialism wants to undo some of the key distinctions that matter for the emergence of the modern state and its legal institutions. The spectacle presents the law as a direct expression of power, a vitalistic presence independent from constitutional procedures or normative debates. Aesthetic politics transposes legal discourse into a voluntary articulation of pure decision and pseudodemocratic acclamation. Situated beyond conventions and legal norms, the spectacle valorizes Nietzschean self-assertions of the will over liberal-bourgeois negotiations of norms, values, means, and ends. The fascist spectacle opens a space in which action no longer means, as Baeumler put it, "'deciding in favor of' . . . for that presupposes that one knows in favor of what one is deciding; rather, action [here] means 'setting off in a direction,' 'taking sides,' by virtue of a mandate of destiny, by virtue of 'one's own right.'"[49]

Political modernity, Benjamin had argued in "Critique of Violence" (1920/21), rests on the institutional separation of lawmaking and law-preserving violence.[50] Accordingly, police violence remains excluded from this crucial process of differentiation: the police force operates in the shadow of the law, often endorsing a peculiar mixture of lawmaking and law-preserving measures.[51] Whether or not we agree with Benjamin's rather peculiar positioning of police violence, it poignantly illuminates his later analysis of fascism. The fascist spectacle no longer distinguishes between lawgiving and law-preserving violence. Relying on a public choreography of exceptionality, fascist politics *is* police politics. It dissolves the peculiarly modern difference between the making of the law and its peculiar execution, between legality and power. Fascist aestheticization implies that the legitimacy of legal institutions derives from the spectacular state of exception. Neither the formality of legal procedures nor the idea of a rational consensus of all citizens may endow law or ruler with legitimation. Thus, the fascist spectacle dispenses with the concept of right altogether. Formal expressions of commitment replace the function performed by rights in a bourgeois democracy.

Benjamin's aestheticization thesis considers this spectacular existentialism of fascism as dual; it is a manipulation of human perception and sentience, and it is an expulsion of spirit and reason from the arenas of political interaction. According to the logic of politics turned spectacular, individuals find redemption from cultural despair whenever they transform themselves into mechanical puppets: fascism equates salvation with the act of subordination. Annihilating the boundaries of the bourgeois subject, fascism reconstitutes subjectivity in the ornamental movements of the masses, movements that are performed in front of the eyes of a charismatic leader. Under the spell of the mass spectacle, the individual surrenders body and reason to the vitalistic logic of the national will. Fascism wants its subjects to believe that Lang's mute Nibelungen soldiers, void of body and mind while standing in the Rhine to build a bridge for their leaders, are completely happy people.

As if contemplating this coming fatal attraction, Benjamin had already in 1920 defined such a simultaneous loss of body and spirit, of sentience and reason, as the root of all horror.[52] The experience of horror, he argued, mutes the subject; it freezes the limbs, paralyzes the body as a receptacle of personal experience, and transforms it into a foreign, exterior object: "[W]ith the depotentialization of the body in the state of horror the counterpole of speech disappears, too, not only the acoustical but language in the broadest meaning of the word, as expression, whose very possibility – as seen from the state of horror – appears as an incomprehensible mercy, whose habit appears as a somnambulic walk on a tight rope" (GS 6:77). What the masses experience in the fascist spectacle as a popular and carnivalistic restoration of emotional authenticity and folk art, in truth only expropriates their own bodies as a unique source of symbolic representation and individual experience. Fascism drives its public exercise of expressive action to such an extreme that it wants to leave human shells devoid of sentiments, devoid of speech, devoid of content. The spectacles of fascist mass culture remake the individual mind and body through prefabricated meanings and standardized experiences that offer something for everyone. A politically inflected version of the culture industry, the fascist spectacle engenders individuals whose critical minds become paralyzed in their own bodies; it casts unlimited horror over the expropriated body politic. In a state of utter self-alienation, Hitler's subjects render their "own destruction as an aesthetic pleasure of the first order" (ILL 242; GS 1:508). What remains in fascism's dark and muted construction of popular culture from above, therefore, is nothing other than silence. And the horror. The Horror.

3

AESTHETIC DICTATORSHIP

One of the most astute analysts of the modern condition, Max Weber understood the rise of bureaucratic institutions and the increasing dissolution of the state into a multiplicity of independent and often bureaucratically structured centers of state-like domination as one hallmark of modernization. Modernity, he argued, disperses power into the hands of a plethora of autonomous, self-organizing power holders that compete with more genuine political institutions such as parliaments or governments. In the eyes of the conservative revolutionaries of the interwar years and the ideologues of the Nazi movement, this peculiarly modern multiplication of power and domination was inadmissible. They strongly opposed the refraction of the state into competing apparatuses of domination. In the view of the extreme Right, the modern state simply represented an effeminate container for a number of disparate and nonpolitical activities, a site that effaced the existential dimension of the political. If politics should once again become Great Politics, it was necessary to recenter the state and emancipate it from the heteronomy of economic, administrative, social, or cultural imperatives. Carl Schmitt's definition of the political in terms of pure friend-foe relations is perhaps the most famous example of how interwar intellectuals sought to reinstate the autonomy of the political and restore the state as the core of all power.

It is no longer a secret that, once in place, the Nazi state did not live up to the political ideals of its own ideologues. Though omnipresent in the sense that Nazi organizations penetrated most aspects of public and private life, the Nazi state entailed an enormous number of competing institutions, conflicting associations, and quasi-Weberian subcenters of bureaucratic domination. As Michael Geyer argues: "National Socialist rule did not create a neat division of labor among bureaucracies, but furthered a burgeoning system of bureaucratic domination composed of shapeless and ill-defined institutions. . . . Centralization of power in a contradictory process on the one hand and extreme dilution of domination into a seemingly endless series of partial state-like organizations on the other hand is the major paradox of the Third Reich."[1] Unwilling to admit its own paradoxes and self-contradictions, Nazi Germany recast politics as the art of maintaining distance between competing agencies of domination. It hoped to recenter the state by personalizing politics and making the head of state, Adolf Hitler, into a charismatic judge whose role consisted in ruling out possible struggles between diffuse centers of power. The closer the Third Reich approached war, the more it presented Hitler as occupying "the nodal points between the partial fields of power, defining ever more precisely what the conditions for domination were and how they were to be achieved."[2] The drive toward war in fact was viewed as an important means to keep the Third Reich's organizational jungle in check. War promised to give politics at least the appearance of unified and resolute action. Combat, military leadership, and imperial exploitation seemed to imply the possibility of satisfying the desire for a recentered state and a rebirth of autonomous politics.

Meanwhile, however, during the years preceding the war, the task of the cultural sector was, among others, to proliferate a sense for the resurgence of Great Politics and the autonomy of the political. The Nazi spectacle offered sights and sounds that diverted from the multiplication of hierarchies and fields of power in the Third Reich. It defined and circulated popular expressions that sanctified the Nazi state as unified and homogenous. In order to maintain the appearance of unbridled political resolution, Nazi rhetoric continuously professed the identity of artistic creativity and political action, the artist's ability to shape clay and the political call to unify the masses in the mold of a resolute state. Though written prior to the Nazi takeover, Joseph Goebbels's novel *Michael* (1929) still provides us with one of the most instructive examples of this ideological trope.

In various passages, Goebbels's semiautobiographical protagonist Michael insists on a fundamental nexus between art and political activity.[3] He even maintains that political leadership is the most distinguished of all aesthetic practices. It is in the realm of political action that men's formative energies accomplish their most impressive results. Resolute leaders, Michael contends, draw from exceptional resources of symbolic expressivity, and thus they simultaneously refine and explode the primary impulse that is at work in any individual artistic activity. Through aesthetic genius, artists express their emotional sensibility; through skillful techniques of domination, politicians generate the forms of public life, order, harmony, and, hence, legitimation: "Art is an expression of feeling. The artist differs from the non-artist in his ability to express what he feels. In some form or other. One artist does it in painting, another in clay, a third in words, and a forth in marble – or even in historical forms. The statesman is also an artist. For him, the nation is exactly what the stone is for the sculptor. Führer and masses, that is as little of a problem as, say, painter and color."[4] For Michael, art materializes whenever gifted individuals inflict symbolic order on the messy appearance of the world. Art expresses the will to form and control, and thus the will to power. While artworks proper depend on the triumph of the artist's will over nature, political legitimation derives from the ability of a strong leader to forge his subjects into the symbolic closure of the state; that is, into "folkhood that has taken form."[5] Goebbels's poetics of leadership thus defines political sovereignty as the ability to model the passions of the people. Sovereign is he who through symbolic spectacles provides best for aesthetic identification, emotional synthesis, and enchanted subordination.

Chapter 2 of *Walter Benjamin and the Aesthetics of Power* analyzed Benjamin's discussion of fascism as a political configuration that domesticates the institutions of modern culture so as to diffuse unrest and engender conformity. Accordingly, the fascist spectacle fuses high and low in a ruthless unity, carnivalizes the state, and circulates kitsch in the hopes of deflecting any comprehension of the political as a nonmetaphysical space in which we may contest the ideas, values, and institutions that organize and ought to organize intersubjective exchange in a modern society. For Benjamin, the beautification of politics in fascism is not simply a traditional form of ideology, an instance of necessary false consciousness. Rather, aesthetic politics transfigures given structures of power through strategic appeals to sense perception, through an affective rhetoric of immediacy and total presence. Though phantasmagorical in nature, the fascist spectacle does not simply reflect ideological misconstructions or mental misperceptions of reality, but a plastic coagulation of aesthetic myths, utopian dreams, and regressive fantasies. Following Benjamin's aestheticization thesis, the transposition of cultic elements into the public sphere in fascism therefore surpasses what traditional Marxism has constructed as the workings of ideology precisely because the fascist spectacle aspires to remove discourse from the arena of politics altogether and exchange it for enactments of powerful leadership, subordination, and communal renewal.

If the preceding chapter sketched the ways in which the fascist spectacle manipulates minds and emotions so as to bar the masses from sober political judgments, chapter 3, by way of contrast, brings into view what can be seen as Benjamin's attack on the pragmatic fallacy of fascism: the transfiguration of political leadership through the image of aesthetic creativity as suggested in Goebbels's above-mentioned novel of the 1920s, the legitimation of power and technology through references to their formative energies, the presentation of political action as the culmination of artistic originality. In his attempt to theorize the political aestheticism of fascism, however, Benjamin is not simply interested in reversing Goebbels's line of argumentation, reinstating principles such as expressivity and originality and reclaiming the secluded sphere of the aesthetic proper. As already indicated, Benjamin believes that both inner and outer aesthetic developments have undone the basis for autonomous art, and consequently he no longer situates his own critical venture within the realm of aesthetic theory. For Benjamin, the aestheticization of politics is less about the blurring of transcendental boundaries between art and the political, and more about fascism's recourse to past aesthetic notions in order to give political action the appearance of autonomy and unity. Therefore, what is primarily at stake for Benjamin is exposure of the invasion of older aesthetic concepts into the modern political arena: the justification of bad politics through bad art, the amalgamation of technological modernity and aesthetic backwardness. Seen through the lenses of Benjamin's aestheticization thesis, Goebbels's fusion of aesthetic genius and modern statesmanship both supports a dubious political project and preserves aesthetic principles that have lost their universal validity in the age of mechanical reproduction. As a result, Benjamin urges us to "brush aside a number of outmoded concepts, such as creativity and genius, eternal value and mystery – concepts whose uncontrolled (and at present almost uncontrollable) application would lead to a processing of data in the fascist sense" (ILL 218; GS 1:473). It is Benjamin's analysis of these concepts, as well their fatal processing in the attempt to reinvent Great Politics, to which we turn in this chapter.

Deeply steeped in the very aesthetic tradition that the artwork essay will later revoke, Benjamin's early essay on Goethe's *Elective Affinities* – written between 1919 and 1922 – introduces a conceptual triad that proves fruitful in order to better understand the role of "outmoded concepts" in the fascist spectacle. The purpose of this triad is to distinguish between three different modes of production – between the forces of creation, formation, and conjuration. Working through each of these three concepts, Benjamin wants to discriminate incompatible forms of action and delimit quasi-autonomous spheres of knowledge and ethical responsibility. Following Benjamin's matrix, creation is located in the sphere of life proper and "brings forth a world from nothingness" (SW 1:340; GS 1:180). Formative energies, on the other hand, erupt in what Benjamin at the time considered the actual universe of autonomous art. In contrast to the power of creation, formation does not start with nothingness, but rather with what Benjamin calls chaos: the unshaped and, hence, meaningless world that is always already there. Conjuration, finally, signifies modes of production that pursue bewitching fusions of creative and formative enterprises, presenting life as art and art as life.

By means of their aesthetic genius and power of formation, artists endow the chaos of the given world with form without ever penetrating its material structure, without making "anything out of this chaos" (SW 1:340; GS 1:180). Formative energies halt the entropy of life and convert chaos into meaningful appearance. The artist's task lies in shaping the meaningless chaos within the boundaries of the aesthetic, transforming it into beautiful appearance. Whereas creation initiates a new temporal and spatial continuity, formation interrupts the flow of time and the metamorphoses of space. Conjuration, by contrast, intends a "negative counterpart to creation" (SW 1:340; GS 1:180), without ever becoming a truly artistic activity. Akin to the force of creation, conjuration claims that it can bring forth a world out of nothing. In truth, however, it only devises a mirage, a phantasmagoria. In opposition to the aestheticist tradition, Benjamin's early aesthetic theory emphasizes the absolute gap between the world of magic and the beautiful appearance of art. While the forces of creation operate in the sphere of life, and formation denotes the impulse to engender art, conjuration tries to collapse both activities into a false synthesis. Employing artistic tricks, the conjurer presents something dead as living. In order to create a simulacrum, to fake life, he utilizes aesthetic means. Conjuration violates, therefore, both activities: it violates the ethics of origin and continuity inherent to creation, and it violates the laws of appearance and interruption that govern the practices of formation.

True works of art, Benjamin argues in his early essay, leap out of the continuum of history, redeeming reality through aesthetic appearance. We would misunderstand the nature of aesthetic creativity if we drew from biological imagery, from the language of organic evolution or incremental growth, to describe its process. Although the creation of great works of art has often been described in likeness to the birth of a human being, this image, Benjamin insists in a *Denkbild* written around 1930, is a dialectical one. It must bring into focus the process of aesthetic formation from two different angles:

One [angle] deals with the creative conception and concerns the feminine in the artist. This femininity exhausts itself with the completion. It gives birth to the work, but then it dies off. What dies in the master with the completed creation is that part in him in which he conceived the creation. Yet this completion of the work – and this leads us to the second aspect of the process – is nothing dead. . . . It takes place inside the work itself. And here, too, we are talking about a birth. The creation, in its state of completion, gives new birth to the creator. Not to his femininity, in which it was conceived, but rather to his male element. Newly inspired, he outdoes nature. . . . He is the male first born of the work that he had once conceived. (GS 4:438)

It is difficult simply to ignore the highly problematic construction of gender difference built into this thought image.[6] Benjamin invokes rather stereotypical gender markers, the binary pairs of passivity and activity, conception and creation, nature and civilization, to describe the coming into being of authentic artworks. Moreover, he also celebrates aesthetic perfection as the triumph of male formation over the merely receptive feminine forces of nature. In order to be reborn and to enter the heavens of true genius, the artist must overcome femininity: woman must die so that art may live.

In spite of this essentializing figuration of femininity, however, Benjamin's thought image provides some useful insights into his early aesthetic theory. This short text not only sheds additional light on the triad of creation, formation, and conjuration, but also helps us understand what is so dangerous about fascism's recycling of aesthetic notions on the grounds of a postautonomous art and mass culture. According to the *Denkbild*, art proper displaces nature and proliferates meaning through form. It also gives birth to new identities, reshaping the self of the artist against the background of the chaos of life. As it disrupts the flow of time and the continuity of space, art reconstitutes identities from its privileged location in the realm of the beautiful, albeit mere appearance. Conjuration, by contrast, simply masks the established laws of identity formation by merging life and art, creation and formation, appearance and essence. Because it lacks the power of interruption, conjuration stakes out a universe of appearances within, not outside, the given continuum. Although he promises to reverse the structures of everyday life, the conjurer in truth only reinforces the order of the day. In opposition to the aesthetic genius, the conjurer presents art as nature and therefore fails to produce the kind of works out of which one may emerge with a new identity. Situated in a separate realm, aesthetic formation requires numerous steps of mediation to resonate in life. Conjuration, on the other hand, corrupts life insofar as it pretends to form it like an artist sculpts clay in the studio. Instead of rupture and discontinuity, comprehensive identification and immanence mark the spectacles of conjuration.

With this in mind, one is tempted to describe the fascist cult of beauty as transgressively taking recourse to the principle of aesthetic formation under the conditions of a postaesthetic culture. As we have seen in the passage from Goebbels's *Michael*, fascism presents political action transfigured through the image of aesthetic production. It appeals to the masses' charismatic hopes and their diffuse desire for political change by presenting political action solely as the skill of forming social chaos, overcoming incoherence, and thus offering new structures of identification and communal fraternization. To halt the bureaucratic differentiation of life and the multiplication of power centers in modernity, fascism invokes the pathos of aesthetic creativity and original conception. Instead of negotiating means and ends, instead of engaging in procedural politics, fascism wants to apply the aesthetic principle of formation directly to the sphere of public and private life. The tropes of nineteenth-century genius aesthetics are meant to give a differentiated apparatus of domination the look of unified and resolute action.

Benjamin's early metaphysics would denounce such an attempt to collapse art and life as a perversion of both spheres – as conjuration. Read in light of this earlier attempt to define the specificity of art, the fascist spectacle undercuts the principles of discontinuity inherent in the act of aesthetic formation: what dominates the politics of the spectacle is not the category of rupture but the conjurer's desire for closure and temporal continuity. As it imposes aesthetic forms directly on the procedures of political communication, fascism blurs the boundaries between appearance and life, thus reproducing the conjurer's exercise in phantasmagorical illusion. Conjurers bewitch the minds of their audiences and betray through phantoms the redemptive hopes of the people. Benjamin's postaesthetic theory of the 1930s will radicalize these insights as Benjamin now no longer sees formation as a critical counterforce to conjuration. Given the changes in modern culture brought about by the latest turns of mechanical reproducibility,

Benjamin's artwork essay in fact claims that any appeal to the principle of formation – whether in politics or in art – has become potentially complicit with conjuration. Couching political action in the dated vocabulary of bourgeois art, the fascist spectacle is simply the apex of what may happen if postauratic culture reinvokes the principle of auratic art – if it infuses the modern popular dimension with the language of what used to be high art. Anachronistic on two accounts at once, the political spectacle of the twentieth century therefore engages in both formation and conjuration alike. Directing the people as bourgeois art directed the movements on a theater stage, fascism "with its *Führer* cult, forces [the masses] to their knees" (IL L241; GS I:506).

In his 1977 essay *Speed and Politics*, Paul Virilio argues that the accelerated experience of the passing of time has become the modern world's destiny and destination, and therefore that the control over social speed and movement has developed into the main resource of power.[7] Virilio contends that modernity perceives stasis as death; therefore, modern political systems must unleash a gradual acceleration of speed to safeguard their stability. Warfare is one of several possible outcomes of this hastening of social mobility because modern combat technologies satisfy the desire for speed in an unprecedented fashion.

At first sight, Benjamin's construction of fascism as a seductive regime of conjuration seems to argue in a very similar direction. First, Benjamin emphasizes that the regulation of movement and time constitutes one of the main pillars of fascist domination. In fact, what one may call the pathos of aesthetic rulership – the pragmatic fallacy of fascism – is just another word for the endeavor to channel formative energies into the scenarios of public life and thereby gain control over the speed of transport, public motion, and communication. Second, Benjamin observes that the acceleration of speed endows modern representations of the masses *eo ipso* with pleasurable qualities: "Mass movements, including war," he argues, "constitute a form of human behavior which particularly favors mechanical reproduction" (ILL 251; GS I:506). In essence, however, Benjamin's theory implicitly rejects Virilio's simple opposition of speed and stasis, showing that the organization of social speed in fascism aims at warfare – and, hence, the stasis of death – already from the outset. Fascism conjures the acceleration of social forms as phantasmagoria to disguise the government of death and stasis at which it ultimately aims. If fascism – like Goebbels's protagonist Michael – equates the political realm with the sphere of genius art, it calls for an acceleration of life only to put to death, to freeze impoverished individuals in the Procrustean bed of stasis.

To undermine this deadly aestheticism of fascism, Benjamin formulates a postaesthetic theory of production and experience that no longer subscribes to the bourgeois aesthetics of genius, empathy, identification, and eternity – that is, to the old aesthetic dream of almighty control, symbolic closure, and exclusion of chance and surprise. Undoing the very ground that allowed Goebbels's *Michael* to apply aesthetic categories to political action, Benjamin advocates postbourgeois concepts of rupture, openness, and collective authorship or reception. According to Benjamin, this new postaesthetic art crystallizes in three different arenas: in the gestural poetics of Brecht, in Paul Valéry's aesthetics of disenchantment, and in the Eisensteinian cinema of montage and noncontemplative reception. Each in his own way and with his own means, Brecht, Valéry, and Eisenstein not only protect their work from any compliance with the political projects of fascism, but in doing so subvert the basis of what Benjamin calls the aestheticization of politics. Whereas the fascist spectacle resorts to the bourgeois "cult of authenticity"[8] so as to claim the existentialist dimension of the political, the modernist projects of Brecht, Valéry, and Eisenstein hope to emancipate their audiences from aesthetic contemplation and identification. To the extent that they experiment with postauratic strategies of interruption, these modernists remind their spectators of the fact that modern culture erases the difference between formation and conjuration, and hence that any undialectical application of the principles of bourgeois art to the spheres of postautonomous industrial culture may result in a world radiating disaster triumphant.

As early as 1935/36 Benjamin had no doubt that the aim of aesthetic politics was warfare. The fascist spectacle is not only supposed to reconcile a deeply shattered society but to mobilize its subjects for imperial war. Fascism renders politics aesthetic so as to gloss over systemic crises that may be controlled only through the production of unproductive goods; that is, war technologies. War offers an outlet for the tensions between technological modernity and the denial of political emancipation. Refocusing the activities of various power holders toward one common target, war solves the endemic predicaments of fascism's reactionary modernism – its radical valorization of technological and economic over political modernization. War is Great Politics par excellence. It shows the political at the height of its formative aspirations.

Benjamin reads this compensatory drive toward war as a sign for political immaturity. In a somewhat astounding move, he fails to discuss in further detail the cultural and spiritual mission fascist ideologues often assigned to the implementation of nonwar technologies – the Autobahn, the Volkswagen, the Italian clearing of the marshes – and instead claims that fascism focuses its technological imagination exclusively on instruments of destruction. Alluding to the standard Marxist argument about the dialectical relationship between productive forces and their social organization, Benjamin contends that war exhausts existing technological possibilities in an unnatural, artificial way. As a matter of fact, Benjamin understands war as the most extreme means of containing the development of productive forces within a given property structure. War and its aestheticization deflect artificially the dialectical course of history: "If the natural utilization of productive forces is impeded by the property system, the increase in technical devices, in speed, and in the sources of energy will press for an unnatural utilization, and this is found in war. The destructiveness of war furnishes proof that society has not been mature enough to incorporate technology as its organ, that technology has not been sufficiently developed to cope with the elemental forces of society" (ILL 242; GS 1:507). According to Benjamin, warfare represents a giant spectacle of displacement. Instead of transforming technology into a tool that could satisfy material needs, fascism accelerates social speed through technology only to aim at a catastrophic explosion of the suspended tensions in war. Just as aesthetics and the domesticated scenes of mass culture are supposed to displace rational political communication, war substitutes for any collective appropriation of technology and, thus, reinforces the existing property structure. Consummating the aesthetic ideology of formation, only warfare can organize the masses in such a way that they are inhibited from any strike against the given distribution of wealth. Instead of "dropping seeds from airplanes" and thus improving the quality of life, fascism "drops incendiary bombs over cities" (ILL 242; GS 1:508).

But the fascist war not only violates nature, it also represses technology itself as it enslaves its own full potential. Warfare epitomizes the systematic castigation of nature and technology in a modern age that fails to live up to its potential. Any future war, Benjamin contends as early as 1930, will therefore also describe a "slave revolt of technology" (TGF 120; GS 3:238), a revolt of modern technology against its bondage through reactionary politics and the suspension of historical dialectics. Yet with cunning, fascism anticipates such counterforces of revenge and directs them against the other objects of repression, the masses, rather than the actual agents of slavery. Analogous to what motivates the public spectacles of pseudo-emancipation, fascist warfare instrumentalizes the powers of revolt only in order to quell their potency. Through war, the fascist state stages an insurrection against itself in order to gain control over all potential forces of subversion: "The horrible features of imperialistic warfare are attributable to the discrepancy between the tremendous means of production and their inadequate utilization in the process of production – in other words, to unemployment and the lack of markets. Imperialistic war is a rebellion of technology which collects, in the form of 'human material,' the claims to which society has denied its natural material" (ILL 242; GS 1:507–8). Presenting war as a self-referential event demanding veneration, submission, and ritual sacrifice, fascism exempts technology from any processes of discursive legitimation.

In his essay on Ernst Jünger et al., Benjamin borrows the concept of "das Geistige" from his own early metaphysical vocabulary to describe this repression of discourse.[9] Capitalist societies, he argues, appropriate the Cartesian split between spirit and materiality so as to bar any critical debate about the use of technology and the equality of progress. "Indeed, according to its economic nature, bourgeois society cannot help insulating everything technological from the so-called spiritual, and it cannot help but resolutely excluding technology's right of co-determination in the social order" (TGF 120; GS 3:238). Fascism's ideology of war perfects this tendency. Just as the stage management of politics replaces rational participation with emotional synchronization, fascist theories of warfare immunize technological modernity against democratic discourses of legitimation and emphasize the ontological abyss between the universe of ideas and the world of technical means. To reject any legitimacy claim, fascism claims that technology does not serve any human purpose. Shaped by great politicians as are statues out of clay, war serves only itself. Technological progress, fascist ideologues of war argue, adheres to an autonomous logic of evolution and renewal, one to which society ought to respond with astonishment rather than critical discussion.

Benjamin quickly denounces what he understands as the cultic legitimation of warfare in fascism as "an uninhibited translation of the principles of *l'art pour l'art* to war itself" (TGF 122; GS 3:240). This figure of thought, though highly intriguing and influential, no doubt requires further explanation. Against the background of comprehensive social changes during the nineteenth century, the *l'art pour l'art* movement articulated the most radical response to the gradual commercialization and decentering of nineteenth-century art – that is to say, the expulsion of the aesthetic from the heavens of uncontested meaning and the exile of artists from the Olympus of social representation.[10] Though anything but unified, European aestheticism sought to redefine this social decline of art as its inner virtue, calling for a total emancipation of art from moral commitment and mimetic veracity. Poised at the threshold of the twentieth century, aestheticism desired, at least theoretically, to transform art into a self-referential system. It conceived of form as the sole content of the artwork and revolted against any attempt to render moral correctness a principle of aesthetic judgment. Aiming at a "theology of art" (ILL 224; GS 1:481), *l'art pour l'art* epitomized the romantic quest for aesthetic absolutes. While it rejected the subjugation of art under the bourgeois principle of utility, aestheticism tried to enshrine art in a hermetic cage.[11] Vis-à-vis the ever expanding commodification of art and the emergence of mass cultural practices, aestheticism believed it could secure the autonomy of art within bourgeois society by transforming the work of art into an object of cultic stature, a luxury object.[12]

In a sense, *l'art pour l'art* no longer locates the source of art's beauty in its actual objects, or *sujets*. Dismissing the classical aesthetics of mimetic authenticity, aestheticism defines the beautiful exclusively in terms of the utilization of available means of formation. In the prologue of his novel *Dorian Gray* (1891), Oscar Wilde has phrased this aestheticist attack on principles of mimetic veracity, moral uplift, and pedagogical utility with great lucidity, even though the plot of his book clearly violates the foreword's programmatic immorality: "The artist is the creator of beautiful things. . . . There is no such thing as a moral or an immoral book. Books are well written, or badly written. That is all. . . . All art is quite useless."[13] Art is no longer supposed to hold up a mirror to reality, let alone contribute to any Schillerian project of aesthetic education. On the contrary, aestheticism considers reality highly inferior to the closed universe of art. To the aestheticist artist, reality is of interest only when reduced to a discount store of impulses in which the aesthete may go shopping to incite his or her inner aesthetic excitement. Aestheticism understands reality as a pool of possible stimulation, not a world in which we can really live, not a world we can shape.

European aestheticism sought to uncouple aesthetic creativity from any moral responsibility. Making form and artistic technique the artwork's sole content, it wanted art to become a miracle again. It is at this point that we can see the rationale behind Benjamin's sweeping comparison of aestheticism and fascist war technology, although Benjamin's unconfronted slippage between artistic technique and technology – rightly criticized by Adorno as undialectical[14] – seems to limit the comparison's explanatory power. Both the aestheticist theology of art and the fascist theology of war claim that their respective objects of fascination – art and war – contain their meaning entirely in themselves. Similar to the way in which turn-of-the-century aestheticism considers artistic techniques free of any moral, political, or social contents, fascism insulates modern technology against any possibility of rational justification or critique. It glorifies war as a vitalistic spectacle of national rebirth, yet in order to do so it presents war's means of destruction as autonomous forces that rage according to their own will and logic. Just as Wilde insisted on the utter uselessness of the artwork and the moral indifference of aesthetic forms, the fascist ideologues of war depict war's advanced technologies of mass destruction not in terms of their effectiveness but rather of their beauty. War is not supposed to be useful; it is first and foremost supposed to be beautiful. And *beautiful* in turn is defined as that which has no function, that which serves no purpose.

Benjamin's analysis of the fascist ideology of war is intriguing, but it also strikes the reader as highly partial. Clearly, fascist ideologues did speak of war not solely in aesthetic terms. They relied on geopolitical arguments concerning the expansion of *Lebensraum* and the need to regain past imperial glory. They propagated war in order to conquer natural resources, capture slave labor, and carry out their anti-Semitic agendas on a global scale. That Benjamin in his critique exclusively focuses on the aestheticizing tropes of fascist war ideologues largely results from the fact that his main witnesses are aesthetically minded intellectuals to begin with, in particular the Italian futurists. To illustrate what he considers the fatal attraction between fascism and aestheticism, Benjamin cites, for instance, in the artwork essay, a futurist manifesto by Filippo Marinetti on the Ethiopian colonial war (1935–36)[15]:

War is beautiful because it establishes man's dominion over the subjugated machinery by means of gas masks, terrifying megaphones, flame throwers, and small tanks. War is beautiful because it initiates the dreamed-of metalization of the human body. War is beautiful because it enriches a flowering meadow with the fiery orchids of machine guns. War is beautiful because it combines the gunfire, the cannonades, the cease-fire, the scents, and the stench of putrefaction into a symphony. War is beautiful because it creates new architecture, like that of the big tanks, the geometrical formation flights, the smoke spirals from burning villages, and many others. (ILL 241–42; GS 1:507)

Marinetti believes war to be beautiful because it provides continuous stimuli for inner experiences. Ironically, however, these experiences emerge from a force field that blurs the boundaries of machinery and the soldier's body. Although war constitutes an arena of unprecedented control over inner and outer nature through technology, it is spectacular insofar as it ultimately extinguishes human identity, culminating in what Marinetti calls the metalization of the body, the transformation of the human body into machinery itself. War intoxicates because it bursts the traditional limits of the self and liberates individuals, through technology, from the alleged cage of bourgeois identity. The fascist war redefines the human body as a prosthetic device. It renders the interface between modern technologies and human bodies as an irreducible mingling of man and machine, a form of identification rather than an exchange of parts or functions. "Within this economy of identification," as Jeffrey Schnapp explains, "machines stand for an ideal: not that of a body without fatigue or of a society without alienation, but instead the distinctively fascist ideal of *constant exertion and fatigue coldly resisted* . . . in other words, metallization."[16] Not any premodern idyll of rural life, not any island in the South Sea, but metal and steel offer the utopian iconography of fascist discourse on war. If the eighteenth and nineteenth century perceived the machine, the human robot, "as a demonic, inexplicable threat and as a harbinger of chaos and destruction,"[17] Marinetti's male fantasy of total power envisions the mechanization of the body as the conclusive triumph of technology over what threatens the fragile modern subject most: nature. Marinetti conceives of the human body in terms of a motor that would never fatigue, a psychotechnical apparatus that defies idleness and is characterized by a seemingly endless reservoir of energy.[18]

According to Benjamin's argument, the aestheticist deification of art and the fascist apology of war share common intellectual ground inasmuch as both no longer situate the beautiful in works and objects that mirror or upgrade nature through aesthetic appearance; rather, in both the aestheticist concept of art and Marinetti's praise of technological warfare, beauty is figured as that which systematically destroys nature, that which fuses appearance and reality into one encapsulated entity. Aestheticism and fascism define beauty as that which emerges whenever resolute human subjects succeed in erasing nature and installing a closed, entirely manmade world of total appearance. While it hopes to amalgamate the human body and machinery "in the face of this 'landscape of total mobilization' " (TGF 126; GS 3:247), fascism thus culminates the decadent aesthete's desire to get rid of nature completely and escape into an artificial and morally neutral space, one that protects from any threatening encounter with otherness.[19]

Returning to Marinetti's manifesto, then, it should become clear that Benjamin – the limitations of his analysis notwithstanding – speaks of the affinity between aestheticism and fascism's apotheosis of war in two senses at once. First, he wants to take issue with Marinetti's attempt to emancipate technology and its potential uses from rational legitimacy claims. The *l'art pour l'art* proclaimed the autonomy of artistic means of formation, presenting art as a self-referential system that ostracizes traditional principles of verisimilitude and moral education. In the fascist cult of war, this excess of art translates itself into a cult of technology: fascism proclaims the independent sovereignty, not of artistic techniques of expression, but of modern technologies of warfare. In so doing, fascism wants to shape attitudes toward technology that resemble the reception of decadent artworks. Shaped by the hands of a resolute political leader, war emerges as a self-referential work that resists discursive questioning as it contains a reality sui generis. It calls for awe and submission, not for normative debates or moral criticism. Secondly, and perhaps more importantly, Benjamin compares aestheticism and fascism because both understand art as a practical expression of power over nature. Dedicated to their respective cults of authenticity, aestheticism uses enigmatic art while fascism employs war technology to overcome the threats of otherness, of nature. Both aestheticism and fascism cultivate beauty, not simply to transfigure the appearance of the given world, but to reshape it into an inorganic architecture of domination and submission, to take pleasure in what putatively has no use and purpose.

Benjamin's recourse to aestheticism when trying to explain the fascist nexus of art, technology, and power surely remains challenging. Postmodern popular and academic cultures still revel in images that show Nazis revering war technology as modernist artworks, as beautiful and self-sustaining gods. What one should not forget, however, is that both German National Socialism and Italian Fascism were characterized not only by futuristic sensibilities but also by highly conventional tastes: the aesthetic culture of Germany and Italy during the 1930s and early 1940s entailed the avant-garde celebration of war machines as much as the numb veneration of premodern traditions. Focusing mostly on the iconography of hi tech, Benjamin's critique of fascist war ideology tends to obscure the way in which modern machines in fascism helped uphold antimodern or reconstruct antiurban experiences. His equation of futurism and fascism should therefore not blind us to the fact that Nazi politics in particular – as emphasized in other sections of Benjamin's work – relied on the co-presence of hi tech and the pastoral, technology and the homeland, the engineer and the peasant. As Jeffrey Herf has shown in minute detail in *Reactionary Modernism*, Nazi ideologues on the one hand venerated advanced technology via premodern principles such as folk and race, but they on the other hand also produced older meanings and antimodern icons with the help of highly modern machines.[20] Just as art under fascism involved more than simply an excess of aestheticist sensibilities, so did National Socialism engender ideological hybrids in which the appeal of modern technology could coexist with an antitechnological jargon of authenticity.

If political action and warfare are to represent the culmination of artistic creativity, and if resolute leadership embodies the most distinguished form of aesthetic expression, can fascism consequently retire all its artists proper? What is left to do for the sculptor, the painter, or the poet, if fascism casts the political spectacle as the ultimate site of aesthetic experience?

Half a century after the end of World War II, National Socialist art is still a great embarrassment to German society and its cultural authorities. Museums have good reasons not to exhibit the works of Arno Breker, Georg Kolbe, or Josef Thorak. Their artifacts remain locked up in storage spaces and thus assume quasi-legendary status. Labeled as kitsch and condemned for its antimodernist iconography, this art is viewed mostly by art historians, not for aesthetic reasons but as historical documents. Although some rightly fear that the idiom of Nazi art may actually appeal to a larger public even today, it is widely recognized that the many works that survived the Nazi era cannot be studied exclusively from an aesthetic standpoint. As Peter Adam aptly summarizes, "The art of the Third Reich is difficult, complex, and controversial. Whether it be in the form of fine arts, architecture, film, literature, or music, it cannot be considered in the same way as the art of other periods. It must be seen as the artistic expression of a barbaric ideology. One can only look at the art of the Third Reich through the lens of Auschwitz."[21]

And yet, even if we rightly reject a view of Nazi art that shuns any reference to the political context, its antimodernist, pastoral, or heroic idiom is much more intricate and ambivalent than many art historians, including

Adam, would like their audiences to believe. To simply call Breker's or Thorak's monumentalism kitsch and thus render it irrelevant obscures the actual problem; for it is the role and cultural dynamic of kitsch itself that needs to be analyzed in the first place. Even in its most reactionary artistic forms, Nazi art on the one hand responded to the dialectics of modern culture, the leveling of former distinctions between high and low, and the rise of modern technologies of representation, while on the other hand endorsing elitist or hierarchical norms that branded modernism as debased, Jewish artists as degenerate, and popular idioms such as jazz as articulations of depraved minds and sick bodies. It has frequently been noted that Nazi painting and sculpture often appear as if photographed – that Nazi sculptures unfold their most stunning effects not as originals but as photographic reproductions. Though meant to reverse the course of modern art, the artistic signature of Nazi sculpture in particular "seems to reckon with technological requirements, as if calculated from the beginning for the purpose of reproduction and mass duplication."[22] Furthermore, monumental sculptures clearly relied on industrial, even Fordist, mechanisms of mass production. Assembled by teams of artists and craftsmen, the most memorable products of Nazi art consisted of individual elements that were designed as exchangeable and multifunctional.

Even some of the most appalling and aesthetically numbing products of Nazi monumentalism, while reveling in premodern effects and longings, thus undeniably relied on modern machines and technologies of seeing. As Karen Fiss argues, Nazi art understood how to weave contradictory threads into seemingly organic cocoons of overwhelming power; it derived its "emotional effects and mobilizing force from the fusion of oppositions such as romantic anticapitalism and technological progress, historical continuity and revolutionary break."[23] Newly available technologies of image reproduction were instrumental in promoting this curious hybrid of myth and modernity. Lavishly produced picture books and popular art journals flourished under Nazi rule.[24] They made available the new aesthetic idiom as spectacular color photography and commodity choice – a testimony to the fact that mechanical reproduction played a key role in what Nazi ideologues propagated as the final return to unmediated experiences of authenticity.

Benjamin, the unsurpassed theorist of mechanical reproduction to our times, strangely avoids any detailed discussion of Nazi art and its intricate negotiation of old and new. His remarks on the role of art proper in fascism are mostly limited to his "Paris letter" (GS 3:482–95), an essay that concerns itself with contemporary French culture rather than Hitler's Germany or Mussolini's Italy.[25] Although in this article Benjamin mentions German artists such as Gottfried Benn and Arnold Bronnen, he primarily focuses his discussion on Thierry Maulnier's assault on the liaison between French surrealism and communism.

"Paris letter"attempts to defend André Gide against what Benjamin considers as his fascist critic Maulnier.[26] In order to do so, Benjamin feels compelled to elaborate on the overall concept of culture that informs artistic activities under fascism. Benjamin situates the origin of such a concept in the early days of fascist movements. Once established and risen from the phase of formation to the one of consolidation, fascism needs to discard its key thinkers because creative brains may disturb cultural life under the new order.[27] What is truly interesting about the fascist concept of culture, however, is not its genesis but rather its definition as a "sum of privileges" (GS 3:493). According to the fascist doctrine, culture reserves and preserves entitlements to the elite, even if – as Benjamin insists – only violence can secure such privileges in the long run. Similar to Herbert Marcuse and his notion of affirmative culture, Benjamin therefore hopes to decipher the signatures of domination that are inscribed into fascism's concepts of culture.[28] He wants to show how fascist art and culture protect what rational arguments no longer can justify – how fascism conceptualizes art and culture as an extension of domination, as violence with other means.

During the dawn of fascism's seizure of power, the "trustees of fascism" (GS 3:486) develop two interconnected arguments in order to buttress this repressive notion of culture. On the one hand, they endorse aestheticist concepts of art purged of any moral liability and reference to the relation of art to other social practices. On the other hand, they denigrate the realm of *Zivilisation* – the arena of material production and reproduction – from the vantage point of *Kultur*, the domain that salvages the individual through spiritual elevation from social discontent. Equipped with the slogan "Civilization is a lie" (GS 3:487), Maulnier denounces mass cultural practices in the hopes of warranting the elite's monopoly over cultural tastes and the realm of symbolic reproduction. Maulnier revaluates nineteenth-century notions of aesthetic and cultural refinement only to mystify material inequality and to offer a vision of universal redemption provided by the symbolic world of spirits and beautiful souls.

An essential part of Benjamin's theory of fascist culture is the contention that art under fascism is locked into a constant struggle between theoretical claims and the demands of reality. "To combine," Benjamin observes, "the decadent theory of art with its monumental practice was left up to fascism. Nothing is more instructive than this contradictory crossing" (GS 3:488). In a theoretical perspective, fascist art is deeply indebted to the aestheticist tradition. It denounces the practical utility or social relevance of art. Like the decadent work of art, fascist art desires esoteric artifacts for a few selected recipients; the implied audience for art-as-theology bears resemblance to cultic circles of initiates. But on the other hand, fascism also renders artworks as instruments of propaganda and, hence, exoterical tools to forge the masses into the molds of racial identity. Despite its intended uselessness, monumental art represents the medium par excellence by which fascism succeeds in "penetrating the entire social life" (GS 3:488) with its political imperatives.

For Benjamin, the elective, if contradictory, affinity between aestheticism and monumentalism results in a strategic hypostatization of the realm of aesthetic appearance, one that impedes the potentially disruptive force of art and tames it through cathartic identification. Instead of providing critic and audience with the means of its own destruction, the fascist artwork aspires to be appearance through and through. Antimodernist in nature, artworks of fascist provenance present themselves as stable incarnations of timeless actuality. By means of symbolic representation and metaphorical continuity, they elevate their subject matter to a level of perfect totality, harmony, and identity. In contradistinction to the allegorical tradition from the baroque to Baudelaire, monumental art is unwilling to overturn the authoritative monuments of history, the triumphant arches of progress. Whereas allegorical modernism commemorates the fragmented, forgotten, untimely, and suppressed, monumental art allies itself with the victors in history. Obstructing any attempt to render art a moment within an emancipatory aesthetics of resistance, the cross-breeding of decadence and monumentality consequently expresses fascism's need to mask what Benjamin in his perhaps most Marxist phase – considering the aesthetic as absolutely heteronomous, as nothing but a function of something outside it – understands as the "functional character of art" (GS 3:488). Under the rule of fascism, art anticipates and organizes the modes of its own reception. It overwhelms the spectator with a multitude of impulses in order to coordinate the very modes of perception according to which it is meant to be seen:

Fascist art is propaganda art. Therefore, it is executed for the masses. Fascist propaganda, moreover, must penetrate all of social life. Fascist art is therefore executed not only *for* the masses but also *by* the masses. Accordingly, one might assume, the masses were dealing with themselves in this art, they would use it as a means of self-communication, they were using the master in their own house: master in their theaters and stadiums, master in their film studios and their publishing houses. Everyone knows that this is not the case. Rather, those who dominate over these sites are "the elite." And this elite does not desire art to provide a means of self-communication for the masses. (GS 3:488)

The primary purpose of fascist art, according to Benjamin's argument, is to deflect genuine forms of proletarian self-representation – the articulation of concrete and group-specific experiences across dominant divisions between private and public. Fascist art proliferates a vitalistic aesthetics of national rebirth and charismatic renewal instead of empowering its disenfranchised constituencies to organize themselves. Fascist art celebrates the beauty of essentialized bodies rather than the defects of the modern body politic; it escapes to premodern countrysides rather than depicting the pathologies of twentieth-century cityscapes. Fascist art reinvokes a disjointed plurality of myths drawn from the past to propagate this project of rejuvenation. Myths of soil reclaim territorial identity; myths of blood advocate ethnic identity. While it endows the present with "features of eternity" (GS 3:489), fascist art replaces psychological interiority with biological determinism, intellect with emotion, history with myth. Naturalizing given power structures, not least of all the patriarchal family and the subordination of women, the veneration of vitalistic beauty thus yields an aesthetics of submission and obedience.

As I have argued in chapter 2, Benjamin's evaluation of the fascist spectacle clearly borrows from Nietzsche's critique of Wagner, and it foreshadows in rudimentary form Adorno's much more extensive thoughts in *In Search of Wagner*, written in 1937/38 and published as a book in 1952. Nietzsche denounced Wagner for his dictatorial modes of compositional address causing the erosion of aesthetic form. Not only does Wagner try to convert his audiences, he also sacrifices artistic authenticity to become a cultural institution of renewal. Wagner's megalomaniac visions of power, Nietzsche argued, force the composer to dictate the ways according to which his works ought to be understood, but they also prompt him to treat his compositional material with violence and, hence, in an unaesthetic fashion. To both Nietzsche and Adorno, Wagner inscribes political imperatives right into the center of his works – and thus destroys their aesthetic integrity. Wagner appeals to the listener's emotions, but at the same time he hits his audience over the head, denies autonomous forms of sense perception, and negates the individual body as a site of desire and spontaneity.

Following Benjamin's argument, Wagner's aspiration to control the emotions of his audience reappears in the monumentalist idiom of the fascist artist. Not only the mass spectacle, but all fascist art relies on an outspoken aesthetics of effects emphasizing the "suggestive energies of [art's] effects at the cost of the intellectual" (GS 3:489). The hybrid of monumentalism and aestheticism negates the possibilities of distance and reflection in face of a work of art. Like Wagner read by Nietzsche and later by Adorno, the fascist artwork endeavors to convert recipients and integrate them into a ritualistic community. In fascist art, the imperative modes of address turn out to be the message. Monumental art constitutes audiences that happily dismiss autonomous agency, self-representation, and rational discussion.

Monumental art in fascism replaces the heroes of nineteenth-century novels of education and development with the corporate-actor *Volk*. Already pressed into conformity as a recipient, the individual must also as a subject of art surrender to the promise of collective renewal at the cost of moral autonomy and psychological interiority. Reduced to a type, to a nameless and faceless identity, the subject blends into the ornamental design of a larger collective, where the human body itself becomes the clay, the material of artistic formation. For Maulnier, this violent reconfiguration of the body through art epitomizes the mission of aesthetic artifacts: to strip objects of their given utility; indeed, even to extinguish them. Maulnier's aestheticism thus complies intimately with Marinetti's apology of war. For it is only in and through war that Maulnier's poetics of extinction can fully unfold its suggestive nihilism: "There is one among the arts that meets Maulnier's definition very precisely. This art is the art of war. It embodies the fascist idea of art both by means of the monumental use of human material and the overall use of technology uncoupled from any profane end. The poetical side of technology that the fascist plays out against the prosaic side – the side the Russians emphasize too much according to the fascist – this poetical side is its murderous one" (GS 3:492). Although Benjamin's theory of art under fascism is highly fragmentary and ignores some of the most challenging paradoxes of, say, Breker's or Thorak's modern antimodernism, it aspires to nothing less than a generic concept of fascist art. However useful the term may appear to us today, fascist aesthetics proper relates directly to the politics of the fascist spectacle.[29] A contradictory fusion of monumentalism and aestheticism, of decadence and violence, fascist art – like the fascist spectacle – deflects proletarian self-representation as it aims at a militant eradication of autonomy, at silenced reception, and at symbolic totalization. Similar to the mass rallies, fascist art manipulates minds and emotions. It engenders through imperative modes of address the very forms of perception according to which it wants to be seen. In the final analysis, both the spectacle and the fascist artwork have death written right across their formal inventories. Fascist art not only endorses an aesthetics of submission disguised in imagery of collective redemption. It also embodies in its very techniques and principles of representation an antici-pation of warfare, an extension of combat by other means. It is through war – this murderous drama of resolute leadership and technological progress – that fascism therefore concludes what fascist art and the aestheticization of politics pursued all along: "'*Fiat ars – pereat mundus*,' says Fascism, and, as Marinetti admits, expects war to supply the artistic gratification of a sense of perception that has been changed by technology. This is evidently the consummation of '*l'art pour l'art*.' Mankind, which in Homer's time was an object of contemplation for the Olympian gods, now is one for itself. Its self-alienation has reached such a degree that it can experience its own de-struction as an aesthetic pleasure of the first order" (ILL 242; GS 1:508).

The cult of creative leadership, the ideology of war, and the monumentalist conception of art: all three work in tandem in fascism in order to give political action the seductive appearance of Great Politics, to endow the political with existentialist relevance. But fascism projects onto the sphere of political action its romantic paradigms of aesthetic genius, expressive-ness, and formation not simply to annihilate the differentiation of separate spheres of action and value in modernity; rather, the ideological application of outmoded bourgeois aesthetic principles to political action attempts to halt the peculiar diffusion of power holders in modernity, to recenter the state in spite of its bureaucratic dilution, and thus to cater to diffuse desires for the autonomy of the political. War is the outspoken telos of this project, for only war can ultimately warrant the suppression of practical reason that drives this peculiar version of modern differentiation and autonomization. Only combat and military leadership – war as a state of permanent excep-tion and emergency – can counteract the inevitable wearing down of Great Politics, of the charisma of the resolute leader who is keeping at a distance the conflicting centers of domination.

Max Weber applied the term charisma to forms of authority that rely en-tirely on the extraordinary, otherworldly qualities of the leader. Charismatic individuals, endowed with quasi-superhuman powers, interrupt the dull continuum of history, appealing to messianic expectations among their followers. According to Weber, charismatic communities are based on "an emotional form of communal relationship," one that implies the surrender of the disciples to the anti-institutional character of charismatic rulership.[30] Promising comprehensive rejuvenation, charismatic leaders defy any institutionalization of norms, legal precedents, and general procedures of decision making. To the degree that they transform politics into a matter of revelation, charismatic individuals create from scratch the very principles according to which the community ought to judge about the legitimacy of their leaders: "The genuine prophet, like the genuine military leader and every true leader in this sense, preaches, creates, or demands *new* obligations – most typically, by virtue of revelation, oracle, inspiration, or of his own will, which are recognized by the members of the religious, military, or party group because they come from such a source."[31]

The fascist propagation of Great Politics clearly reckons with the charismatic expectations of the modern masses, their desire for radically new and different obligations. The charisma of extraordinary leadership and warfare is meant to glorify a strong state and emancipate the political from the iron cage of norms, procedures, and bureaucratic measures. Fascism produces charisma by projecting the romantic image of the artistic genius on the scenes of political action. Geniuses provide, out of nothing, the very resources that are to justify the new order. Likewise, charismatic leadership in fascism is meant radically to dispense with the immediate past, with the liberal-bourgeois depletion of the political as a dimension of existential self-realization. Understanding art as a practical expression of power, a skill to shape chaos into stable forms, fascism invokes the image of the artistic genius to give its dictator the charismatic appearance of unified power. Produced via aesthetic material, charisma thus bestows upon the leader the appearance that he stands above the multiplication of state-like centers of bureaucratic domination in modernity. If eighteenth-century aesthetics attributed divine powers to the aesthetic genius, the political *l'art pour l'art* of fascism introduces its dictator simultaneously as messiah and genius artist, as God the Redeemer and God the Creator.

Invoking a famous line from Eric Charrell's cinematic "superoperetta"[32] *Congress Dances* (1931), Benjamin describes Hitler's aesthetic charisma in 1934 thus: "'That only happens once; it will never happen again.' Hitler did not accept the title of *Reichspräsident*; he sought to imprint on the people the uniqueness of his appearance. This uniqueness derives from the magical elements of his prestige" (GS 6:104). Political action in fascism, according to Benjamin's reading, wants to assume auratic qualities. It presents itself as a unique occurrence in space and time, a magic phenomenon of a distance, however close it may be. Promising release from everyday routine, Hitler dismisses former inventories of signification and symbolization. Like the artistic genius, he seeks to suspend rule-bound practices and normative canons – that is to say, the whole modern apparatus of procedural politics and bureaucratic administration. Instead, he inaugurates spellbinding spectacles of historical extraordinariness, publicly staging his own "supernatural, superhuman, or at least specifically exceptional powers or qualities."[33]

It is important to note that we find this discussion of Hitler's charisma in a fragmentary text juxtaposing Hitler's auratic appearance with the image of none other than Charlie Chaplin. Chaplin had emerged during the 1920s and early 1930s as a discursive site at which the German intelligentsia engaged in fiery debates about the role of art, mass culture, subjectivity, and political empowerment in modernity. A "quasi-religious icon, . . . a composite figure inviting multiple inscriptions,"[34] Chaplin embodied in the eyes of many left-liberal intellectuals of the Weimar Republic what Siegfried Kracauer called a "promise of happiness."[35] Chaplin's cinematic appearance simultaneously appealed to the romantic notion of art as individual self-expression as well as to postbourgeois conceptions of democratic, popular art. It is therefore understandable that Benjamin's fragment compares Hitler and Chaplin not simply with regard to their public appearance but also their modes of address, their aesthetics of effect. Both the politician and the comedian, Benjamin seems to argue, understand the act of reception as an integral part of their overall aesthetics. Furthermore, both Hitler and Chaplin ground their invocation of charismatic extraordinariness and salvation not so much in a resolute display of masculinity, in imageries of phallic strength and authority, as in a feminization of their male bodies. Yet whereas Hitler's femininity, Benjamin indicates, only underscores the perversity of his politics, Chaplin's female elements bear witness to the inscriptions of poverty and social alienation on the body, thus authenticating his rebellious desire for redemption:

Hitler's reduced masculinity –
    to be compared with the feminine elements of the impoverished as represented
    by Chaplin
so much glamour around so much shabbiness
Hitler's following
    to be compared with Chaplin's audience. . . .

Ban of marionettes in Italy, of Chaplin's movies in the Third Reich –
every marionette can imitate Mussolini's chin and every inch of Chaplin the
Führer. . . .
Chaplin shows the comical aspects of Hitler's serenity; whenever he plays the
refined man we know the whole story about the Führer
Chaplin has become the greatest comedian because he incorporates the deepest
horror of his contemporaries. (GS 6:103)

More than half a decade before Chaplin was to ridicule Hitler's spectacles of
charismatic greatness in *The Great Dictator* (1940), Benjamin already emphasizes the strange affinity between the comedian and the politician. Accordingly, Hitler and Chaplin appear as products of the same *Zeitgeist*, yet
they chart the tremors of the present on opposite seismographical scales. As
viewed against the backdrop of Chaplin's melancholic comedies of submission and rebellion, Hitler and his political aesthetics of extraordinariness
emerge as truly farcical – as a bad comedy. Chaplin reveals with every posture that Hitler, not Chaplin, is the greatest, albeit also the vilest, imitator
and impostor of the age: in his cinematic fictions, Chaplin tells the truth
about the fictions of fascist politics. In Benjamin's view, Chaplin brings into
view the anachronism of Hitler's reinvention of aura in the modern age and
shows the ways in which fascism processes outmoded concepts of bourgeois art for the purpose of domination. Hitler, in turn, must ban Chaplin
to protect the decisive principles of fascist domination, the uninhibited
transposition of *l'art pour l'art* into politics, the transfiguration of politics
through the metaphors of artistic creativity. For, all in all, Chaplin does not
only reveal the fact that the fusion of art and power in fascism engenders
bad politics, but also that it draws from and reproduces bad art: Hitler
must censor Chaplin because the art of the latter unmasks the former's project of charismatic renewal as poor theater – as fake.

For Benjamin, then, Hitler and Chaplin symbolize the recto and verso
of one and the same coin, a coin negotiating modern struggles around
bourgeois art, technology, mass culture, proletarianization, and political
charisma. Both Chaplin and Hitler promise redemption from the crises of
modern life: Chaplin through comical laughter, Hitler through imperial
warfare. Both, following Benjamin's emblematic invocation, seem to depend mutually on each other, and yet both also seek the other's destruction:
Chaplin's laughter is to eliminate the atrocity of Hitler's war; Hitler's war is
to silence the critical thrust of Chaplin's satire. What should concern us
here, however, is what Benjamin understands as Hitler's reduced masculin-

ity – Benjamin's insinuation that Hitler's spectacular presence in the public sphere results in a feminization of politics. In radical contrast to the rhetoric of male self-assertion and misogynist bonding that strikes the reader of Goebbels's novel *Michael*, Benjamin seems to consider the relocation of aesthetic formulae to the political arena as an illegitimate intrusion of feminine elements. He does not simply equate fascism with the aestheticization of politics, he also regards the airlifting of nineteenth-century decadence to the political and public sphere of the twentieth century a violation of proper gender boundaries and identities. It is not difficult to see that this critical move rests on a highly traditional and patriarchal construction of gender difference. It assigns the power of rational distinction to the male, while it labels femininity as the site of messiness, of helplessly conflated notions of life and art, knowledge and emotion. In accord with the problematic gender implications of critical theory's assessment of fascism, Benjamin seems to understand the fascist spectacle as a precarious weakening of proletarian virility.[36] Fascism solicits a desire for the repression of desire that Benjamin considers not only as intrinsically totalitarian but also, by implication, as a precarious violation of heterosexual normalcy. Moreover, preoccupied with his generic definition of fascism, Benjamin here also completely eludes the phallic moment that fueled the Nazi jargon of political and existential self-assertion, a rhetoric earmarking Jews as effeminate so as to justify their extinction. Benjamin's claim that the aestheticization of politics equals the feminization of the public sphere thus should make us wonder to what extent Benjamin's understanding of fascism as a spectacle of first rank subterraneously helped to express some of Benjamin's own male anxieties, fears that also reverberate in what the following chapter will picture as his critique of fascist visuality. Although much must remain mere speculation, we have to ask ourselves seriously whether some of the historical shortcomings of Benjamin's critique of fascism – his surprising silence about the racist dimension of National Socialism and the politics of the Holocaust – have as much to do with Benjamin's desire for sweeping generic generalizations as they do with his far from revolutionary gender politics.

4

MEDUSIAN POLITICS

In a diary entry dated 27 April, the hero of Joseph Goebbels's novel *Michael* describes his initiation into the National Socialist movement of the 1920s. Aimlessly strolling through an alien city, the narrator enters a barroom filled with workers, rank-and-file soldiers, and officers, the disoriented and discontented representatives of interwar Germany. Suddenly, Michael beholds the appearance of a speaker in front of these impoverished men, a speaker whose charismatic powers unleash a process of Dionysian fraternization. Endowed with prophetic energies, the speaker displaces quotidian alienation with ritualistic intoxication:

> He is no speaker. He is a prophet!
> Sweat pours from his forehead. Two glowing eyes flash lightning in this gray, pale face. His fists are clenched.
> Word upon word, sentence upon sentence boom like the Last Judgement.
> I no longer know what I am doing.
> I am beside myself.
> I shout, "Hurray!" No one is surprised.
> The man on the podium gazes at me for a moment. Those blue eyes strike me like flaming rays. This is a command!
> I am reborn as of that moment.[1]

Communal fraternization here results from a highly choreographed introduction of optics to politics. The vitalistic ritual of subordination and male bonding culminates when Michael's eyes meet the eyes of the politician-prophet. Enchanted by a mesmerizing gaze that looks back, Michael feels emancipated from his cultural despair, suspended from any reminiscence of the unstable routines in postwar Germany. The speaker's eyes in fact cause Michael to perceive power as a fascinating work of art; they reorganize the political public sphere in terms of a nonattestive culture of vision that – in Yaron Ezrahi's words – induces "wonder and admiration toward the power and magnificence of authority."[2] Scopic perception thus provides the resources for charismatic rejuvenation and community building, simultaneously satisfying the messianic hopes of the masses and warranting structures of dictatorial authority and uncritical subordination.

For the disoriented and politically homeless, the visual experience of charismatic power in Goebbels's novel is meant to promise a new home, to become a conduit to ethnic integration and social hierarchy. What is being described in the novel as the speaker's unique, seemingly auratic presence puts the viewer "beside himself" and reconfigures his identity within the mold of a new collective of initiates. As the "great theorist of the auratic gaze," Benjamin in the artwork essay sets out to challenge such crude attempts to relocate auratic perception to the political public sphere of the twentieth century.[3] Unlike Goebbels, Benjamin explores the auratic as a historical category, and he – successfully or not – endorses its increasing disintegration in modernity as a source of democratic politics. Benjamin defines the auratic gaze as a mode of perception typical for preindustrial communities, a world regulated by the temporality of ceremonies, rituals, and storytelling. Specified as the "unique phenomenon of a distance, however close it may be" (ILL 222; GS I:479), aura signifies forms of ocular perception that provide the cement for contemplative identification and communal integration. For Benjamin, auratic experiences articulate forgotten bonds between the realms of civilization and nature, between the unanimated and the animated. Grounded in circular rather than chronological time, auratic gazes remind us of the human in nature, the natural in humanity.

Although Benjamin's analysis strikes nostalgic chords, he describes the process of modernization as a gradual emancipation from the authority of auratic gazes. In the artwork essay, he argues that modern technologies of mechanical reproduction, in particular the media of film and photography, interrupt the mystical interplay of closeness and distance, contemplation and identification, peculiar to the auratic experience. To the degree that modern life is governed by the desire "to bring things 'closer' spatially and humanly" (ILL 223; GS I:479), modernity proliferates a sense for the universal equality and transitoriness of things and thus subverts auratic appeals to permanence and uniqueness. In his subsequent studies of nineteenth-century Paris, Benjamin extends his initial argument as he now holds the acceleration of life in the modern urban metropolis responsible for the disintegration of aura. In order to protect itself against overwhelming stimuli and discontinuous shock effects, the industrial consciousness armors the eye, and hence censors the kind of radiation and penetration involved in any experience of aura. In the poetry of Baudelaire, Benjamin observes the highly instructive enterprise of exploring these modern modes of postauratic visuality aesthetically; in Baudelaire's poems, Benjamin writes, the auratic "expectation nourished by the look of the human eye is not fulfilled" (ILL 189; GS 1:648). Although Baudelaire, to some degree, redeems the experience of aura through his notion of *correspondences*, he refuses to flee from the postauratic architectures of modern life, a world in which eyes have lost their ability to look and mesmerize each other with flaming authority and violence.

In contrast to Baudelaire's modernism, Goebbels's novel *Michael* disavows the metamorphoses of visual perception in modernity. The quasiauratic experience of Hitler's messianic presence not only promises salvation from specific predicaments of interwar Germany, it is supposed to discontinue historical time and modernity altogether and to reintroduce the temporal rhythms of preindustrial life, the time of ceremonies and rituals. Although a highly instructive document regarding the rise and self-conceptualization of German fascism, Goebbels's novel provides us with only half the truth about the visual politics of fascism. After all, it was Goebbels himself, as minister of propaganda, who was to advocate a powerful amalgamation of specifically modern technologies of mass communication *and* auratic modes of visual perception in order to construct the home, the allegedly magical community of the folk. Once risen to power, German National Socialism utilized film as the most effective hardware of modern communication and amusement to proliferate mesmerizing representations of authority and thus reproduce massively the aura and specular submission incited by Hitler's charismatic performance in *Michael*.

This chapter discusses in further detail Benjamin's critique of visual culture under fascism. As I unfold in what follows, Benjamin argues that fascism imbues postauratic technologies of reproduction, in particular film, with auratic meaning, thus providing for cathartic submission and drowning possible discontent in a manipulative flood of images. What is at stake for Benjamin, however, is not to indict the overall proliferation of images and ocular exchanges in all branches of modern life; he does not consider the visibility of power and politics per se as a sign of evil politics. Rather, Benjamin's critical project is to expose the way in which fascism selectively uses modern visual media in order to glorify power and extend the bygone rhetoric of art-for-art's-sake to the realm of the political. Accordingly, fascists aestheticize politics to the extent that they truncate the full possibilities of modern visual representation and experience. Fascism utilizes voyeuristic impulses while it represses the emancipatory potential of cinematic address and exchange; it employs modern visual culture to celebrate power rather than to help people negotiate the norms and attest the institutions of collective life. In contrast to populist media critics today, who argue that visual media per se corrupt modern politics, Benjamin insists on the democratic, albeit systematically suppressed potential of modern visual culture.[4] For Benjamin, fascism's technologically mediated iconography relies on a perversely curtailed version of modern visuality, one that incites scopophilic desires and masochistic fantasies for the cause of mute subordination and political self-monumentalization.

Benjamin's preoccupation with the role of sight and visual culture in fascism is not surprising. Images exercised powerful and persuasive effects in National Socialist Germany particularly. They hit people over the head, but also – as Eric Rentschler has recently argued – "soothed egos and massaged the masses, blending fustian and soma."[5] Nazi visual culture has often been seen as a showcase of beautiful bodies and armor-plated subjects, of metalization and mobilization, of ornamental masses and emotional violence, of heroism and transfigured death. Nazi propaganda films captivated viewers so strongly that they surrendered mindlessly to Nazi ideology. The cinema of the Third Reich, writes Marc Silberman, presented "an extreme moment of state authority in the film industry, a moment where art and social need were to coalesce in an affirmative ideology. This ideology aimed at empowering a particular social reality to establish the authority of the system and to justify a group identity that would differentiate or exclude the Other."[6] But Nazi cinema at the same time also simply tried to capture dormant utopias and animate primal emotions. It emulated Hollywood narratives and patterns of recognition, seeking to provide its consumers with exotic attractions and unpolitical distractions, with escapist vehicles that moved the hearts and minds of the masses. In contrast to explicit or thinly disguised movement films, the majority of the era's many genre films – melo-dramas, light comedies, even homemade Westerns – intentionally omitted direct references to Nazi agendas or specific party icons. "Goebbels eschewed overt agitation; he wanted films with formal assurance and popular appeal, fantasy productions that would expand German market shares and alleviate the need for foreign imports. He sought to create a star system; he cultivated script writers and directors. Like any Hollywood entrepreneur, he checked box-office returns and stressed the crucial role of advertising and publicity in generating product recognition. From the start Goebbels articulated the desire to create a cinema that could both satisfy the domestic market and function as a foreign emissary."[7] In creating a German Hollywood, the administrators of Nazi cinema sought to capture the popular demand for Americanist diversions with an army of seemingly innocent entertainment vehicles. Long neglected as an entity by the scholars of Nazi culture – yet ominously popular on the screens of German postwar TV – Nazi cinema aspired to become German cinema's golden era.

It is interesting to note that Benjamin's comments on visual culture under fascist rule entirely ignore this role of entertainment films in Nazi mass culture. Although seemingly unpolitical feature films constituted the overwhelming majority of Nazi film productions, Benjamin's interest lies instead with the visual regime of overt propaganda films, with the operatic staging and filming of mass rallies and political parades à la Leni Riefenstahl. Strangely enough, however, though composing the artwork essay in the immediate aftermath of the release of *Triumph of the Will*, Benjamin does not mention the name of Riefenstahl at all. Such surprising omissions might best be explained by referring to what Miriam Hansen has called the belated status of the artwork essay. Unlike Adorno's work on mass culture, Benjamin's theory of film still participates in the avant-garde perspective of the Weimar period. It derives some of its crucial insights against the backdrop of cinematic practices and forms of viewership during the 1920s, insights that kept Benjamin from discussing in further detail the filmic material at hand during the 1930s. It is this moment of unsynchronicity that may also account for what many of Benjamin's students, understandably, consider counterintuitive or grossly inaccurate about his film theory in general. The artwork essay's curiously refracted gaze "enhances the utopian modality of its statements, shifting the emphasis from a definition of what film *is* to its failed opportunities and unrealized promises."[8] Because Benjamin's critique of aesthetic politics is inextricably bound up with his theory of cinema, the present chapter will engage with some of the crucial incongruities of the artwork essay: the rendition of montage as cinema's exclusively emancipatory and empowering principle; the rather unclear relation of film, photography, and (epic) theater; the limited treatment of visual pleasure; the definition of cinema's generic specificity in a perspective that is too narrow to explore the technological and cultural possibilities of film; and last but not least, the ambiguous notion of aura that is meant to explain the changes of modern perception.

At first sight, the sheer force of these critical shortcomings seems to grind

Benjamin's account of fascist visuality into pieces. If Benjamin's theory of film indeed fails to convince its readers of the liberatory potential inherent in the very form of cinematic address and exchange, then it seems to forfeit its task to counter the perversion of modern vision in fascism. However, as I will argue at the end of this chapter and in chapter 5, it is in Benjamin's later studies on nineteenth-century Paris, in the context of his materialist anthropology of capitalist modernization, that we may explore a more elaborate account of the metamorphoses of visuality in modernity, one in which film occupies only one among many other scenarios of looking. In contrast to his fragile theory of film, Benjamin's ethnography of modernity and modern experience in the *Arcades Project* defines more reliable categories to debunk the scopophilic politics of fascism, the reduction of politics to a vitalist spectacle of visual amusement and consumption.

Although the artwork essay displays crucial shortcomings, the present chapter shall nevertheless recapitulate Benjamin's phenomenology of fascist film, seeking to rethink Benjamin's initial critique of scopic politics in fascism in light of recent film theory and some of Benjamin's general remarks about visuality. Informed by concepts of visual pleasure developed in the study of narrative film, I will reconceptualize Benjamin's notion of ocular-centric politics as a simultaneous attempt to (1) appeal to an Oedipal rhetoric of phallic self-assertion, and (2) arrest the spectator in pre-Oedipal, nonphallic games of pleasurable disappointment and masochistic disavowal. In so doing, the present chapter not only suggests a theoretical formula stronger and more complex than Benjamin's own in order to understand the workings of what Benjamin – however one-sidedly – considers generically as Nazi or fascist cinema; it also seeks to undo some of the phallocentric principles that Benjamin subterraneously shares with his object of criticism; namely, the construction of cinematic spectatorship in terms of an all too narrow Oedipal logic that vacillates between castration anxiety and male self-affirmation.

In a fragment written in 1918, Benjamin draws attention to what he considers the demonic visuality of Adalbert Stifter's narrative style.[9] Stifter's writing, Benjamin contends, is predicated upon the absence of acoustical sensations – of sound. Even actual speech acts appear restricted in Stifter's prose to the visual "exhibition of feelings and thoughts in an acoustically insulated space" (SW 1:112; GS 2:609). Exclusively devoted to what is visible regarding human forms of expression and communication, Stifter's works ultimately aim at a pacified, restful silence. Although full of sympathy for details, for the fragmented and the marginal, Stifter's ecphrastic style, his photographic positivism, forfeits any sense of moral righteousness and human justice. In fact, precisely by erasing the difference between the margin and the center, between the "small" and the "big," Stifter tends to collapse nature and human fate, myth and history. "He is spiritually mute – that is to say, he lacks that contact with the essence of the world, with language, from which speech arises" (sw 1:112; GS 2:610). Because Stifter is incapable of representing emotional states of shock and consternation, states that require language to find articulation, his characters appear enmeshed in demonic forces, controlled by that which never becomes visible. Stifter wants to salvage both his heroes and his readers from the excruciating cascades of time. For him, optics and silence provide the power to join a history that has ceased to move, a history no longer steered by human interests, activities, and visions. In his obsession with visuality, Stifter, therefore, enchants the reader through his narrative voyeurism as much as he effaces the moral autonomy of his characters.

Following Benjamin's argument in the artwork essay, fascism rearticulates Stifter's demonic visuality as it employs peculiarly modern paths of optical representation and communication to contain political unrest and integrate the individual into the transhistorical community of the folk. Whereas Stifter's ecphrastic style was to redeem the bourgeois subject from the authority of urban temporalization, fascist cinematography transfigures the modern masses while it transfixes the spectator in isolated passivity in front of the screen. Although the masses, through cinematic newsreel spectacles, "are brought face to face with themselves" (ILL 251; GS 1:506), they are denied an exploration of the cinema as a space of political self-representation and critical exchange: fascist cinematography paralyzes emancipatory desires to the extent that it forces the audience into speechless, submissive forms of spectatorship. Fascist cinematography transforms the masses into an audience that casts auratic gazes at itself and thus extinguishes the very emancipatory power it could exercise in and unleash from the public sphere of the movie theater.

Contrary to the claims made about film and spectatorship by later French theorists such as Jean-Louis Baudry or Christian Metz,[10] theorists who understand the cinematic apparatus and the projection situation themselves as crucibles of occultation and regression, Benjamin does not believe that all films necessarily homogenize spectatorial responses or render natural that which in fact is an ideological production. Not film per se but only its wrong use will result in the production of ideology and imaginary subject positions – in the kind of "phantasmatization of the subject" that Baudry views as the underlying principle of all forms of film exhibition that rely on elements such as projection, darkened auditorium, and spectatorial immobility.[11] By no means an apparatus theoretician in the sense of 1970s Lacanian and Althusserian film criticism, Benjamin in fact enthusiastically embraces film as a popular training ground for new modes of sense perception and novel forms of mass enlightenment, as a site that enables the proletarian masses to articulate experience and contest individual and collective meanings across dominant divisions of public and private. Unlike Adorno and Horkheimer, who by and large disavowed film because it failed to foster the desired powers of negation, Benjamin is at pains to formulate a postaesthetic theory of the new media, one that accounts for the fact that film directors rather than poets, cameras rather than pens, seem to determine the scenes of art in the twentieth century.[12] As a result, Benjamin maintains that cinematic representations of the masses do not necessarily need to transfigure processes of political legitimation through the power of bewitching imagery. In fact, film – by means of what Kracauer in his *Theory of Film* was to call its "revealing function"[13] – proves particularly able to encompass the kind of human crowds that entered the stages of history in the course of the nineteenth century. Just as close-ups allow us to picture things normally unseen, and thus revolutionize our perception and entire notion of reality, so do aerial wide-angle shots surpass the perceptual capacities of the human eye, rendering large objects, in particular masses of humans, in a way that is new and insightful to any spectator.

Mass reproduction is aided especially by the reproduction of masses. In big parades and monster rallies, in sports events, and in war, all of which nowadays are captured by the camera and sound recording, the masses are brought face to face with themselves. This process, whose significance need not be stressed, is intimately connected with the development of the techniques of reproduction and photography. Mass movements are usually discerned more clearly by a camera than by the naked eye. A bird's-eye view best captures gatherings of hundreds of thousands. And even though such a view may be accessible to the human eye as it is to the camera, the image received by the eye cannot be enlarged the way a negative is enlarged. This means that mass movements, including war, constitute a form of human behavior which particularly favors mechanical equipment. (ILL 251; GS 1:506)

In emphasizing the elective affinity between cinematic mass reproduction and the reproduction of masses, crowds of people, Benjamin hopes to extrapolate from the formal structure of the medium film its appropriate subject matter and thereby to distinguish film from other domains of representation. Benjamin believes, however, that not every cinematic representation of mass events is of equal caliber. Although he fails to refer to any concrete examples, and although his silence about the transformations of Soviet cinema during the 1930s remains deeply problematic, Benjamin implies that there are crucial differences between Nazi propaganda film and the rendition of collective action in Soviet avant-garde film, between *Triumph of the Will* (1935) and, say, *October: Ten Days That Shook the World* (1927). In Benjamin's view, Russian cinema of the 1920s, through elaborate montage technique, intended to both address and exercise collective, anti-illusionary, and critical modes of spectatorship. Fully exploiting the technological possibilities of editing, it "sought to show that history was made by collective action."[14] Fascism, on the other hand, engages in a politically regressive use of the new medium. It embraces film to silence the critical impulses of the spectator and, in newsreel spectacles and pseudo-documentaries, it propagates the mythic belief that history makes masses – that collective action is initiated and steered by forceful leaders alone. Whereas Eisenstein's or Vertov's camera assumed a bird's-eye view to illuminate and reassure the emancipatory power of collective action, Riefenstahl's aerial perspective is one of auratic distance, one that strips the masses of their desire to make history, putting them at the mercy of dictatorial politics.

Instead of giving the masses power, fascist cinema in Benjamin's understanding bestows and entertains the masses with the viewpoint of a charismatic leader. Film under fascism sanctifies the putative reemergence of Great Politics and unified political action. It displaces the realm of normative debates, regulative principles, and everyday routines; it cloaks politics in alluring cinematic shapes so as to exalt in the image of a recentered and autonomous state. Fascist newsreels represent the masses as forged into human ornaments and public ceremonies. They picture anonymous individuals contained in solid architectures of power, struck by the dictates of domination and submission. As they consume the visual display of abstract human patterns, the masses in the auditorium indeed face themselves, yet what they encounter is no longer a living organism but a deanimated entity, seen from the auratic vantage point of power. Fascist cinematography thus addresses voyeuristic impulses while it entices the audience to experience its own mortification on the cinematic screen as the highest form of pleasure. In its scopic celebration of surrender and mortification, fascist cinematography actualizes the ancient myth about Medusa, the infamous Gorgon who fossilized all human life by means of her deadly gaze.

Benjamin, to be sure, at no point explicitly mentions Medusa's petrifying vision as a chiffre for what he understands as fascist cinema. Yet it is this mythological image and its Freudian reading that may offer interesting insights into some of the underlying assumptions of Benjamin's theory of fascist visual culture, insights that might help not only better understand his critique of the nexus of power and vision in Nazi cinema, but also to highlight the limitations of his own critical approach to fascism. The notion of Medusian visuality emphasizes what Benjamin considers as one of the keys of the fascist spectacle. Aesthetic politics, according to Benjamin, strips the masculine power of autonomous agency and self-assertion away from the masses and transfers it to the charismatic figure of the political leader. The spectacle glorifies virile posing and mindless surrender, yet solely by feminizing or castrating the bodies of those that observe and make possible the spectacle in the first place; it promises to make men into men, yet in truth emasculates them.

In the following pages, Medusa's gaze – petrifying visuality coded female – serves as an image to illustrate Benjamin's critique of cinematic spectatorship in fascism and to indicate Benjamin's own male investments into his understanding of modern visuality. It indicates his theoretical construction of the cinematic apparatus, progressive or regressive, as an Oedipal catalyst of either knowledge and insight or feminized transfixation. In a second step, however, I will challenge both fascism's Oedipal rhetoric as well as the hidden gender discourse of Benjamin's theory of film. Departing from phallocentric Freudian or Lacanian theories of spectatorship, I will reconsider Benjamin's notion of aura and its reproduction in fascist cinematography as a masochistic disavowal that recycles pre-Oedipal scenarios of dependence – scenarios that exist prior to any sexual differentiation.

In a short text written in 1922, Freud read the story of Medusa as a mythological chiffre for male castration anxiety: Medusa's terrifying appearance reproduces the boy's horror when initially facing the female genital, most likely the mother's.[15] Just as the mother's lack of a penis strikes the boy with panic, Medusa's gaze inflicts upon its object the fear of death and castration, one to which the male spectator ironically responds with petrification in order to reassure his sexual identity and potency: "The sight of Medusa's head paralyzes with horror, transforms the spectator into stone. The same origin in the castration complex and the same change of affects! For the stiffness symbolizes the erection, that is, consoles the spectator in the original situation. He still has a penis, assures himself of the penis's existence through its becoming stiff."[16] Whenever artists, Freud argues, invoke Medusa and her deadly gaze, they not only seek to displace symboli-cally the female genital, but also to isolate horror from pleasure while expe-riencing the other, the penis-less sex. According to Freud's phallus-centered narrative, the image of Medusa thus serves as an apotropaical symbol, a sig-nifier that exorcises the possible disaster of death and castration. By expos-ing himself to Medusian imagery, the spectator hopes to inflict castration anxiety on his enemy; the displaced erection in the Medusian experience is supposed to efface terror by transferring it to others. "What excites horror in oneself, can yield a similar effect in the enemy that is to be ward off."[17]

For Benjamin, fascism translates Freud's account of Medusian displace-ment into a political formula: it inflicts upon the audience symbolic death and Medusian paralyzation so as to strike the foes with terror and castra-tion. Similar to the Gorgon's deadly gaze, fascist cinema plays out scenarios of male castration anxiety as it transfixes its audience in gestures of assent and surrender, hoping that the spectator's temporary petrification – and feminization – may reassure his militaristic vitality and masculine virility. The scopic politics of fascism renders spectatorial petrification and sub-ordination a long-term means of mobilization, a spectacle of phallic re-juvenation. On the one hand, aerial reproductions of mass formations are supposed to freeze the individual in the simulated community of the state. On the other hand, the image of such human ornaments evokes a mode of cinematic spectatorship that translates Medusian fear into a phallic erection in order both to impress the future enemy with renewed bellicose mas-culinity and paralyze it with castration anxiety. In order to pursue this Oedi-pal plot, fascist cinematography reinvokes outmoded aesthetic principles of cathartic illusion and identification. To transfer castration fear to the enemy and deflect disaster, fascist film involves its audience in a spectacular dialec-tic of horror and emotional cleansing, one that precisely effaces what Ben-jamin considers the key component of the new medium, film – its tactile, disruptive qualities.

Following Benjamin, Russian avant-garde film – as I will detail later – uses the art of editing to disseminate physical shocks, to interrupt through montage the spectator's process of association and emotional identifica-tion, and thus – like the dadaists – transform art into "an instrument of bal-listics" (ILL 238; GS 1:502). Fascist film, on the other hand, addresses and utilizes voyeuristic desires, at once inciting and organizing purely emo-tional responses of the spectator. In contrast to the distracted, tactile recep-tion produced by Russian montage film and its strategic attacks on the psyche of the spectator,[18] fascist cinematography masks the disruptive quality of film, engendering visual spectacles that arrest their objects in static displays and absorb spectators rather than allowing them to absorb the work (ILL 239; GS 1:504). In order to augment its rhetoric of phallic self-assertion, fascism tends to project the visual and temporal logic of early photography onto the modes of cinematic communication.

Benjamin, in his "Brief History of Photography,"[19] maintained that early photography preserved the auratic moment of traditional art because crude technologies of exposure made it necessary to position the human object in secluded, undistorted environments.[20] In these early photographic images, everything was made to last, and therefore the procedures of exposure prompted models "to grow, as it were, into the picture" (GS 2:373) rather than to face the fleeting, transitory nature of photographic representation. Instead of momentarily interrupting the flow of time, early photography sought to transcend time altogether and thus recreate the kind of cultic timelessness and contemplation typical for what Benjamin considers auratic art. In *On Photography*, Susan Sontag has gone even further than Benjamin, claiming that not only early but all photography is implicated in such a language of pathos and contemplative transcendence. Far from ever fully endorsing the transitoriness of things, photography is intrinsically elegiac, constantly mourning the passing of time and desiring to halt the maelstrom of history: "Photography is an elegiac art, a twilight art. Most subjects photographed are, just by virtue of being photographed, touched with pathos. . . . All photographs are *memento mori*. To take a photograph is to participate in another person's (or thing's) mortality, vulnerability, mutability. Precisely by slicing out this moment and freezing it, all photographs testify to time's relentless melt."[21] To the degree that they present past moments as objects of "tender regard," photographic images evoke a melancholic awareness of passing time, a pathos of looking at times past, thereby undercutting any historical or moral judgment.[22] An advocate of what Nietzsche called the antiquarian mode of historiography, photography renders the passing of time a spectacle of triumphs and losses in which each moment appears equally close to God (that is, the camera).[23]

Just as photography tends to rescue contemplative modes of visual consumption in the age of mechanical reproduction, fascist cinematography appeals, according to Benjamin, to auratic experiences in order to truncate the democratic potential of film and the popular. Through its peculiar way of capturing monster rallies, fascist cinematography wants to freeze both its human referent and the spectator in the hopes of disempowering possible unrest and scrambling rational judgments. Like early photography, cinematic representation in fascism prompts model and spectator to grow into the picture rather than to appropriate it for the cause of political self-representation. In so doing, fascists hope at once to homogenize the masses and to prepare them for the next war, to utilize and exorcise castration anxiety, to administer symbolic death and masculine resurrection. If Russians, according to Benjamin, understand film as a tool to dispense tangible shocks and interrupt the spectator's identification, fascist films are memento mori that suture their audiences into enchanting spectacles and thus entertain the masses with their own mortification. Whereas Russian montage cinema explores the full possibilities of cinematic representation to undercut the demonic aspects of pure visual consumption, fascist cinematography represses the anti-illusionary dimension of film to glorify power and suture the individual into public rituals of total mobilization.

Drawing from the psychoanalytical vocabulary of Freud and Lacan, Laura Mulvey in her seminal essay on "Visual Pleasure and Narrative Cinema" (1975) has indicated two contradictory aspects of scopophilia, the pleasurable structure of looking inherent in cinematic spectatorship. On the one hand, most mainstream films portray "a hermetically sealed world which unwinds magically, indifferent to the presence of the audience, producing for them a sense of separation and playing on their voyeuristic fantasy."[24] Encased in the darkness of the auditorium and enchanted by the shifting images on the screen, the spectator is immersed in the illusion of gazing at a private world, a world constituted of what is normally hidden and forbidden, a world that thus emerges as an object of the spectator's pleasurable look. In the scopophilic drive, the desire to see without being seen coincides with the illusion of exercising control over the represented object: scopophilic dispositions both mark a repression of the spectator's own exhibitionism and project repressed fantasies on the actor. On the other hand, cinema not only gratifies primordial wishes for pleasurable looking, it also addresses the spectator's narcissistic desire for identification and, hence, ego-constitution: the pleasurable look in cinema repeats the matrix of recognition and misrecognition, of identification and subject-formation typical for what Lacan has described as the mirror state. Following Mulvey, the cinema proliferates forms of visual enchantment that provide for both a temporary loss of ego identity and a reconstitution of the self in the imaginary realm of ego ideals and human forms. Forgetting their own world in face of the cinematic dream screen, the fascinated spectators recognize themselves in the other, the actor, the star. Although both moments of pleasurable looking in cinema, voyeuristic distance and narcissistic identification, instinctual drive and self-preservation, seem to contradict each other at first, Mulvey concludes that the tension and interaction between both aspects is at the core of visual pleasure in any conventional cinematic situation.[25]

Benjamin's artwork essay, though of course preceding the rise of psychoanalytic film theory, dedicates considerable space to the position of pleasurable looking in cinematic spectatorship. Surprising though it may seem, however, Benjamin makes no distinction whatsoever between the ways in which we view narrative or non-narrative films. Unlike more recent film theory, he discusses both viewing pleasures and positions under the same rubric. As a result, Benjamin allows for visual pleasure only to the extent that it is fused with critical reading practices, with intellectual distance and rational judgment. "The greater the decrease in the social significance of an art form, the sharper the distinction between criticism and enjoyment by the public. The conventional is uncritically enjoyed, and the truly new is criticized with aversion. With regard to the screen, the critical and the receptive attitudes of the public coincide" (ILL 234; GS 1:497). Progressive cinema, Benjamin suggests in a rather utopian turn of thought, should enable spectatorial responses that combine visual pleasure and the orientation of the expert, that marry enjoyment and critique. Fascist cinema, by contrast, to the degree that it grafts auratic moments onto postauratic visuality, separates visual pleasure and critical attitude in a repressive fashion. As it uncouples the triad of perceptual, emotional, and intellectual excitement and exclusively plays on the affectual registers of the spectator, Medusian cinematography solicits total identification with the represented masses on the screen, one that locates political submission in the very structures of visual perception and spectatorial response.

Benjamin suggests that the isolation of visual pleasure – typical for what he considers fascist cinema – describes a measure of political homogenization and terror in itself, a premise that is clearly too sweeping in order to study film in general and the politics of visual representation in fascism in particular. Against the background of Mulvey's argument, however, one might be able to draw out the further consequences of Benjamin's analysis. On the one hand, the representation of staged mass events and public ceremonies in fascist cinema activates the scopophilic desires of the spectator, giving visual outlets for the spectator's repressed exhibitionism, for our desire to express ourselves. To be sure, in contrast to Freud's notion of scopophilia, the presented world is not the realm of the hidden and the forbidden, not a private world but the sphere of public mass events. However, as I have argued in the foregoing, fascist cinema depicts mass events from the vantage point of the charismatic leader; it visually constructs political rallies from a quasi-voyeuristic perspective in which detached observation and visual control seem to coincide. Inescapably adopting the camera's gaze, the leader's gaze, the spectator in the auditorium experiences a displaced act of voyeuristic pleasure, one that through a procedure of double projection reinscribes the subjugation of the masses – and, hence, the audience – under the existing architecture of power.

On the other hand, the representation of mass events in fascist cinema, to the degree that it effaces the tactile qualities of film and capitalizes on optical excitement, designates an object of narcissistic identification. In front of the screen and its elaborately shifting patterns of light and shade, the spectator recognizes the geometrical appearance of the masses as ego ideal, or idealized form of collective action, in whose imaginary domain one can joyfully reconstitute one's temporarily lost identity. In contrast to what Benjamin considers as the emancipatory powers of Russian montage cinema, the fascist representation of crowd scenes involves structures of emotional fascination strong enough to provide a momentary loss of self-identity while simultaneously preparing the thus decentered subject for its resurrection in the aesthetic ideal form of the community of the folk. Fascism renders the spectators of Nazi rallies as the actual spectacle. It appeals at once to the pleasures of seeing and the pleasures of being seen, a connection Thomas Elsaesser has expressed as follows: "Might not the pleasure of fascism, its fascination have been less the sadism and brutality of SS officers than the pleasure of being seen, of placing oneself in view of the all-seeing eye of the State? Fascism in its Imaginary encouraged amoral exhibitionism, as it encouraged denunciation and mutual surveillance. Hitler appealed to the Volk but always by picturing the German nation, standing there, observed by 'the eye of the world.'" [26]

Read in light of Mulvey, Freud, and Lacan, Benjamin suggests that fascist cinema solicits forms of visual pleasure that include both a scopophilic displacement of exhibitionist fantasies and a narcissistic desire for ego-constitution in the imaginary realm of public festivals. Truncating what Benjamin considers a progressive alliance of intellectual judgment and visual pleasure, fascist cinema uses specular excitement to summon acts of collective subordination. Vis-à-vis the representation of staged mass spectacles, sight here becomes repressive; it invites standardized forms of behavior that celebrate the Medusian petrification of the masses as a thrill of first rank. Fascist cinematography organizes audiences that are blind to the fact that the fascinating grammar of cinematic looking may administer death, that it paralyzes in order to guarantee political stability; that cinema may transfix the viewer as a rigid spectator only to mobilize him for the next war, to transfer castration anxiety to the enemy and thus impress the foe with the display of resurrected military strength and potent masculinity. Subjugation to the spectacularized state constitutes a feminine experience that is meant to reverse dialectically into, as Linda Schulte-Sasse has put it in a different context, "a 'hardening' of the male subject, a masculinization and abjection of the female Other, either within or outside of the self."[27]

While Benjamin's notion of petrifying visuality is meant to denounce the effects of fascist cinematography, it simultaneously indicates the male anxieties in Benjamin's own theoretical construction of cinema. Understood through the lenses of Mulvey's argument, Benjamin reads fascist cinema as a regime of Medusian gazes that transfixes the spectator through regulated scopophilia. Whereas Russian montage cinema of the 1920s, according to Benjamin, provides knowledge, collective action, and emancipation from pure scopic desires, fascist cinematography ensnares the spectator in positions of passionate identification and consumption, positions that Benjamin clearly encodes as female. Actualizing the myth about Medusa's petrifying gaze, fascist cinematography, while glorifying the political as a site of masculine self-assertion, yields a temporal feminization of the cinematic audience. Fascist cinema for Benjamin opens a cultural space at which femininizing forces undermine proletarian virility, (male) rationality, and critical distance. Although Benjamin believes he can unhinge the workings of fascist cinematography, he in fact remains caught in the same set of phallocentric assumptions that fuel the very operations of what I have called here Medusian cinematography. Benjamin's montage cinema may on the other hand overcome the pleasurable transfixation in front of the screen, but – according to Benjamin's theoretical model – it can do so only at the cost of defeating the threat of femininity – erasing sexual difference. In the eyes of today's reader, Benjamin's juxtaposition will thus appear hardly viable any longer. Neither can Benjamin's conception persuade theoretically; nor is it able to marshal convincing historical arguments. Celebrated by Benjamin as a powerful alternative to fascist film, Russian montage cinema – as I will detail in a moment – was far from joining pleasure and insight in the ways Benjamin suggested; nor was it able to foster critical audiences that would have prevented the rise of Stalinism. As I will argue in the following, however, we may rescue Benjamin's approach to film and visual pleasure if we rethink his notion of auratic and postauratic spectatorship in terms of visual theories that undermine his Oedipal theme, replacing the theoretical figure of castration anxiety with the one of masochistic disavowal.

Two years before the artwork essay, Benjamin speculated in a short text entitled "The Distance and the Images"[28] (1933) about the relation between visual pleasure and contemplative behavior, optical enchantment and the suspension of chronological time:

> Perhaps the delight in the world of images is nurtured by a murky defiance of knowledge? I look out into the landscape: here lies the ocean in its bay as smooth as glass; forests rise as an immobile, mute mass at the top of the hill; up above dilapidated ruins of a castle, as they were standing already centuries ago; the sky radiates without any clouds, in eternal blueness. This is what the dreamer desires. That this ocean rises and falls in billions after billions of waves, that the forests tremble in every moment from their roots up to the last leaf, that an uninterrupted trickling and falling prevails in the stones of the ruin, that in the sky gases, before they form clouds, fight invisibly in order to surge together – all this, the dreamer must forget to abandon himself for the sake of the images. With them, he has rest and eternity. . . . To thus halt nature in the frame of faded images, is the pleasure of the dreamer. To captivate it through original apostrophe, the skill of the poets. (GS 4:427)

The dreamer's delight in the world of pure images erases his awareness of both the spatial reality of specific objects and their being in time, their temporal existence. Benjamin's dreamer experiences scopic pleasure to the extent that he renders a natural setting as a painted canvas; that is to say, emancipates the objects of his gaze from their spatial and temporal coordinates and thus transforms them into aesthetic appearance. Ironically, however, as his delightful perception rests on the power of forgetting, on the denial of insight and knowledge, the dreamer also forgets about his own temporal and spatial location, his corporeal existence, and thus prepares himself for what Benjamin calls absorption through the object of delight. The dreamer's auratic gaze describes not only a structure of visual pleasure but also an act of corporeal self-denial, and, hence, subordination under the authority of beautiful surfaces.

Benjamin believes that cinematic visuality potentially destroys the bewitching aspects of auratic gazing. As long as it does not curtail the possibilities of technological reproduction, film has the "tendency to promote the mutual penetration of art and science" (ILL 236; GS 1:499). By means of cutting, close-ups, wide-angle shots, and slow motion, cinematic representation defamiliarizes the things around us, endowing the spectator with completely new insights in the physical structure of his environment. In contrast to the auratic mode of looking, film has the potential to couple visual pleasure and intellectual excitement. Unlike the dreamer's eye in "The Distance and the Images," the camera solicits visual pleasure only to pierce the appearance of the given world, at once stimulating and satisfying the spectator's scientific curiosity. The cinematographer reminds Benjamin of a surgeon "who greatly diminishes the distance between himself and the patient by penetrating into the patient's body" (ILL 233; GS 1:496).

Although film – as I will detail in chapter 8 – clearly harbors positive mimetic qualities for Benjamin, its primary task is not simply to reproduce or redeem the natural environment in the form of an image or to invite identification with an autonomously unfolding spectacle; rather, by permeating the existing order of things, cinema displaces the familiar and engenders a new nature. In the film studio, Benjamin maintains, "the mechanical equipment has penetrated so deeply into reality" that it provides an "equipment-free aspect of reality" (ILL 233; GS 1:495). Cinematic images embody an inseparable fusion of technology and nature; they engender a nature of second degree in front of which both visual pleasure and scientific interest join each other and obliterate traditional forms of aesthetic experience. According to Benjamin, then, the quasi-scientific position of the cameraman yields revolutionary results for the structures of aesthetic reception and spectatorial response. For insofar as the cinematic audience associates itself with the scientific gaze of the camera, it emancipates itself from the authority of auratic identification and thereby overcomes the temporal and spatial blindness of traditional spectatorship in the art museum, the classical theater, or in the face of a pacified landscape. Film, properly used, pierces seductive surfaces and reconstitutes our perception of the physical world. Proper cinematic representation shows the world not as a natural fact but as a product of history and human activity; it thereby appeals to the pleasures of destroying the old and instituting a new order of things. Auratic visuality, on the other hand, involves forms of specular pleasure that naturalize the world beyond the camera; it exalts in the captivating force of aesthetic semblance and arrests the spectator in a constant desire for masochistic distanciation and deferral.

In a pioneering study, Gaylyn Studlar has recently analyzed in further detail the role of masochistic pleasure in the cinematic situation, not only to raise fundamental questions about the mechanism of cinematic pleasure production, but also to present a counterapproach to earlier feminist theories about scopic pleasure and the spectatorial positioning of women.[29]

Since traditional film theory, including Mulvey, remained bound to Freudian scenarios of castration anxiety and thus – willingly or not – reiterated phallocentric models of sexual differentiation, it tended to duplicate the subjugation of woman in mainstream film in the realm of theoretical speculation as well. Drawing from Gilles Deleuze's inquiry into masochism,[30] Studlar offers alternatives to both the patriarchal construction of woman on the cinematic screen as well as to theories of spectatorship that explain specular pleasure exclusively in terms of Freud's Oedipal complex or Lacan's mirror stage.[31] As I will argue, her approach not only yields further insights into Benjamin's ideas about the positioning of the spectator in fascist cinema; it also undoes the phallocentric credos that fuel the operations of what I earlier called Medusian politics; that is to say, fascism's rhetorical appeal to scopophilic pleasure in order to exorcise castration anxiety.

Studlar locates the origin of masochistic desires in the pre-Oedipal, oral stage, prior to the establishment of sexual differentiation, and thus prior to both Freud's tragedies of castration fear and Lacan's drama of narcissistic self-recognition. Masochistic desires emerge whenever the infant rejects identifications with the phallic power of the father and finds its ego ideal in the mother. The desired reunion with the mother during the phase of pregenital sexuality, however, remains a highly ambivalent one. The subject is positioned in a state of constant vacillation between recovery and loss, suspense, delay, fantasy, and punishment: the very separation between subject and desired object, between wish and fullfilment, guarantees the continuation of the pain/pleasure structure. Recast as a form of cinematic spectatorship, masochism lives from heightened emotionality vis-à-vis idealized vignettes of suffering. Violence appears muted, sexuality diffused, suffering aestheticized in spectacles of disappointment: the necessary suspension of gratification manifests itself in quasi-institutionalized games of waiting, surprise gestures of tenderness and cruelty, performative masquerades that delay consummation.[32]

It will surely serve us well not to draw all too swift parallels between Studlar's masochistic style of narrative cinema and the visual logic of nonnarrative newsreel shows. But while its monumentalism appeals to popular demand for resolute action and phallic revitalization, fascist cinema in Benjamin's understanding seems to invoke the same masochistic pleasures that Studlar describes in her analysis of the von Sternberg/Dietrich productions. Fascist cinema positions the spectator as an inactive receptacle. It arouses scopic pleasure through repeated acts of self-denial, allowing the experience of continuous suspension of emancipation and power as an object of emotional excitement. To the extent that fascist cinema plots mass events from the privileged perspective of the leader, it recasts the social space cinema as a nurturing environment, a site of emotional homogenization, instead of a location of spectatorial self-enlightenment and proletarian empowerment, as Benjamin wants it. Overwhelming the viewer with a well-orchestrated series of ever-changing sights and sounds, the spectacular reproduction of mass events pictures modern politics as an arena of strong and decisive action beyond fact and value. Lacking any representational depth, fascist cinematography solely venerates the geometric appearance of the masses and denies any further motivations aside from aesthetic ones. Riefenstahl delights in showing what is already a performance, a dramatic simulation of authenticity, and thus repeats the intricate procedures of aesthetic stylization and infinite displacement that mark the masochistic aesthetic.

Fascist film subscribes to what Studlar calls an iconic mode of representation whose devotion to pure surfaces simultaneously attracts and rejects: what you see is what you get, but what you get always remains a pleasurable ritual of disappointment, or as Benjamin put it in one of his most famous formulas, what you get is a chance to express yourself but not an inalienable right. Similar to films that incorporate the masochistic aesthetic, fascist cinematography therefore tends to evoke highly stylized universes that unfold autonomous orders of space and time.[33] It displays simultaneous enactments of stasis and movement only to collapse linear progress in structures of ritual repetition and thus, of course, to suspend chronological time altogether.[34] The image of monstersized parades in fascist cinema draws all things political into the light of public visibility, not only to revere stylized symbols of self-sacrifice, but also to solicit pleasurable looks at one's own submission and thus infinitely to repeat the masochistic scheme of painful pleasure and pleasurable pain.

Both Deleuze and Studlar have shown how post-oral fantasies often are brought regressively into a relationship with the oral phase. Masochists, they argue, use Oedipal schemes as a masquerade in order to express their wish for suspended symbiosis with even greater vigor. Likewise, in fascist cinema the above-mentioned phallic, Oedipal plot of Medusian fear and affirmation serves only to promote masochistic, pre-Oedipal activities of disavowal and fetishization; fascist cinema simulates phallic resurrection to increase pleasurable disappointment and submission – that is to impose nonphallic infancy on the cinematic audience. Staging self-sacrifice and symbolic death, fascism thus deploys the rhetoric of Medusian self-assertion and the iconicity of its masochistic aesthetic to hide, according to Benjamin, the truths about its socioeconomic foundations: Riefenstahl couches the triumph of the will in seductive imagery so as to obscure whose will actually triumphs. While the pathos of total visibility results in a totalitarian control of life, iconic modes of representation cause the spectator to forget about the facts beneath the dazzling surface, the world on the other side of the camera. Venerating the orgiastic forms of moving bodies and submissive behavior, fascist cinematography proffers an oceanic jargon of total presence and authenticity, not only to drive politics beyond any normative encoding and thus recenter the state but also to efface the fact that ordinary people and bodies can make history.

Recent film theory has in so many ways pointed out that narrative cinema is implicated in an intricate network of gazes: the characters look at each other, the camera looks at the actors, the spectator looks at the screen. Dominant cinema, it has been argued, tends to neglect the last two looks, deflecting from the active role of both the viewer and the camera. In the conventional cinematic situation – Teresa de Lauretis, for example, writes – "the spectators are not aware of their own look, of themselves as looking on, as being voyeuristically complicit in the pleasures built into the image; second they are not aware of the look of the camera, so that they have the impression that the events, people, and places figured on the screen exist somewhere, in an objective – if fictional – world created by the filmmaker, the director, the artist."[35] Whenever it denies the spectatorial activity of the recipient and the camera, mainstream cinema tends toward phantasmagoria: it presents the diegetic text as a self-producing and self-sustaining world that exists independently of the camera and the spectator's gaze. Benjamin, in turn, believes that cinema ought to provide the very tools to discontinue such phantasmagorical illusions and enable the spectator to understand the triple structure of looking in cinema. What Benjamin considers progressive film, such as the Russian montage cinema, reveals the active role of the camera in constructing the image figured on the screen while it sharpens the spectators' understanding of their own spectatorial activity. Montage cinema repeatedly breaks down the unified diegetic world and narrative coherence, disorienting viewers and, thus, forcing them "to recognize a reworking of the raw event through constant editing gaps and mismatches."[36] Resisting the temptation to suture the recipient into voyeuristic inactivity, Benjamin's avant-garde cinema reveals the manifold structure of looking in cinema so as to overcome masochistic identification and to put – as Benjamin maintains – "the public in the position of the critic" (ILL 240; GS 1:505), a sober-minded examiner and tester.

The spearhead of modern mass culture, film for Benjamin marks at once the end of bourgeois art and a revolutionary interpenetration of scientific insight and symbolic representation. Film expresses the peculiarly modern desire to establish fundamentally new perceptions and conceptualizations of reality that, in turn, allow for powerful reorganizations of social space and time. To the extent that cinema espouses constructivist methods of representation, stimulating the spectator's flow of association through discontinuous montage shots as well as multiple perspectives, it defamiliarizes the customary construction of space and time and thus obliterates what has always been particular to auratic art: illusion, absorption, transfixation. With film, Benjamin believes, "art has left the realm of the 'beautiful semblance' [schöne Schein] which, so far, had been taken to be the only sphere where art could thrive" (ILL 230; GS 1:491). Whereas Hegel in his famous thesis about the end of art thought that philosophy and Wissenschaft – science in the broadest of senses – simply replaced and expanded the focal position of art and religion in premodern societies, Benjamin contends that modern technologies of aesthetic representation themselves destroy the realm of aesthetic appearance – that the emergence of film in and of itself prompts a fusion of art and science.[37] Not external competition, in other words, but the inner progress of technologies of representation causes art to outstrip its own auratic heritage, erase bourgeois aesthetic practices, and address the desire to destroy the commanding authority of the beautiful appearance.

Furthermore, Benjamin believes that the revolution of the means of aesthetic representation not only solicits new and critical modes of spectatorial response, but also inaugurates the advent of both new audiences for and subject matters of symbolic expression. As it eradicates the auratic distance between spectator and aesthetic representation, film breaks down traditional barriers between producer and recipient. The cinema empowers the common spectator to become an actor, and the actors to become their own spectators. Accordingly, Russian montage cinema – like modern mass sports – positions the recipient as a possible participant and expert. In the cinema of Eisenstein or Pudovkin of the 1920s, film renounces aesthetic fixations on bourgeois individuality, promoting the collective to the hero proper and, thereby, giving voice to the profane concerns of everyday life: "Some of the players whom we meet in Russian films are not actors in our sense but people who portray themselves – and primarily in their own work process. In Western Europe the capitalistic exploitation of the film denies consideration to modern man's legitimate claim to being reproduced. Under these circumstances the film industry is trying hard to spur the interest of the masses through illusion-promoting spectacles and dubious speculations" (ILL 232; GS 1:494).

The populist jargon of Benjamin's endorsement of Russian film is no doubt problematic. The avant-garde's promotion of the masses to be the hero of films should clearly not be confused with an automatic achievement of democratic and rational will formation. At times, the artwork essay's description of Soviet cinema in fact comes much closer to a politics of plebiscitarian acclamation and the proto-totalitarianism of Rousseau's general will than Benjamin could have intended. But what in the eyes of Benjamin distinguishes the mass appeal of avant-garde films from irrational politics is their Brechtian aesthetics of affective distanciation and self-restraint. Insisting on an integration of physiological, emotional, and intellectual responses to the cinematic image, Benjamin conceives of the movie theater as a training ground for collective, noncontemplative, and postmasochistic forms of perception. Just as the cinematic apparatus interrupts the flow of action through shot and editing techniques, so the individual viewer – surrounded by the crowd of fellow spectators – learns to control his own emotional response, discontinuing pure scopic pleasure to embark on critical discussions about the film and its representation of everyday life.

It is obvious that the development of both Soviet cinema and mainstream film production and distribution throughout the last sixty years has systematically frustrated Benjamin's figuration of cinema as a proletarian public sphere. Instead of provoking recipients to emancipate themselves from and appropriate the images on the screen, dominant cinema – Benjamin would argue – has chosen to absorb the viewer, arresting and disempowering him as a mute voyeur. Considering the fact that Benjamin's utopia of filmic address and specular exchange so clearly contradicts any actual cinematic experience, both with respect to the 1930s as well as today, one should ask oneself to what extent Benjamin's theory owes its utopianism to flawed analyses of cinematic representation in the first place, fallacious assumptions about the principle of montage, its power of disruption as well as its ensuing social relevance. Given the ease with which Eisenstein at the end of the 1930s was able to translate his 1920s aesthetics of montage into a quasi-Wagnerian poetics of total cinema,[38] we need to question whether Benjamin's theory of film rests on too narrow a concept of both cinematic representation and spectatorial activity: if the Russian concept of montage indeed can engender and legitimize the politics of both *Battleship*

Potemkin (1925) and *Ivan the Terrible* (1944–46), then Benjamin's dualistic, undialectical categories of absorption and appropriation, auratic distance and tactile closeness, are not really sufficient to describe cinematic spectatorship and suggest alternatives to fascism's masochistic aesthetic.

For the early Eisenstein, montage devised a dynamic system of filmic language that allowed him to connect film to the philosophical framework of dialectical materialism. Accordingly, possible collisions of shots, of cinematic cells – understood as collisions of planes, volumes, spatial configurations, temporality, light and shade, depth and foreground, sound and image, or intellectual content – constantly administer shocks to the audience. Audiences are thus provoked to activate their hermeneutic faculties, to fill in the gaps between individual units, and to endow the disruptive sequence of images with synthetic meaning: "[W]hat we do in the cinema," Eisenstein wrote in a 1929 essay, is "combining shots that are *depictive*, single in meaning, neutral in content – into *intellectual* contexts and series."[39] For the later Eisenstein, however, montage will no longer denote a technique of triggering intellectual responses through visual provocation. Instead, it will describe a polyphonic style that organizes all possible planes of cinematic representation in one organic whole. According to the later Eisenstein, the method of montage permits the director to fabricate intricate, cross-referential networks of artistic expression and stylization that unify the existing arts in one single work. In contrast to the earlier rendition, montage now reinvokes romantic conceptions of artistic genius, expressivity, and empathy, as it is supposed to transform the cinema into "a site of an emotional communion between artist and perceiver."[40]

Although Benjamin never discusses particular Russian avant-garde films in further detail, his understanding of cinematic communication as a process of shock, disruption, and spectatorial stimulation clearly draws from Eisenstein's early notions of montage cinema. Like Eisenstein, Benjamin conceives of montage as a technique that defines the specificity of cinematic representation against the other art forms, a method of expression and address that at once interrupts a continuous flow of associations and incites the viewer to intellectual responses. Consequently, Benjamin believes he can reveal the political agenda of any given film by analyzing its use of existing cinematographic techniques – that is, its use of montage. Benjamin renders a film's political position as a function of how it seeks to exhaust the inner logic of cinematic representation itself, the specificity of the medium film. If Russian montage film, then, is progressive because it enables viewers to overcome pure visual consumption and establish themselves as critical readers of discontinuous shot sequences, fascist cinematography is regressive because it denies open processes of spectatorial synthesis and thus yields repressive modes of visuality.

The deterministic elements of Benjamin's 1935/36 theorizing about the politics of film put him in a position that, not only from today's perspective, must be seen as both politically and formalistically naive. As early as the second half of the 1920s, the debates about Walter Ruttmann's *Berlin: Symphony of a Great City* (1927) had indicated that montage, shock, collision, and discontinuity might very well be used for dictating desired interpretations of given shots and thus anestheticize the viewer's critical activity. Ruttmann's montage sequences present pure patterns of movement. They cast urban speed into a rhythmic, quasi-symphonic text that seems to distract from social problems prevailing underneath the surface of metropolitan life.[41] Although influenced by Dziga Vertov's experiments with the optical rhythm of everyday life, Ruttmann's montage film differs vastly from Vertov's own *Man with a Movie Camera* (1929). Whereas Ruttmann depicts Berlin life as an aesthetic spectacle seen from the detached vantage point of an auteur director, Vertov engages with the political process of postrevolutionary Moscow. Whereas Ruttmann emphasizes tempo as a formal quality, Vertov praises metropolitan speed as a means to accelerate the construction of a new society. Relying on similar techniques of editing and cinematic representation, then, both films not only construct urban life according to immensely different political positions, they also infuse their respective modes of address with competing ideological agendas: "Had Ruttmann," Kracauer speculated twenty years later, "been prompted by Vertov's revolutionary convictions, he would have had to indict the inherent anarchy of Berlin. He would have been forced to emphasize content rather than rhythm. His penchant for rhythmic 'montage' reveals that he actually tends to avoid any critical comment on the reality with which he is faced. Vertov implies content; Ruttmann shuns it."[42]

Though deeply indebted to the critical debates of the 1920s, Benjamin avoids any closer inquiry into the possible ambiguities of cinematic montage. The differences between Ruttmann's and Vertov's work, however, clearly belie Benjamin's belief that avant-garde forms of film editing per se yield what he considered as politically correct effects. Montage by no means relies – as Eisenstein wants it to do – necessarily on a collision of visually neutral shots, disruptive constellations of cinematic cells the spectator-reader needs to synthesize in order to endow the sequence of images with meaning. Rather, if Eisenstein, in *October*, intercuts between Kerenski, the chair of the provisional government, and the image of a pheasant, it is the director, not the spectator, who comments on the action and through montage dismantles the politician's narcissism and vanity. Although *October* shows the technique of montage as its best, it too seeks to dictate to the spectator its own interpretation, in particular if one considers that the speed of Eisenstein's intellectual montage tends to numb the hermeneutic activity of the viewer, producing pictorial explosions that are unreadable to those who are not in control of the editing board, the projector, or the pause button of a VCR.

It is worth noting that Benjamin circumvents any detailed discussion of competing montage techniques not simply because of his own political agenda, his valorization of the Soviet avant-garde of the 1920s as a mass cultural weapon against the atrocities of German National Socialism. Instead, Benjamin's undifferentiated evaluation of montage must also be understood as a result of his reductionist conceptualization of film in general. Based on the rather unspecified juxtaposition of auratic and postauratic visuality, absorption, and appropriation, Benjamin's conceptual apparatus leads him to evaluate spectatorial activities within too narrow a framework in order to account for the manifold activities the spectator must exercise even in front of a streamlined Hollywood product. Benjamin, in other words, favors montage as the exclusive stimulus for critical spectatorship only because his overall matrix proves to be too constricted to understand sufficiently what we do when we embark on the quite complicated adventure of watching and comprehending a film. Informed by Eisenstein and his attempt to integrate physiological, emotional, and intellectual forms of response, Benjamin renders montage as the only vessel to activate the viewer and to position him as a critical reader rather than a detached consumer of images. Yet as David Bordwell, for instance, has shown, even classical Hollywood cinema relies on a whole set of expected activities the spectator must execute to construct narrative causality: "creating and checking first impressions; linking actions by their anticipated consequences; weighing and testing alternative hypotheses about causality, time, and space. Brick by brick, scene by scene, and inference by inference, the classical film impels the spectator to undertake a particular but not naive work."[43] Apodictically distinguishing between contemplative distance and critical appropriation, Benjamin's matrix of spectatorship overlooks the existence of cinematic viewing techniques other than the ones incited by the shocklike collision of two shots. Neither does he acknowledge the work necessary to comprehend, for instance, certain plot and character constellation in genre movies, in which the viewer needs to recall previous acts of reception to understand the action on the screen. Nor does he consider that while scanning individual images on a large screen our eye executes certain activities already before montage and cutting interrupt the alleged sleep of visual consumption. Whereas Benjamin discovers the critical potential of film in the actual caesura between two shots, one might as well argue with André Bazin that critical, antivoyeuristic, disruptive faculties are exercised in the act of scanning one and the same image, in identifying and synthesizing the multiple layers of deep-focus representation, in choosing what to see and use as a source of meaning.[44]

In his attempt to discontinue masochistic forms of visual consumption, Benjamin reconceptualizes cinematic viewing as an act of reading. A cultural space collapsing art and science, Benjamin's alternative cinema recasts film, in a seemingly Schillerian move, as a public form of mass communication, a communal playground on which to practice unhampered forms of communicative exchange. For Benjamin, Russian montage cinema unveils the intricate work of looking, and thus reflects and enables reflection about the location of cinema within the larger framework of society. Whereas fascism utilizes cinema to freeze the spectator in political conformity, Benjamin's alternative cinema is one that problematizes its own devices of phantasmagorical illusion and thus empowers its viewers to exercise their theoretical and practical reason. Secretly redressing the scenes of modern visual culture in the garments of his literary predilections, Benjamin tends to evacuate visual pleasure altogether. But can we call a cinema without visual pleasure – a cinema of readers rather than viewers – cinema at all?

It has become commonplace to point out that Benjamin's theory of film relies heavily on a Brechtian model. Like Brecht's theater of *Verfremdung*, Benjamin's cinema is supposed to dismantle traditional barriers between spectator and production, not to transform society into a grand spectacle but to obliterate empathy, catharsis, and identification – that is, the alleged sources of political conformity and subordination. Written during a period of intense exchange between Brecht and Benjamin, the artwork essay in fact was meant to excel the force of critical disruption Brecht located in epic theater,[45] and it is this ambition – as Dieter Wellershoff, for instance, has argued – that caused Benjamin to misconstrue the formal properties of film: "Apparently Benjamin relocated the critical theatergoer, who according to

Brecht would follow the performance in a relaxed and distanced fashion and who would not be overwhelmed by empathy, to the cinema auditorium. And despite the unconsciousness, he described with his notion of distraction, Benjamin observed aspects of a 'testing attitude' among the audience."[46]

Imprinting Brecht's signature on film as the flagship of modern industrial culture, Benjamin constructs cinematic spectatorship as a tool of mass information and rational self-enlightenment. To the extent that film exposes the grammar of gazing, to the extent that it merges art and science, it emancipates the spectator from mesmerized passivity and, like Brecht's epic theater, paves the way for critical discussion among the members of the audience. In contrast to Brecht, however, Benjamin employs the concepts of defamiliarization, distance, and disruption not merely to establish a functional alternative to traditional theatrical practices; instead, Benjamin wants to define the specificity of film as a medium itself in likeness to what Brecht called epic theater. Therefore, Benjamin must claim that films already transgress their inner form whenever they involve the viewer in spectacles of scopic empathy. As he equates a priori the Brechtian theater with the formal nature of cinematic communication, he maintains that film results in both bad art and bad politics if it violates the rational task inscribed into the technological structure of the cinematic apparatus. Fascist cinema corrupts the integrity of film; in a sense, it produces films that are not films at all.

It is not without any irony that Benjamin's effort to graft Brecht's epic theater onto the structures of cinematic communication found one of its most critical readers in Brecht himself. Although agreeing with Benjamin about the need to explore new strategies of aesthetic address and reception, Brecht polemically objects to the conceptual tools Benjamin employed to do so. For Brecht, the centerpiece of Benjamin's theory of film, the category of aura and the thesis about its decay in modernity, is simply adolescent mysticism. During Benjamin's visit to Svendborg/Denmark in 1938, Brecht records in his *Arbeitsjournal*:

[H]e [Benjamin] assumes something he calls *aura*, which has to do with our dreaming (the daydreaming). he says: if you feel a glance directed at you, even in the back, we return it (!). the expectation that what one is looking at will return the look creates the aura. supposedly, it is in the process of disintegration lately, in conjunction with the cultic. B[enjamin] has discovered this while analyzing film, where aura disintegrates by means of the reproducibility of artworks. nothing but mysticism, cou-

pled with an antimystical stance. in such a way he adapts the materialistic conception of history! it is pretty dreadful![47]

Brecht faults Benjamin's theory because it inculcates materialist critique
with mystical murkiness, and thus regresses to a fuzzy version of anticapitalism. What one may hold against Brecht's polemic is that theoretical work
does not necessarily forfeit its critical aspirations if it, as Michael Löwy has
argued recently, borrows terminology from "the vast semantic field of religions, myths, literature and even esoteric traditions to enrich the language
of the social sciences."[48] But Brecht's injunction nonetheless urges us to reconsider the status of "aura" in the artwork essay, a tool of reflection that
becomes accessible only in the moment of its actual evanescence.[49] In one
of his few attempts to define this category, Benjamin tellingly invokes natural imagery, a landscape as if seen through the eyes of a painter, not a
preindustrial peasant: "If, while resting on a summer afternoon, you follow
with your eyes a mountain range on the horizon or a branch which casts its
shadow over you, you experience the aura of those mountains, of that
branch" (ILL 222–23; GS 1:479). Benjamin's image recalls Goethe's bourgeois hero Werther, when imposing Homeric imagery on the peasants in
the fields while having a cup of coffee in a rural inn. It is worth mentioning
that Benjamin's description of aura cites, as Marleen Stoessel has revealed,[50]
a passage from Alois Riegl's *Mood as the Content of Modern Art*: Benjamin's
appeal to contemplative visual uniqueness appears already dispersed in the
prism of preceding textual experiences. In effect, then, Benjamin introduces aura as a mode of perception already trained through the study of
traditional artworks, in particular the study of paintings. Auratic gazes perceive natural settings or social relations as aesthetic artifacts; they mark the
world with signatures of the desire for beautification and aesthetic harmony. Therefore, any attempt to employ the category of aura in order to
conceptualize traditional art and, in turn, theorize the transformation of
aesthetic perception through film must border on the tautological; it explains and exposes what it presupposes to begin with. Unless filled with
more substantial content within the context of a material anthropology,
Benjamin's theory of seeing in the artwork essay tends to impede its own
critical aspiration. While he defines modernity as the age that calls into
question the authority of aura, Benjamin in the artwork essay fails to provide a solid basis for what caused the change from traditional to modern
perception in the first place. Such defects in the conceptual groundwork,

however, in turn tend to thwart the explanatory power of his attack on scopophilic politics overall on a number of levels.

First, it seems that Benjamin's conceptualization of filmic representation – as seen from today's perspective – describes modes of spectatorship typical not for cinematic audiences, but for couch potatoes in front of TV screens. In contrast to the centered, enclosed, and isolated forms of spectatorship in cinema, the customs of TV viewing are implicated in a "lower level of sustained concentration on the image"[51] – one that allows for distracted distance and a limitation of scopophilia. Stripping the image of any unnecessary detail, TV broadcasts often have the effect of greater immediacy and actuality, and therefore suggest a larger sense of complicity between spectator and sender. "TV's regime of vision is less intense than cinema's: it is a regime of the glance rather than the gaze. The gaze implies a concentration of the spectator's activity into that of looking, the glance implies that no extraordinary effort is being invested in the activity of looking. . . . In psychoanalytic terms, when compared to cinema, TV demonstrates a displacement from the invocatory drive of scopophilia (looking) to the closest related of the invocatory drives, that of hearing. Hence the crucial role of sound in ensuring continuity of attention and producing the utterances of direct address ('I' to 'you')."[52] It goes without saying that TV spectatorship, though decentered and distracted, often collective and nonscopophilic (the frequent in-between walk to the fridge!), has hardly ever produced the kind of critical viewer Benjamin identified in front of the cinematic screen, a viewer who uses distraction to tear down the authority of surfaces and symbolic totalizations.[53] As a matter of fact, commercial TV tends to use its atmosphere of immediacy and tactile structure of address to even further distraction, maintaining systems of amusement that prepare the spectator to become a good, that is economically effective, shopper.[54]

Second, the all too undialectical opposition of auratic identification and Brechtian distance entices Benjamin on the one hand to deny spectatorial activities we perform in front of traditional artworks, and on the other hand to overestimate the technological aspects of postauratic culture.[55] Benjamin, as Heidi Schlüpmann and Miriam Hansen have argued, "assumes too close and immediate an affinity between patterns of mass-cultural reception and the standards of and methods of rationalized, mechanical modes of production."[56] His theory of film falsely hypostatizes the advances of technological and instrumental rationality as signs of an inclusive unfolding of reason in modernity; it fails to develop more differentiated concepts of political, social, and cultural rationalization that would enable us to understand the dialectical course of reason in all its different guises. It is this theoretical blind spot, on the other hand, that bears responsibility for the artwork essay's final and most infamous proclamation, the juxtaposition of aesthetic politics and politicized art, of Marinetti's apotheosis of techno-logical warfare and modern Russian film art, fascism and communism, a juxtaposition that has raised more questions than it can in fact answer. Mo-tivated by too formal and one-dimensional an account of aesthetic percep-tion, Benjamin suggests an authoritative but in this context no doubt dangling chiasmus of political art and aesthetic politics that seems to en-dorse an alternative to fascism that is no less problematic – one that, in one way or another, prepared the ground for the disputable achievements of so-cialist realism.

Third, and foremost, however, the reductionist conceptualization of modern visual experience in the artwork essay undermines Benjamin's cri-tique of fascism itself as it lacks some crucial criteria of difference. Although one may derive fruitful notions of submissive spectatorship, Benjamin's theory of film and scopophilic politics is too broad in order to account for the historical uniqueness of German National Socialism and its scopic pol-itics. It lumps the spectatorial response to traditional artworks, mainstream narrative cinema, and fascist spectacle into one category of auratic (and masochistic) looking, and thus seems to generate all too simplifying formulas. It also fails to theorize adequately the overall obsession of nineteenth- and twentieth-century politics with symbolic modes of self-representation, spectacles in the context of which political processes and in-stitutions are no longer legitimized through public debates but merely through drama and appealing visual appearances.

In order to respond to and rectify some of the reductionist tendencies of Benjamin's theory of scopic politics in the artwork essay, chapter 5 will re-configure his 1935/36 argument within the material anthropology of Ben-jamin's later works, in particular his unfinished *Arcades Project* and his essay on Baudelaire. As I will argue, Benjamin's later works not only shed addi-tional light on the aestheticization thesis, they also ground the account of political visuality in a more solid theoretical foundation. Outlining a much more complex and variegated theory of modern experience, Benjamin's works after about 1935 provide notions of visuality that overcome the am-biguities coupled with the original notion of aura. They help unbind his critique of aesthetic politics from the shortcomings built into the schematic definition of auratic and postauratic perception in the artwork essay.

Benjamin in his later texts rethinks the aestheticization thesis with regard to newly emerging structures of experience in industrial mass society since the middle of the nineteenth century. On the one hand, he brings into focus a peculiarly modern replacement of verbal communication with visual, voyeuristic modes of experience that undermine the possibility of social discourse and rational critique. Urban life changes our modes of perception and, in so doing, undoes traditional foundations of social integration. On the other hand, retracing the steps of capitalist modernization, Benjamin observes the emergence of political practices that deliberately address the peculiarly modern will to scopophilia and voyeurism. Benjamin is especially interested in the sensational, transfigured display of newly produced commodities, displays that bind and organize the masses by appealing to their drive for optical entertainment. Prefiguring the Nazi spectacle, nineteenth-century modernity transforms the present into a stage full of simultaneous references to all kinds of historical and mythical pasts. It silences social unrest through pleasurable looking and thus describes a blueprint for the later practices of fascist domination and political homogenization.

5

MODERN VISUAL CULTURE AND THE POLITICS OF PHANTASMAGORIA

The third section of Benjamin's artwork essay calls for a theoretical armature historicizing our modes of sense perception and experience. Benjamin
in this passage rejects any Kantian attempt to map our ways of seeing and
experiencing the world solely by means of transcendental categories. He instead proposes a perspective that deciphers how particular historical conditions shape our patterns of apprehension, experience, and representation:
"During long periods of history, the mode of human sense perception
changes with humanity's entire mode of existence. The manner in which
human sense perception is organized, the medium in which it is accom-
plished, is determined not only by nature but by historical circumstances as
well" (ILL 222; GS 1:478). Human sense perception is deeply ingrained in
the course of history and technological progress; its development bears testimony to groundbreaking social changes. Although Benjamin refers
to Alois Riegl and Franz Wickhoff, the neoromantic art historians of the
Viennese school, his insistence on the historicity of sense perception rings
Marxian indeed. For Karl Marx, in his early anthropological writings, in
particular his *Economic & Philosophic Manuscripts* (1844), had sought already
to ground idealist constructions of sense perception à la Kant and Hegel in
the materiality of history: "The *formation [Bildung]* of the five senses is a
work of the entire previous world history."[1]

Though insisting on the historicity of the human senses, Benjamin's artwork essay falls short of accounting for what solicits historically specific
modes of perception. Central to his argument on the scopic politics of fascism, the genesis and content of what Benjamin defines as auratic art and
postauratic visuality, respectively, remain obscure. The artwork essay describes the transition from auratic to postauratic visuality, from contemplative to distracted modes of seeing, in terms of a universal process of
secularization, instead of following Benjamin's own program and analyzing

the material conditions that engender modern vision and experience. Not the advent of, say, modern traffic technologies or the feverish logic of the capitalist market economy beget the modern drive for distraction, but the rather unqualified uncoupling of art from cultic practices and the ensuing opening of the aesthetic toward the masses – that is, film. In the final analysis, Benjamin's artwork essay answers the question, "Why does auratic perception disintegrate?" by saying it does so "[b]ecause of secularized man's desire to bring things closer," an answer that fails to live up to Benjamin's own critical aspirations and thus undermines the historical and theoretical viability of the aestheticization thesis. Outlining a theory that maps historical developments in diachronical paradigms, Benjamin's artwork essay tends to reinscribe idealist moments into its putatively materialistic doctrine of art. It ends up claiming that secularization happens because of the intellectual desire for secularization.

It is in the context of the *Arcades Project* and the related essays on Charles Baudelaire that Benjamin delivers a historically more specific model of sense perception – one that relates long-term processes of secularization to the institutions, technologies, and material living conditions that have structured everyday existence since the middle of the nineteenth century. In contrast to Benjamin, who believed that the artwork essay would cast light on his magnum opus,[2] in the following I suggest, conversely, that it is the *Arcades Project* that allows us to better understand the artwork essay. As it distinguishes between the formal opportunities and the failed promises of modernity, the *Arcades Project* helps us substantiate the artwork essay's argument on modern visual culture and on how postauratic visuality may become complicit with antimodern political projects. In contrast to the artwork essay, the *Arcades Project* no longer conceives of the predominance of visual distraction in modernity as a quasi-automatic corollary of modern secular life. Instead, Benjamin now explains postauratic diversion and the pictorial turn of modern society as a direct response to the material environment and the perceptual challenges in industrial societies. Modernity is preoccupied with looking because the eye allows for a peculiar form of protection against the technological configurations of the urban environment, the acceleration of communication speeds, and the overabundance of discontinuous stimuli on the streets and in the factory halls. Social modernization coincides with, indeed even expedites, nineteenth-century cultural and aesthetic modernization. It evokes in the sphere of everyday life unprecedented aesthetic attitudes – scopophilic exhilaration *and* distanciation – necessary to preserve and reinvent individual and collective identities against the grain of technological progress and institutional differentiation. Benjamin's *Arcades Project* develops a material anthropology that not only clarifies concepts such as auratic and postauratic experience, but in doing so also allows us to better understand the peculiar role of visual culture in fascism. Surely, similar to the artwork essay, the *Arcades Project* seems to ignore the fact that vision was not the only sense fascism exploited. Though written almost a decade after the introduction of the talkies, the artwork essay completely elided any awareness of how the advent of synchronized sound in the late 1920s had changed film exhibition, style, and consumption, how it had generated new patterns of identification and had resulted in an increasing standardization of perception. Curiously out of synch with the developments of film technology, Benjamin favored Soviet montage cinema of the 1920s over Riefenstahl's mass spectacles because montage allegedly infused our ways of looking with the critical – and one might suspect more respectable – power of hermeneutic reading. In doing so, Benjamin ended up ignoring the many ways in which film practitioners in the 1930s could rely on aural effects in order to intensify meanings or, conversely, complicate viewing positions. Benjamin's silence on sound evidenced a crucial failure to address how the breakthrough of the talkies played right into the hands of Nazi film practice and its quasi-Wagnerian attempt to satisfy that "old Germanic longing to include the whole world into one artwork."[3] This silence corresponded with Benjamin's negligence about the fact that new aural technologies such as the radio added important dimensions to aesthetic politics.

Notwithstanding this striking lack of attention to the aural, Benjamin's thoughts on modern perception as suggested by the *Arcades Project* remain important in understanding how the Nazi spectacle sought to orchestrate emotions and anesthetized sense perception. To Benjamin, fascism is obsessed with visuality, with images, with signs and symbols, and this obsession emerges as a wicked twist within the larger history of modern sensuality and ideological captivation. Benjamin argues that nineteenth-century capitalist societies, to the extent that they transfigure commodities, labor, and domination by means of what he calls phantasmagoria, strategically address the modern desire for innerworldly, visual diversion. The advocates of social modernization understand not only how to engender new aesthetic experiences beyond the domain of autonomous art, but also how to utilize scopophilic impulses in order to justify the breakthrough of capitalism and seduce the masses into delightful conformity. If fascist politics gives individuals symbolic expression instead of power, nineteenth-century capitalism organizes public spectacles in which mass entertainment coincides with assent and submission. The phantasmagorias of capitalist modernization enthrone newly produced commodities as objects of fetishistic worship so as to reintroduce cultic elements to modern society and shape a homogenous body politic. A symptom and catalyst of postauratic visuality, the nineteenth-century phantasmagoria thus preludes the ways in which fascism makes use of industrial culture in order to recreate lost rituals and reproduce the sacred as simulacrum and simulation.

Benjamin's history of modern sense perception begins with a trauma; namely, the disturbance of the gaze during the first railway trips, the dissolution of traditional vision and identity in the face of nineteenth-century urban masses, the mechanization of the body in front of new automatized manufacturing technologies. At first these traumas of modernity, while undermining the circular rhythms of preindustrial life, may also obliterate the possibility of aesthetic experience altogether. The mind's nervousness produced vis-à-vis a rapidly passing landscape or the amorphous movements of urban life seems to undermine once and for all the preconditions of traditional pleasure, whether in the art museum or in reading a romantic novel. But upon closer inspection, Benjamin argues, the various ways of coping with the trauma of modern speed in fact add a new chapter to the history of aesthetic experience – in fact revise the entire concept of the aesthetic. Culture – understood as the system of perceptions, norms, values, and expressions – responds to social modernization, to nineteenth-century acceleration and mechanization, with innovations of its own kind. In order to protect the individual from traumatic disruptions, humanity learns how to transform speed into a source of pleasure and, thus, to emancipate aesthetic modes of seeing the world from traditional loci of bourgeois art. As a response to the physiological challenges of urbanity, humanity relocates aesthetic experiences to the scenes of modern everyday life, not simply to transfigure and hence deflect the precarious effects of new technological achievements but rather to reinvent individual and collective identities – that is to say, flee into, not out of, modernity.

According to Benjamin, modern sense perception is primarily characterized by the notion of shock, a category that is meant to connect the technological transformations of the urban environment with the subjective apparatus of visual and physiological experience. The concept of "shock" derived from Middle Dutch and originally denoted the clash of military troops after the dissolution of individualized combat techniques that were typical during the Middle Ages.[4] In his account of modern life as a scenario of shock experiences, Benjamin, as we will see in a moment, clearly alludes to the combative aspects invested in the original meaning of shock; his analysis of Paris and his readings of Baudelaire's poetry abound with quasi-militaristic metaphors. Yet it is neither etymological speculation nor a retrospective glance at early modern military discourse that fuels Benjamin's theoretical construct of shock; it is, rather, his readings of two seminal turn-of-the-century theorists of the modern, Georg Simmel and Sigmund Freud.

Simmel, in his famous essay "The Metropolis and Mental Life," theorized the impact of nineteenth-century urbanization in terms of an "acceleration of nerve-life."[5] Confronting a heretofore unknown abundance of visual stimuli in the heart of the growing urban centers, modern man turns into an impressionist, virtually unable to process the available masses of impulses and information, and therefore constantly threatened with decentering intoxication and exteriorization – that is to say, nervousness. But Simmel's original contribution was not to identify affinities between social modernization and increased numbers of nervous breakdowns – nervosity clearly marks one of the key words in a variety of aesthetic discourses around 1900[6] – but to investigate certain mechanism of defense, deployed to protect the individual against the overwhelming flood of punctualized impulses. Following Simmel, the modern subject sees salvation from the trauma of modernity in raising the level of consciousness. As they sharpen their visual perception and presence of mind, the urban dwellers discover a "shield to protect subjective life against the rape through the metropolis."[7] Exposed to the peril of nervous fragmentation, urban subjects respond to visual excitement with what Simmel calls the intellectualization of perception; they anticipate the shock in thought so that it won't hit them so hard! This mobilization of awareness, of intellectual defense shields, however, leads to the atomization of the urban inhabitant amid the crowds on the streets. For in order to preserve traditional boundaries of identity and self-hood, the individual espouses highly stylized modes of self-demarcation, a pompous rhetoric and theatricality of distanciation and self-representation. This excess of urban narcissism and self-stylization interrupts the possibility of unhampered communication and meaningful exchange. All eyes, and in desperate need for visible criteria of distinction, Simmel's modern city dwellers turn into bohemians, aestheticists, and exhibitionists.

Informed by Simmel's account of urban life, Benjamin explores the impact of nervousness and increased visual awareness on the workings of individual and collective memory – the accumulated symbolic orders in the context of which meaning and social practices are constructed and negotiated.[8] For Benjamin, the intellectualization of urban perception and the resulting exercises in self-stylization undo the conditions of lived experience. They relegate the individual to the discontinuous thrill of voyeuristic amusements rather than the long breath of tradition, and therefore undermine the production of meaning and communication. For lived experience and, hence, meaningful identities are, as Benjamin argues, "indeed a matter of tradition, in collective existence as well as private life. It is less the product of facts firmly anchored in memory than of a convergence in memory of accumulated and frequently unconscious data" (ILL 157; GS 1:608). Meaningful experiences and identities are possible only if subjects succeed in reconstructing their life history in narrative form, but also – unknowingly – store memory particles in the unconscious. In order to protect themselves against the shocks of urban life, the modern city dweller, by contrast, not only raises his level of awareness, but thus also sequesters the storehouse of remembrance with an impenetrable shield of intellectualized perception: no shock, but also no real memory. Thrown into the urban flood of discontinuous provocations, the nervous individual fails to synthesize individual data of perception with an overarching stream of experience, rendering punctualized events as a source of visual pleasure rather than a well of knowledge or wisdom.

The greater the share of the shock factor in particular impressions, the more constantly consciousness has to be alert as a screen against stimuli; the more efficiently it does so, the less do these impressions enter experience *(Erfahrung)*, tending to remain in the sphere of a certain hour in one's life *(Erlebnis)*. Perhaps the special achievement of shock defense may be seen in its function of assigning to an incident a precise point in time in consciousness at the cost of the integrity of its contents. This would be a peak achievement of the intellect; it would turn the incident into a moment that has been lived *(Erlebnis)*. (ILL 163; GS 1:615)

Nineteenth-century industrialization repositions the body vis-à-vis the built environment. It entreats the subject to map the external world in radically new ways. To the extent that modern speed destabilizes traditional conceptions of spatial unity and continuity, the urban subject needs to explore in hitherto unknown ways the temporal vectors of perception. Thus, the act of mapping the environment becomes a matter not of timeless contemplation but instantaneous recognition and maneuvering. Because in Benjamin's modernity, time dominates over space, individuals will master the shocks of modern life only if they succeed in becoming complicit with the regime of transitory movements; that is to say, render fleeting images attractive and, hence, develop what Wolfgang Schivelbusch calls forms of panoramic perception. Initially shocked by the speed of the railway, the industrialized consciousness learns quickly to enjoy train rides, once passengers cease to mourn what Schivelbusch has analyzed as the loss of a foreground, the evanescence of distinctions, and the deterritorialization of the spectator.[9] Sense perception enters modernity whenever it learns how to construct, say, the window of a railway car as a screen where one may encounter spectacles of transitory nature – a kind of nature, however, that has only little to do with older perceptions of landscapes as it appears produced by the railway coach in the first place.

The material configurations of modern life, then, require constant activities of distanciation and technological mimicry. The individual needs to learn how to outspeed the pace of urban existence. In the eyes of Benjamin, this acceleration of being and perception obliterates the grounds for individual and collective memory and, hence, thwarts traditional forms of self-representation and social integration. Developed to map the new organization of space and time in the urban environment, intellectualized perception screens out whatever could leave a real trace – a trace of experience. In a sense, these screens of optical protection embody a novel mediation between the subjective and objective world, both internalizing the exterior world into the spectator and marking the incorporation of the subject into a depthless world of stimulus and response games. Benjamin, in his essay on Baudelaire's poetry, borrows from Freud in order to elucidate this reconfiguration of the body amid the technological environment of modernity. Hardly ever present in Benjamin's overall work, psychoanalysis is here supposed to account for the traumatic absence of memory traces, the blurring of traditional boundaries between the subjective and objective world, the displacement of unconscious knowledge with surface distraction and entertainment in modern life.[10]

Benjamin is mostly interested in Freud's analysis of remembrance as outlined in *Interpretation of Dreams* (1900), but also in the psychoanalytic examination of traumatic neuroses – the shocks of patients involved in railway accidents – in *Beyond the Pleasure Principle* (1920). In the earlier work, Freud examined the unconscious moment inherent in the construction and accumulation of individual memory and, hence, experience. Our memories, Freud wrote, are "unconscious in themselves; those that are most deeply impressed form no exception. They can be made conscious, but there is no doubt that they unfold all their activities in the unconscious state. What we term our character is based, indeed, on the memory-traces of our impressions, and it is precisely those impressions that have affected us most strongly, those of our early youth, which hardly ever become conscious."[11] If remembrance is indeed a matter of storing impressions in the treasure box of the unconscious, the modern formation of protective shields interrupts the very possibility of such experiences. Under the auspices of urban modernity, the unconscious becomes sealed off from what our eyes register and, thus, degenerates to a tabula rasa, empty of impressions, empty of the writings of experience. The spectacular scenes of modernity may penetrate our minds'Random Access Memory, but they fail to ever touch, let alone fill, the hard drives of true knowledge and experiential wisdom. Because, as Benjamin quotes Freud, "consciousness comes into being at the site of a memory trace" (ILL 160; GS 1:612), the modern regime of RAM – not unlike Freud's *Wunderblock*[12] – mandates the erasure of all signatures in the psychic apparatus, even those of the most immediate past, in order prepare the mind for the next challenge. Keen to protect the ego from further visual shocks, intellectualized perception elevates its protective shields, the psychophysical armor, to a new, peculiarly modern demarcation of individual identity. Modernity sharpens our senses, but it also disintegrates memory and transforms corporeal experience into a combat zone. In the amnesic spaces of modernity, the eyes serve as tools for simultaneous enactments of visual defense, pleasure, and voyeuristic distanciation.

Coalescing Freud and Simmel into an effective theory of modern experience of the senses, Benjamin reads Baudelaire's work as testimony to a mode of perception "for which the shock experience has become the norm" (ILL 162; GS 1:614). The flâneur Baudelaire understands how to parry the multiplicity of stimuli in urban life. He also knows how to use the transformation of the cortex as a source of aesthetic pleasure and artistic productivity. Benjamin considers Baudelaire's poetic production as a form of heroism in an age that no longer seems to entice or tolerate heroic gestures; for Baudelaire responded to the revolutions within the fields of perception, which seem to disempower the resources of traditional art and artistic production, with a book of poetry itself, a modernization of art that unlocks the aesthetic toward experiences of the transitory and fleeting. As a point in fact, Baudelaire, in one of his texts, casts the repositioning of aesthetic experience in modern urban society, the grounding of modern art in everyday environments of shock stimuli, in a telling, not surprisingly belligerent allegory: "He speaks of a duel in which the artist, just before being beaten, screams in fright. This duel is the creative process itself. Thus Baudelaire placed the shock experience at the very center of his artistic work" (ILL 163; GS 1:615–16).

If urban life, sense perception, and modern poetry all become sites of a kind of dueling, then communicative exchange transmogrifies into an instantaneous execution of visual spontaneity and receptivity. As the modern metropolis favors the eye as the primary organ of relating to the world, the poet Baudelaire constructs love as an ocular phenomenon whose sole origin lies in the shortest of all time spans, the *Augenblick*. Baudelaire's sonnet "A une passante" bears testimony to this peculiar metamorphosis of social intercourse. In this poem, a random encounter of poet and widow suffices to inflame a passionate response in the lyric I: for an abrupt moment, absolute presence and eternity seem to coincide amid the transitory movements on the boulevard. To the extent that the eye becomes the primary sense of social interaction, even love mutates into a shock experience, one that erupts and consumes itself in one and the same moment, one that appears in its very transitoriness absolute, but also absolutely without any further consequences: "What this sonnet communicates is simply this: Far from experiencing the crowd as an opposed, antagonistic element, this very crowd brings to the city dweller the figure that fascinates. The delight of the urban poet is love – not at first sight, but at last sight. It is a farewell forever which coincides in the poem with the moment of enchantment. Thus the sonnet supplies the figure of shock, indeed of catastrophe" (ILL 169; GS 1:623). The nineteenth century thus gives birth to the scopic regime of last sights. Because the multitude of stimuli threatens the individual with psychic disintegration, the subject not only covers itself with protective shields but also imbues discontinuous shock experiences with the glimmer of eternal meaning, with aesthetic stature. Yet in contrast to, say, the classicist artist who desires timeless tranquility beyond the worldly order of time, the flâneur seeks to escape the accelerated speed of modern time through time itself. An allegory for the sharpened modes of urban perception, then, Baudelaire's image of the duelist articulates the modern desire to submerge into sudden, self-consuming events – the gaze of the widow – only to bereave them of their temporal index, and hence, render them epiphanic presences that overthrow the routines of time altogether. The flâneur, prototypically embodying the scopic regimes of modern life, finds his eternity and aesthetic exhilaration not beyond but in the very heart of modernity's accelerated temporality.

Informed by Simmel's theory of metropolitan life, Benjamin reads Baudelaire and the figure of the flâneur as testimony to the vicissitudes of visual perception in modernity, the protective function, transfigurative task, and overexertion of the eye vis-à-vis the trauma of postrural existence. Because – as Simmel writes, quoted by Benjamin – the "jostling and colorful mess of metropolitan traffic would be unbearable without any psychological distantiation" (GS 5:561), the eye functions as an organon of self-preservation and detachment. Just as Simmel believes that the monetarization of human relationships inserts functional breathing spaces between the life spheres of urban individuals and prevents the city dweller from suffocating closeness, so does the increased activity of the eye serve as a measure of protection and delimitation. Yet this visual disengagement no longer operates in terms of restful contemplation – that is, auratic distanciation. The modern gaze is totally tactile. It keeps one's distance from possible shock impressions, but – in Benjamin's parlance – there is "no daydreaming surrender to faraway things in the protective eye. It may even cause one to feel something like pleasure in the degradation of such abandonment" (ILL 191; GS 5:650).

If modernity, indeed, describes a social configuration in which the eye takes over, in which postcontemplative, tactile visuality, dating from long before the advent of film, structures our ways of looking, what happens to the word – to verbal communication? Benjamin's answer to this question is twofold: on the one hand, he claims that the end of contemplative distance coincides with the disintegration of traditional narrativity and the vaporization of storytelling as a social institution; on the other hand, Benjamin correlates the peculiar regime of visuality in modern life with the breakthrough of what he calls information – the reduction of communicative substance to snapshot-like bits and pieces of exchange, discontinuous messages that tend to consume themselves.

Following Benjamin's argument in his seminal essay "The Storyteller" (ILL 83–109; GS 2:438–65), epic narration constitutes a preindustrial institution of social integration and communicative exchange. Mediating knowledge and wisdom, stories and storytellers solicit new, and tighten existing, communal networks. For Benjamin, storytelling represents a craft rather than a specialized artform. Though told only by specific individuals, stories are deeply rooted in the fabrics of everyday life and therefore precede the incarceration of art in the private spaces of bourgeois reader- and spectatorship. Untouched by the temporal imperatives of modern urbanity, story-telling emerges as "an artisan form of communication" (ILL 91; GS 2:447), as a site of gaining and trading lived experience located in the domains of oral culture: "If peasants and seamen were past masters of storytelling, the artisan class was its university. In it was combined the lore of faraway places, such as a much-traveled man brings home, with the lore of the past, as it best reveals itself to natives of a place" (ILL 85; GS 2:440).

Whereas the nineteenth-century realist novel was immensely important in the constitution of nation-states, empires, and imperial attitudes,[13] Benjamin's preindustrial storytellers provide narrations that guarantee communal identity in societies ruled by the rhythms of nature and ritual. To the extent that stories establish temporal and spatial continuities, their function is one of positioning the local social body in the fields of both tradition and geography: just as is a nation, communities *are* narrations. The words of Benjamin's stories narrate their listeners into the textures of circular time and topographical location. Far from offering objects of mere entertainment, storytellers embody a public institution of remembrance. They incarnate society's conscious and unconscious mirrors of reflection, and their primary function is to explore their privileged access to the cultural memory banks in order to give advise and counsel.

Modern life undoes the authority of the past over the present, and in so doing it silences the voice of the storytellers and dissolves their public task to strengthen communal impulses and bonds. Social modernization displaces epic breadth with accelerated nervousness, public craft with bourgeois interiority, *Gemeinschaft* with *Gesellschaft*, oral culture with visual culture. In this way, it also dismisses the preindustrial catalyst of experience and wisdom: "The art of storytelling is reaching its end because the epic side of truth, wisdom, is dying out. This, however, is a process that has been going on for a long time. And nothing would be more fatuous than to want to see in it merely a 'symptom of decay,' let alone a 'modern' symptom. It is, rather, only a concomitant symptom of the secular productive forces of history, a concomitant that has quite gradually removed narrative from the realm of living speech and at the same time is making it possible to see a new beauty in what is vanishing" (ILL 87; GS 2:442). The nostalgia of Benjamin's account cannot be missed. He at times seems to endorse the disintegration of narrative communities, even though, at other times, he is at pains to airlift epic communities to the field of modern society in order to overcome modernity's decentering and alienating powers. Suffice it to say that Benjamin's critical film community, for example, modernizes and secularizes the crowd gathered around the storyteller: film, properly used, proves powerful enough to Benjamin to inherit the storyteller's function of community building after the death of oral culture.

Modern technology, however, not only gave birth to film as a revolutionary new form of cultural expression, it also devised mass-circulating newspapers that – according to Benjamin – explore new modes of representation in accordance with the rule of visual elements in nineteenth- and twentieth-century culture. The mass press subscribes to modernity's ocularcentrism by elevating photojournalism to one of its centerpieces, and thus, in its daily design, increasingly replaces textual with visual forms of representation; it reports with illustrations. More importantly, Benjamin argues that the peculiarly modern absence of epic breadth and narrative patience, the regime of shock and discontinuous distraction, directly affect the structures of communicative language in the press – the written word. Provoked by the accelerated logic of modern life, newspaper language grafts pictorial elements right onto the traditional use of syntax and grammar, a process Benjamin describes in terms of a valorization of information over narration. Modernity strips words and larger forms of verbal expression of their semantic plentitude as it transforms them into depthless images – tools of quick, economical exchange.

For Benjamin, the concept of information – in accord with his account of modernity as a regimen of shock events – designates forms of communication whose ultimate function rests in isolating "what happens from the realm in which it could affect the experience of the reader" (ILL 158; GS 1:610). Information, paralleling the tasks of the eye in urban life, operates as a protective shield. It registers the accelerated chunk of news in the global village Earth with ever greater pleasure but deliberately fails to synthesize individual, discontinuous news items with larger narrations, with experience. If the storyteller was fully devoted to what makes curious incidents representative for overarching traditions and customs, Benjamin's journalist and newspaper reader delight in atomized, self-consuming, and hence spectacular sensations. "Information receives its reward instantaneously, not only in that very moment when it was new. It lives only during that moment. It must succumb completely to this moment and devote itself to it without wasting any time. Narration is different: it does not consume itself. It preserves its force in its interior and is able to unfold after a long time" (GS 4:437). Devoted to information's pathos of self-consuming presence, modern journalism embraces global news as entertaining sensations and thus reverses the storyteller's desire for temporal and spatial continuity.

No matter what happens, the relevance of reported incidents no longer derives from their relation to the stock of tradition or the paths of historical evolution, but rather their momentary entertainment value. Whereas the story was supposed to map one's own position within the uniform coordinates of time and space, nineteenth- and early twentieth-century journalism pictures and fragments the world through snapshot-like information in order to divert the reader. If the fact becomes a spectacle, print the spectacle.

Modern societies, then, sever communication from its substance as they render it a sensation, a shock event, a source of pleasure. In a highly interesting fragment, Benjamin links this structure of modern communication and its resistance against overarching meaning to the role of the newspaper as a commodity. This fragment entails *in nuce* a complete theory of the structural transformation of the public sphere during the nineteenth century: "Regarding information, advertisement, and feuilleton: the idler needs to be provided with sensation, the merchant with customers, and the man of the street with a philosophy" (GS 5:484). To the extent that the imperatives of market exchange penetrate the existing forms of bourgeois publicity, newspapers convert from a medium of, no doubt precarious, cultural reflection into one of cultural consumption. In the wake of the commodification of public language, literary and political raisonement increasingly lose their anchor beyond the domestic sphere as they become replaced with privatized modes of textual appropriation. Benjamin's category of information represents one of the main catalysts of this structural transformation. It signifies forms of communication no longer capable of critique, reflection, and collective will-formation. Once drawn into the scenarios of market exchange, language, in other words, emerges as a commodity itself. As an object of pleasure and a stimulus for distraction, it simultaneously, however, provides the reader with world images, ideologies that – following Benjamin – are to counteract social fragmentation and privatization. In fact, in the age of accelerated global information, communication itself becomes an ideology, a fetish. As it addresses the specifically modern desire for diversion, information provides spectacles of systematically distorted communication that help stabilize given hierarchies of power: "The newspaper is an instrument of power. It can derive its value only from the character of the power it serves; not only in what it represents, but also in what it does, it is the expression of this power" (REF 249; GS 2:344).

In his seminal essay on Karl Kraus, Benjamin hailed the Viennese writer as an exemplary critic of such deformations of modern language as caused by the imperatives of power and information.[14] Accordingly, Kraus's insistence on unhampered communication culminates in his attacks on prevalent forms of journalism, which are seen as nothing other than "the expression of the changed function of language in the world of high capitalism" (REF 242; GS 2:337). Obliged to present the ever-newest news items, modern journalism corrupts the inner wealth of language as it degrades it to an organon of sensationalism. In the cultural institution of the feuilleton Kraus observes a strategic obfuscation of proper boundaries between expressive and denotative uses of language, between poetic and informative modes of writing, between art and ethics. To raise sales figures and entertain the distracted subjects of modernity, the feuilleton transforms culture into a market object while it promotes language to a fetish, an ornament that ceases to mean anything at all: "The hack journalist is in his heart at one with the ornamentalist. Kraus did not tire of denouncing Heine as an ornamentalist, as one who blurred the boundary between journalism and literature, as the creator of the *feuilleton* in poetry and prose; indeed, he later placed even Nietzsche beside Heine as the betrayer of the aphorism to the impression. . . . The empty phrase of the kind so relentlessly pursued by Kraus is the label that makes a thought marketable, the way flowery language, as ornament, gives it value for the connoisseur" (REF 241–42; GS 2:336–37). Like Kraus, Benjamin believes that the prevalence of self-consuming information and the ornamentalization of language, the regime of the empty phrase, constitute two faces of one and the same coin. Propelled by the structural transformation of the public sphere during the nineteenth century, the logic of visual communication so deeply penetrated the domains of oral and written expression that it left language deeply marked by the logo of commodity exchange. As a result, journalist sensationalism has curtailed the communicative substance of language, bereaved the tools of expression of semantic depth and historical reference. The feuilleton emancipates the word from its function of coordinating collective action, disseminating wisdom, linking past and present, while it recasts language into an object of market strategies, a currency. Under the rule of distraction and shock, language thus loses its ability to unveil critically the workings of domination. Instead, it operates as an ideology that not only hides the existing distribution of power but effaces its own function within society.

During the last years of his life, Benjamin vacillated between, on the one hand, a preservative position, in which he mourned the acceleration of urban life as a loss of semantic resources, and, on the other hand, a liquidi-tionist stance, in which he espoused the evanescence of traditional experi-ence as a necessary step toward emancipating humanity from the orthodoxies of the past. Benjamin's account of the triumph of visual over oral culture in modernity is deeply enmeshed in this basic ambivalence – in the antinomies of tradition in modern life.[15] Modern visual culture, according to Ben-jamin, is double-edged. It erases what over centuries has kept humanity under the yoke of traditionalism. Fueled with utopian promises – the promise of fulfilled presence – it opens a new chapter in the history of the human senses and, thus, empowers fresh gazes toward renewal. At the same time, however, modern visuality may also yield new forms of assent and submission. Attracted to what diverts and astonishes, the modern amnesic voyeur may just as well turn to the thrill of political spectacles that taboo ex-isting frameworks of power and engender mass conformity.

It is in his *Arcades Project* that Benjamin examines this regressive and dis-empowering potential of modern visuality in further detail. The key cate-gory of this critical undertaking is the one of phantasmagoria. It describes forms of political and social representation that address and symbolically satisfy the new urban will to scopic pleasure and diversion. Benjamin's con-cept of phantasmagoria is part of a theory of public expression that rethinks traditional Marxist concepts of alienation in terms of a Freudian grammar of dream-work. It brings into view capitalist modernity as a dream in which self-representation, individual or collective, appears distorted under the sway of symbolic condensation and displacement. Marx originally intro-duced the concept of phantasmagoria to describe the mystic workings of what he labeled commodity fetishism. Phantasmagorias, for Marx, mirror pathologies of human interaction. They have nothing to do with the com-modity's physical nature but, on the contrary, "represent the specific social relations of humans, which for them here take the phantasmagorical form of a relation of things."[16] In Benjamin's considerably different understand-ing, phantasmagorias, by contrast, emerge whenever a society by means of cultural material tries to abstract from the existing conditions of produc-tion, thereby obscuring the fact that objects and commodities are products of collective work in the first place. Benjamin's phantasmagorias are delu-sions, mirages, deceptions *built already into the very form and outlook of cul-tural manifestations*. They do not merely denote – as Marx thought – the results of collective blindness, but are visible and tactile entities, part of the material inventory by which capitalist society presents itself and addresses the senses of its citizens. Phantasmagorias deflect qua culture and physical appeal from unequal distributions of power, labor, and wealth. Plastic figurations of ideology, phantasmagorias embody utopian dreams and wish-images that simultaneously incite the modern will to diversion, provide symbolic satisfaction, and quell possible unrest.

Visual culture under the regime of capitalist modernization helps present the achievements of urban modernity as spectacle; it links technological progress to a peculiar aesthetics of attraction. Benjamin, on the other hand, responds to these transfigurative practices with a canny exercise in critical physiognomy. Equipped with his microscope gaze, he sorts through the material inventory of the nineteenth century, celebrated achievements or trash, in order to uncover the signatures of a society caught in a collective dream-sleep of consumption. In what Benjamin reads as phantasmagorical configurations, modern visual culture becomes the site at which impressive appearances and great expectations, technological progress, and mythic fantasy intersect. Benjamin's phantasmagorias absorb the gaze of the flâneur, the prototypical representative of modern sense perception, as they emancipate objects from their functional positions and install them, as spectacles, in public showcases. Through phantasmagorias, modern society not only wants to forget that commodities are products of human labor, but also celebrates new technologies and commodities as possible objects of entertainment and specular pleasure. Deifying technological progress, exhibiting national grandeur, revering the rhythms of fashion as ritual recurrences of the always new, the culture of phantasmagoria is one of self-congratulatory hypnosis that reintroduces mythic and cultic elements to modern secular time.

Aside from the Paris arcades, the world fairs are treated by Benjamin as the most instructive nineteenth-century phantasmagoria: capitalism as a theme park. "Sites of pilgrimages to the commodity fetish" (REF 151; GS 5:50), world exhibitions enthroned merchandise and technological accomplishments as cultic icons. They allowed the urban masses to subject themselves to spellbinding iconographies and thereby partake of new forms of social homogenization: the individual experiencing itself as part of an anonymous but joyful crowd of visual consumers. "The world exhibitions glorify the exchange value of commodities. They create a framework in which commodities' intrinsic value is eclipsed. They open up a phantasmagoria that people enter to be amused. The entertainment industry facilitates this by elevating people to the level of commodities. They submit to being manipulated while enjoying their alienation from themselves and others" (REF 152; GS 5:50–51). World exhibitions simulated a society in which each and every one might be empowered to indulge in the pleasures of unrestricted consumption and thus, through delight as a shopper, actualize the utopian desire for unlimited material endowments, the dream of the *Schlaraffenland*. Benjamin reads the world fairs as a meeting ground of a new crowd, one that experiences visual distraction as a common denominator, as the primary mode of social integration. "World exhibitions were the haute école in which the masses excluded from consumption could learn empathy with the exchange value. 'Look at everything, do not touch anything'" (GS 5:267). Anticipating twentieth-century advertising in material form, world fairs opened adventure spaces in which distracted subjects could exercise their voyeuristic dispositions, bring objects to a close distance, and travel visually through time and space. As they embarked on spectacular rides through the landscapes of industrial productivity, the masses were forged into a new community, a community of hypnotics that dreamed the pleasurable dream of endless consumption.

Phantasmagorias solicit spectatorial positions that perceive consumer goods as self-producing entities, objects without authors. Phantasmagorical creations efface any trace of their own coming into being, negate the hand that made them, and thus deny any notion that humans and bodies could make history. With his notion of phantasmagoria, Benjamin describes nineteenth-century technologies of power that – as Jonathan Crary put it in a different context – generated possibilities "for imposing visual attentiveness . . . and managing perception."[17] Phantasmagorias recode the newly emerged liberation of the eye, regiment the alleged freedom of ocular distraction, and thus couple visual consumption with strategies of internalizing power. As they encounter the achievements of industrial productivity like artworks, the distracted masses of the nineteenth century enter a realm of mythic inevitability. While they allude to the oldest myths and incite the spectators' utopian fantasy, phantasmagorias picture the new as old only to colonize the unconscious and solicit uncritical applause to the spectacle of modernity: "Corresponding in the collective consciousness to the forms of the new means of production, which at first were still dominated by the old (Marx), are images in which the new is intermingled with the old. These images are wishful fantasies, and in them the collective seeks both to preserve and to transfigure the inchoateness of the social product and the deficiencies in the social system of production" (REF 148; GS 5:46–47).

Appealing to new modes of sense perception and experience, nineteenth-century capitalism unleashes cultural material in order to put the masses to sleep. Phantasmagorias move hearts and minds, but they also discipline emotions and overwhelm critical perceptions. In contrast to Marx's concept of ideology, Benjamin's notion of phantasmagoria, therefore, does not simply denote systematically distorted forms of consciousness, blind spots in the heart of the perceptual apparatus as it were; nor does it invoke a concept of modern society as an ensemble of public lies, as nineteenth-century critics such as August Strindberg wanted to have it.[18] Rather, phantasmagorias in Benjamin's sense embody a bizarre but effective discombobulation of political, economic, and aesthetic practices. They present sites at which one can experience ideologies as plastic realities, as images that address and involve the sharpened senses and industrialized modes of perception particular to urban life. In contrast to vulgar notions of ideology, Benjamin insists that there is no true order of things underneath the bewitching surface of phantasmagorical configurations. One cannot simply crush their glamorous appearance in order to make things look as they ought to look. Yet although phantasmagorias may be seen as simulacra, as copies without original, to Benjamin – in contrast to Baudrillard – they attenuate relations to something quite real. As they efface social relations and labor through strategies of transfiguration, condensation, and displacement, phantasmagorias glorify modernity upon arrival. They sell modernity as a spectacular ride, a cult and ritual that puts modern amnesia and the will to scopic pleasure in the service of producing conformity and diffuse, but effective, forms of political legitimation.

Like Benjamin's nineteenth century, fascism was both image made and image mad. It relied on a highly sophisticated media industry that overwhelmed the individual with an endless flood of mass-produced images, not only to entertain its subjects but also to hit them over the head and distract them from its unstable ideological core. Modern visual culture in fascism became a laboratory in which a new mass subject could be shaped and new forms of mass organization were introduced. Much more than simply an instrument of overt propaganda, the visual established ample "relays from the imaginary to the real" and thus enlisted postauratic perception in the service of fascism's peculiar approach to subject formation.[19] Nazi visual culture helped provide imaginary solutions to real contradictions. Reckoning with distracted, industrialized modes of looking, with the amnesia of the modern urban subject, fascist visual culture appealed to the collective in its unconscious, dreaming state. While fascism condemned, as Susan Buck-Morss has argued, "the contents of modern culture, it found in the dreaming collective created by consumer capitalism a ready-at-hand receptacle for its own political phantasmagorias. The psychic porosity of the *un*awakened masses absorbed the staged extravaganzas of mass meetings as readily as did mass culture."[20] Fascism drew heavily from the redefinition of sensual pleasure during the nineteenth century, casting the mass of dreaming consumers into the no less dreamlike, albeit more violent, scenes of the community of the folk. Not unlike the world exhibitions or the arcades, the aestheticization of politics in fascism relied on a phantasmagorical transfiguration of life, one that however directed the modern regime of last sights not at the trophies of liberal capitalism but at mass rallies and war machines.

National Socialism has often been seen as opposed to culture and civilization, a view that crudely underestimates the extent to which German fascism made use of cultural material in order to mold a new subject and collective. Yet cultural modernization in fascism – like the nineteenth-century phantasmagoria – in many respects culminated in a rejection of symmetrical forms of intersubjectivity, an articulation of banality leading up to a disaster that left posteriority speechless forever. Public language in Nazi Germany was meant to bond the subject to nationally and racially homogenous experiences.[21] Capitalizing on that which knows no real referent in language – the material rhythm, texture, and color of verbal expressions – the use of linguistic expressions was aimed at the utopia of a mythic community integrated via the tessitura of the German language. Contrary to what is often said about the Third Reich, the Nazis did not refuse speech altogether; they promoted primarily one version of it – the dictator's harangue. Language in the Third Reich served – in Victor Klemperer's words – primarily the purpose of conjuration and incantation transforming all linguistic expressions into public speeches and ritualized events.[22] Nazi language inundated the listener with a multitude of sounds that deflected the possibility of autonomous thought and rational communication. It appealed to the listener's emotions not simply to entertain and distract but to erase former boundaries between private spaces and public agendas. Steeped in the repertoires of mechanical reproduction, visual culture was meant to occupy and intensify this inner silence and affective monologism of the Nazi state. It offered images that glorified unalienated immediacy and heroic authenticity. Image-hungry consumers could find abundant reproductions that supplanted direct experience. The visual thus became a crucible of preconceptual, affective integration: "Crowds watching films learn from the screen to know themselves as a crowd: moviegoing becomes a group rite, or a place where strangers meet to dream together. The crowd comes to know itself as film."[23]

Nazi intellectuals, though often taking recourse to self-contradictory arguments, did not hesitate to support this favoring of the visual and imaginary over the word. Consider Alfred Baeumler's metaphysical sketch of contemporary culture as torn between two interrelated principles, between the symbol and the word, between image and language, between – in post-Lacanian parlance – the imaginary and the symbolic. For Baeumler, symbols warrant essential forms of social unity that are always already there, as part of a collective's unconscious – its destiny. Appealing to our senses, symbols are mythic repositories of cultural homogeneity, unquestioned solidarity, and physical immediacy, of meanings that remain outside and beyond the bounds of history. The word, by contrast, operates as the instrument of dissecting rationality, of civilization and history. It engenders separation and individuation, relegating the individual's mind to rules, norms, and organized patterns of thought. "All efforts to communicate are vain if we do not take strong roots in the world of the symbol. . . . We no longer understand each other today if we do not transcend the empire of existing words, we misunderstand reality if we do not immerse ourselves into the world of the symbol. . . . It is simply impossible to understand National Socialism through the word; for our age is a time of the disempowerment of the word."[24] It is the call of every nation, Baeumler argues, finally to arrive at the word, in spite of the pictorial turn in modern history. But this journey will succeed only if we anchor the word in the unifying power of the symbol – if the homogenizing force of the imaginary keeps the centrifugal force of language in check. For Baeumler, National Socialism aims at nothing less than this reenchantment of the word, at a new sacred. National Socialism endorses the rootedness of language in the all-encompassing authority of the visual, of cult and myth. Dedicated to the reconciliation of reason and emotion, history and myth, language and image, fascism unifies the divided tracks of human cognition and experience by means of the affective logic of the symbol, the imaginary.

Myth, cult, destiny, affective integration: all four categories also occupy a central place in Benjamin's material history of the modern senses, his ethnography not only of fascist visuality but the role of modern visual culture in general. Benjamin's *Arcades Project* understands nineteenth-century industrialization as an ambivalent process of cultural modernization and disenchantment that generated mythic powers and fueled secularized society with rejuvenated cultic impulses. In the new metropoles, everyday life encountered a multitude of visual references to a mythical world that had subterraneously survived eighteenth-century Enlightenment. Poised at the threshold of a fundamentally new order of life, the old society seemed to hesitate for a moment, hiding the unfamiliar face of technology behind the iconography of classical myth.[25] But in addition, and in contrast to Max Weber's equation of capitalist rationality and secularization, nineteenth-century culture also institutionalized hitherto unknown environments of cultic worship and integration as it installed technological achievements and material goods as iconic objects, objects that engrossed the scopic desires of the modern city dweller and sutured him into the quasi-egalitarian, affective community of window-shoppers.

Like nineteenth-century culture, fascism, too, curtails the emancipatory power of modern visual experience. Postauratic modes of looking in fascism help recuperate with modern means humanity's lost rituals. Favoring the image over the word, the mass rallies in fascism functionalize the modern appetite for scopic pleasure and instantaneous sensual gratification, not in order to undo the authority of tradition, but rather to reconstruct cultic spaces of social integration, to stir hopes for innerworldly redemption, and thus to recast the political as a site at which unestranged authenticity comes into being. Similar to the nineteenth-century reinvention of myth and religiosity, fascism resorts to modern visual experience so as to reawaken religious sentiments, rekindle messianic hopes, and thus lay out unquestioned paths of social and political homogenization. Fascist visual culture fills the amnesic spaces of modernity with spectacular events; it addresses the modern viewing subject with engrossing simulations of the past, of identity, of certified meaning, of religious experience. In a 1921 fragment[26] Benjamin thought that a "religion may be discerned in capitalism – that is to say, capitalism serves essentially to allay the same anxieties, torments, and disturbances to which the so-called religions offered answers" (SW 1:288; GS 6:100). Read through the lenses of Benjamin's materialist anthropology of modern experience, fascist visual culture emerges as a last step within this modern reinvention of the sacred, of myth and religion. Fascism is what happens when political leaders impose themselves as replacements of God and create – qua mechanical reproduction – religious feelings as simulacra. Fascism rearticulates the sacred as an agenda of a modern society; it enlists visual culture to demand devotion, induce intellectual assent, and enforce emotional commitment.[27] Its cult not only aims at a final redemption of being in warfare, it also tries to solicit this salvation as a pleasure of first rank.

It has often been rightly pointed out that Benjamin's thought throughout the 1920s and 1930s had a curious affinity for some of the antiliberal ideas of his enemies on the Right. Like Baeumler in the above-mentioned passage, Benjamin, too rejected a world of mere linguistic communications and instrumental transactions. Similar to Baeumler and other right-wing political existentialists such as Schmitt or Jünger, Benjamin, too, at certain points in his career hoped to free modern existence from the burdens of bourgeois normality and routine, of regulation and standardization, in order to reenchant the world and overcome the impoverishment of experience and communal bonds in modernity. Although it would be foolish to deny that left- and right-wing antiliberalism in early twentieth-century Germany shared many of their critical vocabularies, it would be equally foolish to conclude that both entertained the same utopian visions. His often romanticizing views of political alternatives notwithstanding, Benjamin's recurring call for a resurrection of the mythic and prediscursive emphasized – unlike the fascist variants – the necessity of historical mediation.[28] To Benjamin, the charm and legibility of more archaic experiences remained a function of history itself, whereas his right-wing enemies propagated the new as an unmediated return of the old and the cultic as an extrahistorical source of meaning and identity. For Benjamin, the reconstruction of the mythic through modern technologies implied the – however precarious – possibility of liberating the senses and restoring individual experience in its most emphatic sense; for his adversaries on the Right, it offered means to homogenize sense perception and negate the body as the site of autonomous experience and spontaneity.

Consider Albert Speer's infamous lightdomes as the perhaps most striking example for the disciplining elements inherent to fascism's postauratic restoration of religion and cult, fascism's political theology. Its most memorable staging has been recorded at the end of the second part of Leni Riefenstahl's *Olympia: Festival of Beauty* (1938). It is supposed to testify in this film to the successful cinematic forging of beautiful bodies into the organized clusters of mass ornaments, the reactionary fusion of spontaneity and discipline. Speer's lightdomes mobilized advanced technology and a futuristic rhetoric of progress in order to convert modern visual culture into a sacred space, one that transformed the bodies of the participants into props and extras. Addressing peculiarly modern desires for voyeuristic distraction, Speer's lightdomes promised redemption from the predicaments of social modernity, the loss of memory and meaningful identity, the pains of social fragmentation, and the perils of communicative (as well as material) impoverishment. "It is my belief," a participant tellingly described the effects of Speer's political cult, "that our Führer Adolf Hitler was given from the heavenly light to the German volk as the messiah of light over the darkness."[29] Speer's luminary spectacles offered phantasmagorias of social equality that – not unlike the cult of nineteenth-century modernization – constructed collective identity with no reference to existing contradictions; they established political homogeneity beyond the continuing fault lines of class, gender, and political conviction. Prioritizing the imaginary over the real, the image over the word, visual culture here helped stage a cultic festival of self-denial *and* messianic redemption. But it would be perverse not to remember and emphasize that Speer's lightdome at the 1936 Olympics, in colonizing modern amnesia and distraction, in disciplining perception and organizing bodily expression from above, also opened up a training ground for those who only a few years later found themselves in the battlefield trenches, the ultimate catacombs of modern life.

6

PERSEUS'S PARADOX

Jacob Burckhardt – a master in representing the past in paratactical cross-sections rather than diachronic narratives – once cast his notion of historical agency in a maritime metaphor: "The bright and bellying sail conceives itself to be the cause of the ship's motion, but it only catches the wind, which may change or drop at any moment."[1] For the pessimistic realist Burckhardt, the art of making history relied on the skill of utilizing the storms that blast in unpredictable cycles over the oceans of any given culture.[2] Like sober-minded sailors, the agents of history understand how to set sail at the right moment in time; they know how to exhaust those rare periods in history when cultural energies thrive and yearn toward change. Having written movement, renewal, and progress across their sails, Burckhardt's sailors never desire for utopian islands where they can rest and retire from their journeys through time. Instead, they primarily employ the winds of history so as to discontinue the quotidian regime of the always same and thus to contain the agonizing forces that threaten all members of their crew: "Who speaks of victory? To survive is everything."[3]

More than half a century later, and under fundamentally different historical conditions, Benjamin took up Burckhardt's nautical image in a late fragment of 1939 or 1940. In contrast to the conservative historian Burckhardt, Benjamin now employs the sailboat metaphor to encode not the possibilities of historical action, but the exercise of what he considers dialectical historiography: "What is at stake for the dialectician is to have the winds of world history in the sails. To think means for him to set the sails. *How* they are set, that is what is important. For him, words are merely sails. How they are set is what transforms them into a concept" (GS 1:674). In the face of German National Socialism and its aesthetic politics of authenticity, Benjamin's dialectician searches for redemptive powers in the realms of representation and reflection before entering the arenas of so-called immediate action. Whereas Burckhardt's sailors used the winds of history to escape the agonies of routinization, Benjamin's historiographical navigator – somewhat apocalyptically (and, ultimately, nearsightedly) assuming that there is one and only one direction of world history – sets sail to interrupt the hellish logic of *this* modernity; for "[that] it 'keeps going on like this' *is* the catastrophe" (GS 5:591).

It should come as no surprise that Benjamin, not unlike Burckhardt, takes recourse to metaphorical imagery when describing the task of the historian. After all, Benjamin's own thought and writing were firmly rooted in the visual culture of modernity since the middle of the nineteenth century. Exploring the political agendas and ramifications of competing regimes of visuality, Benjamin's "metaphorical materialism,"[4] in particular his theory of the dialectical image,[5] draws heavily on the peculiarly modern favoring of the eye over speech, the image over the concept, this modern preoccupation with ocularcentric modes of social integration. In a sense, the pivotal role of images and metaphors in Benjamin's oeuvre might be understood as a subtle exercise in eristics. Vis-à-vis the visual culture of modernity and its cataclysmic functionalization in Nazi Germany, Benjamin charges his own thought with visual powers, not only to distinguish between regressive and emancipatory modes of visuality, but to strike his adversaries with their own weapons. Benjamin, as Norbert Bolz has argued, "receives the energies of the opponent for the sake of [the opponent's] immanent destruction."[6]

Embedded in peculiar hermeneutic practices, Benjamin's devotion to the visual bears testimony to some of his most esoteric aspirations.[7] Not least of all, Benjamin's pictorial thinking results from his desire for a medium of reflection and expression that emancipates the word from its status as a conventional, arbitrary sign. Benjamin's metaphors and images challenge the putative violence inscribed in instrumental conceptions of language; they are meant to circumvent the void of meaning implicit in what Benjamin denounces as the modern, communicative languages. For Benjamin, images and metaphors promise to restore semantic plentitude and mimetic power to modern reflection. Yet although dedicated to the particular and fragmented, Benjamin's hermetic exercises in pictorial thinking do not seek to displace conceptualization and abstraction altogether. Instead, as Heinrich Kaulen has argued, Benjamin envisions access to concepts and objective truths by means of a cunning detour through the realm of images, one that does not render mute the particularity of the object of investigation: "It [Benjamin's thinking in images] is so arrested and almost compulsively pushed forward by the power of visual apperception, the non-conceptual, non-discursive aspects of recognition, that in the end a conceptual interpretation all by itself springs from the cracks of the image, as it were."[8]

Challenging the sacrifice of the particular on the altar of totalizing systems and discursive reason, Benjamin's pictorial style marks an intellectual practice that mimics the surrealist obsession with the visual – indeed even posits philosophical reasoning as the highest manifestation of surrealism, thereby establishing – as Adorno once put it – "a philosophy cleansed of any argument."[9] The pathos of seeing in surrealism served as an injunction against modern instrumental reason and bureaucratic domination. Surrealists endorsed an excess of the visual in order to explore uncharted territories of the unconscious, and thus map new possibilities for the formation of individual as well as collective identity. In his *Le Paysan de Paris*, Louis Aragon in fact depicted the surrealist call for images and the explosion of the given realm of representation as the decisive step toward a revolutionary change of society: "[F]or every image, whenever it strikes, forces you to revise the entire universe. And every man has an image which, in coming to light, will obliterate the entire Universe."[10]

As he aims at theoretical constructs that, as he recorded in the *Arcades Project*, have "nothing to say. Only to show" (GS 5:574), Benjamin is no stranger to Aragon's pictorial ambitions. Like Aragon, Benjamin's metaphorical materialism deploys visual forms of thought and expression in order to attack the manifestations of instrumental reason in modernity and to solicit revised views of the world that give voice to what has always been censured and silenced. Moreover, while he critiques the ocularcentric modes of social integration in fascism, Benjamin, too, searches for an image powerful enough to obliterate the present universe, that is to say, the Medusian petrification of life under the sign of fascism, the displacement of politics with homogenizing spectacles. It is particularly Benjamin's last text, the 1940 "Theses on the Philosophy of History," written after the Hitler-Stalin pact, that reflects this search for subversive images. True to his metaphorical style, Benjamin unfolds his final theology of history by appealing to numerous images and associations, resisting the imperatives of discursive unequivocalness, and in fact even undermining any attempt to establish a consistent, comprehensive interpretation.[11] More importantly, however, in its allegorical centerpiece, the famous ninth thesis, Benjamin's text also contemplates the inner dilemmas and aporias of a theory that responds to the scopic politics of fascism with quasi-surrealist explosions of the visual. Like the melancholic angels in Wim Wenders's *Faraway, So Close* (1993), Benjamin's angel of history embodies not a redemptive message in itself, but rather a divine messenger and observer. Unlike Wenders's angelic interceptors, however, Benjamin's angel is struck with silence, bereft of speech and, thus, deprived of any redeeming message:

A Klee painting named "Angelus Novus" shows an angel looking as though he is about to move away from something he is fixed contemplating. His eyes are staring, his mouth is open, his wings are spread. This is how one pictures the angel of history. His face is turned toward the past. Where we perceive a chain of events, he sees one single catastrophe which keeps piling wreckage upon wreckage and hurls it in front of his feet. The angel would like to stay, awaken the dead, and make whole what has been smashed. But a storm is blowing from Paradise; it has got caught in his wings with such violence that the angel can no longer close them. This storm irresistibly propels him into the future to which his back is turned, while the pile of debris before him grows skyward. This storm is what we call progress. (ILL 257–58; GS 1:697–98)

Both Gershom Scholem and Rolf Tiedemann in their respective readings of Benjamin's last text have convincingly shown that the allegorical figure of the angel cannot encode the Messiah, who – after all – should be able to awaken death and reconfigure the broken vessels of history into a state of original wholeness.[12] Rather, the angel's gaze denotes nothing other than the perspective of what Benjamin considers the one of the historical materialist, struck with silence in the face of the world historical spectacle of destruction and disintegration. Out of sympathy with the defeated, the angel wants to halt the catastrophic progress of time, but what "he must see, seems to render him speechless."[13] While the storms called progress and chronological time hurl the angel into the future, the angel's gaze remains directed toward the catastrophic panoramas of the past, trying to prevent possible blind spots in our historical vision and memory, chiasmas that would deny ubiquitous suffering.

In contradistinction to the claim of the sixth thesis, which describes the historian's task as "fanning the spark of hope in the past" (ILL 255; GS 1:695) and relocates it into the present, Benjamin's allegorical angel in the ninth thesis appears transfixed by the debris of history, transformed into an institution of melancholic remembrance rather than active intervention. Couched in the allegorical language of Klee's drawing, Benjamin's angel of historiography no longer succeeds in importing political explosives from the past into the present. The angel may see more and more clearly than those whose gaze is exclusively directed toward the future and thus sacrifices the victims of history once more within the realm of remembrance. But Benjamin's angel, unable to distance itself from what it sees, has also something grotesque and terrifying. While the wings appear petrified, the gaze seems as dead and deanimated as its object and, hence, incapable of giving either history or his own trajectory a decisive turn. To return to the aforementioned sailboat metaphor: arrested in mute horror, Benjamin's angel of history forfeits the task of the dialectician to set sail since he appears to be incapable of positioning his wings and his gaze in such a way that he could transform images into concepts and thus fuel the fights of the present with new hope and energy. Whereas the navigator-dialectician actively searched for and utilized the winds of history, the atmospheric currents of history – time and progress – are not on the side of the angel-historian: Benjamin's angelic sailor is held captive by the imagery of destruction and, hence, fails to transpose his empathy with the victims into liberating concepts.

In likeness to the distracted subjects of modernity, Benjamin's angel experiences the world primarily in the mode of looking. Yet, in contrast to the views of the flâneurs, the players, and the nervous city dwellers, the angel's gaze is not captivated by the visual phantasmagorias of modern culture, but rather focused on the imagery of destruction, violence, and suffering that exists beyond plastic veneers of transfiguration and spectacle. As it reads the modern regimes of visual pleasure against their grain, Benjamin's angel reveals the immanent terror of scopic politics. In so doing, however, in administering this reconstructive look, the angel performs what Benjamin, during the final years of his life, considered the last remaining notion of revolutionary activity. Significantly, the "Theses on the Philosophy of History" invoke the original, seemingly unpolitical notion of revolution as crystallized in the discourse of Renaissance astronomy, more particularly in the works of Copernicus, who defined revolution as the rotation of the stars and the restoration of an old law.[14] Unable to incite a discontinuous leap out of history, Benjamin's angel nonetheless aspires a forward move toward the origins, one that rectifies the broken vessels of historical time, reinstates the old law, and thus resurrects a text and order that have been written long ago yet rendered unreadable throughout the course of time. Although he thus seems to relocate Copernicus's astronomical concept of revolution into the realm of politics, Benjamin's notion of revolution remains theological through and through. Messianic redemption and reawakening rather than democratization and emancipation, cessation of profane time rather than material change, emerge now as the ultimate goals of any future revolution: "Marx says that revolutions are the engines of world history. But perhaps things are completely different. Perhaps, revolutions are humanity's grasp for the emergency break of humanity while travelling in the train of world history" (GS 1:1232).

Whereas Jacob Burckhardt pictured history in terms of an endless oscillation between stagnation and vitalist renewal, Benjamin's angel refrains from trusting the forces of tradition or those of rejuvenation and progress. In fact, Benjamin's last text wants to undo the pathos of progress as inscribed even in traditional Marxist and Socialist ideologies. For Benjamin, the Social Democratic dogmas of social evolution in particular have tended to incapacitate rather than strengthen the utopian energies and emancipatory potentials in modern society. "Progress as pictured in the minds of Social Democrats was, first of all, the progress of mankind itself (and not just advances in men's ability and knowledge). Secondly, it was something boundless, in keeping with the infinite perfectibility of mankind. Thirdly, progress was regarded as irresistible, something that automatically pursued a straight or spiral course" (ILL 260; GS 1:700). Benjamin considers all of these predicates to be problematic because all of them are rooted in the conception of historical time as an empty and homogenous continuum. Benjamin instead advocates a theory of discontinuous "now-times" that renounces any attempt to synthesize particular historical moments with overarching master narratives and networks of meaning. In contradistinction to Hegelian or Marxist dogmas of automatic progress, Benjamin refuses to subscribe to the idea that "every historical event derives out of necessity from another and all of them constitute a progressive movement."[15] Challenging totalizing paradigms of historical meaning, he desires to evacuate hypotactical notions of cause/effect from the narrations of historiography and to replace them with paratactical, discontinuous representations à la Burckhardt.

Benjamin's anti-evolutionary and catastrophic construction of history is no doubt itself a product of very peculiar historical developments. Against the background of both the aestheticized terror of fascism and the bureaucratic fossilization of communism under Stalin, Benjamin depicts the course of human history as a path through ever-increasing scenarios of domination and suffering. Advised by his messianic pessimism, Benjamin's

final text suspends, as Habermas has argued, any meaningful notion of political action, and thus in the absence of powerful democratic forces tends
to sever theory from practice altogether.

In this totalizing perspective, the cumulative development of the productive forces
and the directional change of the structures of interaction are wound into an undifferentiated reproduction of the always-the-same. Before Benjamin's Manichean
gaze, progress can be perceived only at the solar prominences of happiness; history
spreads out like the orbiting of a dead planet upon which, now and then, lightning
flashes down. This forces us to construe the economic and political systems in concepts that would really only be adequate to cultural processes: Within the ubiquity
of the context of guilt, evolutions are submerged beyond recognition – evolutions
that, for all their questionable partiality, take place not only in the dimensions of the
forces of production and of social wealth but even in the dimensions in which distinctions are infinitely difficult to make in the face of the weight of repression. (I
mean progress, which is certainly precarious and permanently threatened by reversal, in the products of legality if not in the formal structures of morality.) In the
melancholy of remembering what has been missed and in conjuring up moments of
happiness that are in the process of being extinguished, the historical sense of secular progress is in danger of atrophy. No doubt these advances generate their regres-
sions, but this is where political action starts.[16]

Out of sympathy with the victims of history, the gaze of Benjamin's angel
recognizes only the losses on the large scale, not the no doubt often precarious, profane victories on a small scale – victories that simply do not exist
for Benjamin. Benjamin's Manichean critique of progress therefore implies
the notion of an ultimately meaningless and unhappy innerwordly emancipation. As a result of his leveling assault on conceptions of linear progress,
Benjamin, in other words, envisions the image of a liberated collective that,
in the face of the towering debris of history, has lost the semantic resources
for an understanding of its own existence as a meaningful, a happy one: no
more violence, but also no more content. Perhaps, it is most of all the fear
about such a senseless emancipation that strikes Benjamin's angel with silence and forces him to turn categorically away from the future. To the eyes
of the angel, history presents itself as a horrible spectacle of violence that in
a fundamental way escapes any linguistic mediation. It is "essentially only
as an image" that the angel may succeed in representing the catastrophes of
the past and present, and thus in expressing his terror in a world devoid of
meaning.[17] Fixed in mute horror and petrification, Benjamin's angel sees
history as an endgame. No word could ever suffice to vocalize, let alone

subvert, this totalitarian cosmos of power, phantasmagorical illusion, and subordination – that is, the Medusian failure of modernity.

Adorno once contended that the glance of Benjamin's philosophy is Medusian – that it is characterized by a "fixating gaze."[18] Adorno's well-chosen metaphor points toward the intricate status of the category of visuality in Benjamin's critique of aesthetic politics. Benjamin, in particular during the very last years of his life, somehow hoped he could outpetrify the petrifying power of fascism and aesthetic politics. Fascism, he believed, gives modern politics the spectacular appearance of heroic, self-contained action and thus drives it beyond fact and value. It glorifies the image of the powerful state, presents the figure of the politician as a genius artist, and thus forces the masses into emasculated, petrified positions of assent and submission. Aesthetic politics redefines political action and history in terms of natural history, as destiny, as a terrain neither made nor marked by ordinary humans. Benjamin, on the other hand, hoped to reverse this spell of transfixation back to its point of origin. He sought to transfix the transfixers – to wrestle away the visual and popular from those who manipulated modern images and modes of looking in the hopes of domesticating hearts and minds and engendering uncritical conformity.

His Medusian philosophy and metaphorical materialism notwithstanding, Benjamin – as I argued in the preceding two chapters – remained highly ambivalent about the pictorial turn of modern history and experience. Though often hailed in recent years as a master theorist of modern visual culture, Benjamin in fact at times endorsed a much older intellectual tradition that understands visuality and visual pleasure as a threat, a force of castrating, feminizing consumption. Throughout the 1930s, Benjamin's judgments about the power of images echo negative attitudes toward the visual that were shaped in German intellectual life during the eighteenth century. Although the European Enlightenment by and large – as Martin Jay has shown in minute detail in *Downcast Eyes* – embraced the visual as an organon of intensified insight and knowledge,[19] the German variant in many respects denigrated the consumption of images from the vista of the written and spoken word. Philosophers such as Alexander Gottlieb Baumgarten demoted visual communication and perceptual apprehension as an inferior gnosis, a spell cast upon the individual by affective and irrational modes of experience.[20] Images were not only seen as merely ornamental, as sources of deception and blindness, in constant need of textual interpretation and control; they were also excluded from what was supposed to fuel the project of bourgeois emancipation and political reform. Visuality was thus discursively constructed as a form of seduction and manipulation, a power that sutures the individual into political spectacles of false collectivity and terrorist homogenization. Clearly indebted to this line of thought, Benjamin in his writings on film favors montage in Eisenstein because montage disrupts the deceptive veneer of images – their appeal to merely emotive registers of reception. As a technique of cross-cutting contrasting images, montage transforms images into text. It keeps in check the affective force of the visual, renders it discursive, and in so doing infuses our ways of looking with the critical power of hermeneutic reading. Moreover, montage and postauratic tactile looking undercuts and controls what Benjamin believes to be the feminizing aspects of visual experience. To avow – like "communism" in the artwork essay – distracted, readerly looking as the centerpiece of modern experience, for Benjamin, means to empower the (male) collective to make history. Fascism, on the other hand, embraces but at the same time disavows postauratic visuality. It endorses modern visual culture for the sake of a curious project of reauratization, and in this way undermines the virility of the proletarian masses while hiding what is essentially feminine – the decadent and aestheticist political leader – in the guise of fake masculinity. Benjamin engenders as feminine what fascist visual culture does to the modern masses, whereas he considers the synthetic aura of the fascist leader as merely a simulation of authentic masculinity.

Benjamin believes that aesthetic politics plays out and displaces male castration anxieties; it illegitimately transfers masculinity from the masses to the leader via the channels of industrial culture. The fascist spectacle, in his understanding, turns out to be a political actualization of the myth of Medusa – of that horrible, phallic woman who cast heroic men into passivity and symbolically castrated them. Recalling the ancient myth, it was of course the hero Perseus who – according to both Lucian and Ovid – finally set out to slay the terrifying Medusa. Wandering along remote and pathless ways through the foothills of the Atlas mountains, Ovid's Perseus, when approaching the Gorgon's home, sees himself relocated into a grotesque, open-air museum: "Everywhere, all through the fields and along the roadways he saw statues of men and beasts, whom the sight of the Gorgon had changed from their true selves into stone."[21] Not only does Medusa bereave her victims of life, she interrupts the flow of chronological time. Not unlike, say, a sculptor or a photographer, she arrests the objects of her gaze in a single, but eternal moment – in timeless, albeit deanimated presence. According to Ovid, Perseus overcame Medusa's violent aestheticism by using his shield in such a way that he could escape her sight, approach her, and cut off her head: "[H]e himself looked at dread Medusa's form as it was reflected in the bronze of the shield which he carried on his left arm. While she and her snakes were wrapped in deep slumber, he severed her head from her shoulders."[22] In Ovid's version, Perseus's shield operates as a mirror whose power of reflection potentially breaks the Gorgon's petrifying, aestheticizing force and thus allows the hero to approach Medusa safely. In Lucian's version, however, Perseus uses his bronze shield not as *his* screen of reflection but instead, guided by Athena, he presents the Gorgon with her own mirror image: facing herself, Medusa undergoes the fate of her previous victims and changes from her true self into stone.

The two versions of course contradict each other with logical necessity. In the first version, Medusa's reflected image lacks the power of petrification; visual reflection emerges as a cunning tool to undo the mortal effects of the monster. By contrast, in the second version, the mirror image is still charged with petrifying powers and thus allows for the application of the beautiful terror of transfixation on the Gorgon herself. If Ovid, in other words, thinks the mirror image interrupts strategies of petrification, Lucian believes that it causes Medusa to petrify herself.[23] It is worth noting, however, that both accounts themselves never render problematic the function of the shield; they depict Perseus as a courageous hero who never questions his devices of cunning imaging and reflection. Yet given the contradictory nature of the mirror in Ovid's and Lucian's respective accounts, how can any modern reader feel anything but surprise at Perseus's unquestioned belief in the power of reflection; how can we avoid bewilderment about the hero's trust in the shield as an instrument to fight the horror of Medusian petrification and aestheticization?

In contrast to his mythic ancestor, the modern Perseus Walter Benjamin, equipped with the shield of metaphorical materialism to slay fascism's Medusian politics, clearly doubted the potency of his critical shield and his images of reflection. In a sense, the ninth thesis of Benjamin's last text vocalizes these doubts in an allegorical image and perhaps even expresses Benjamin's horror of getting trapped in his own imagery, his own ambivalent endorsement of modern visual culture. With the figure of the paralyzed angel-historian, Benjamin points at the possibility that Perseus, misjudging the salvaging powers of his shield, may turn into stone himself. In the ninth thesis of Benjamin's last text, the angel of history – the critical historian of modern history – seems struck by the effects of Medusian petrification. Deeply engrossed in forms of pictorial thinking and metaphorical expression, Benjamin sets out to debunk the Medusian effects of aesthetic politics only to find that none of his dialectical thought-images and critical interventions could ever suffice to obliterate this hellish universe. Not only does the double imagery of catastrophic disempowerment and spectacular political self-representation render the observer silent; in the final analysis, the historian himself seems arrested in a state of paralyzation that disallows any powerful vision into the future. The angel's staring gaze resembles one of those tragic heroes who in the very moment of recognizing the third of the Gorgons was struck by her deadly powers: a despaired, indeed already broken and deanimated gaze. At the end of his life, Perseus Benjamin, therefore, no longer envisioned a triumphant victory over the modern powers of petrification; instead, he sought to collect and preserve the debris produced by the aestheticization of politics, the phantasmagorias of power, the amalgamation of beauty and terror in a failed modernity. Yet even that task was more than one single individual could ever accomplish. Not in the Atlas mountains but in Port Bou, in the Pyrenees, Medusa's gaze struck back.

TWO

RETHINKING
THE SPECTACLE

INTRODUCTION TO PART 2

Benjamin's thought is inseparably linked to the idea of historical actuality. A monumentalizing gaze at the past, according to Benjamin, produces blind spots similar to an antiquarian one. The dialectical historian, in contrast, professes to undo any false heroization of historical events: the task is to shatter the burdens of tradition and canonization, to emancipate the symbolic expressions of former generations from fixed interpretations or facile narratives of continuity, and thus to bring past and present into a volatile dialogue. Benjamin's critique of historicism rallies against the idea that we could own the contents of historical recollection like material objects that the time travelers of historiography can put in their pockets and take home to the future. In the view of the historicist, what is mediated in fact expresses immediacy; historicism signifies the flip side of commodity fetishism. It derives from the chimera that the past can be shipped like a product between the markets of space and time – from the chimera that historical events can be traded in the form of distinct, uncontested, and unchangeable containers of meaning. To insist on actuality, then, means not simply to resist the drive toward canonization and unified interpretation; rather, it means that every generation needs to struggle over the meaning of time in the first place – needs to define anew and in light of an ever-changing present which kinds of collective memories are of greater or lesser significance. Benjamin's ethics of actuality consequently defies the contemporary rhetoric of cultural memory banks. We cannot store memories in a timeless archive unless we desire to divest the past of the possibility to speak to us. To quote the past in fact makes sense only if it establishes the condition for the possibility of knowing the present. Advocates of actuality decipher the legacy of the past in the present but also unearth what prefigures the present in the past. Canons, uncontested traditions, and linear narratives of historical progress or decline tend to obscure rather than illuminate the past and any adequate sense for the logic of temporality. The true historian explodes the continuum of historical time, the fetishes of tradition, in order to unearth a past that may change the understanding of our present. Given this emphatic insistence on actuality and nonlinear historical temporality, it is not without irony that Benjamin's notion of aesthetic politics – understood as a critique of the spectacular fusion of modernist aesthetic practices and antimodern ideologies in European fascism – holds a rather uncontested place within the postwar pantheon of cultural criticism and historiography. Sixty years of scholarship, analyzing the location of culture in German National Socialism or Italian Fascism, has elevated the keyword of the aestheticization of politics to an unquestioned token of critical discourse. Thanks to Benjamin, it has become a truism to say that we cannot speak about fascism without speaking about the role of the aesthetic – about the beautification of social infrastructures and the concomitant translation of decadent idioms of nineteenth-century art into a mesmerizing language of power. Preoccupied with theorizing aesthetic incursions to the political, postwar criticism has domesticated Benjamin's remarks in its attempt to analyze fascism simply as a monumental art exhibition and beguiling showcase of power, as a tyranny of decadent art over procedural politics. Any application of Benjamin's model, however, as Andrew Hewitt has rightly argued, "without continued interference to social and economic determinants must itself fall prey to a form of aestheticization."[1] Converted into a valuable academic commodity, Benjamin's aestheticization thesis has thus often helped support arguments that themselves tend to aestheticize. Stripped of their complexity and scope, isolated quotes from the artwork essay have been used to verify global claims about the nature of fascism. Without further empirical research or comparative analyses, such claims fail to overcome the very terms according to which fascism in fact staged itself.

To describe fascism in its entirety as an aesthetic event of first order, as a comprehensive exercise in monumental seduction, grossly neglects the fact that the beautification of power, state, and life rested on a racist, radical project of inclusion and exclusion, of separating between friend and foe. Fascism did not beautify power and recast politics as a Wagnerian drama of affective excess simply in order to entertain the megalomaniac desires of some perverse would-be-artists-turned-politicians. Rather, beautification served ideological politics; its telos was nothing other than war, exterminism, and genocide. While it diffused the hopes of Germans or Italians to govern themselves, aesthetic politics promised active participation in a charismatic project of national rebirth: a phoenixlike rising of the community of the folk over the dead bodies of subjugated peoples and nations. The epilogue of Benjamin's artwork essay, proposing a theory of generic fascism, therefore understood aestheticization as the inseparable fusion of allure and violence, entertainment and terror, social pacification and total mobilization. Accordingly, aesthetic politics – in its most extreme formulation – is war with other means. It prefigures and prepares for coming attractions, for imperial warfare as the most extreme means of solving the inner economic and political dilemmas of the fascist state. Both war and aesthetic politics, for Benjamin, define the generic core of fascist ideology and practice; both target social reconstruction through racial and national purification.

As outlined in the preceding chapters, Benjamin does not imagine politics in fascism becoming aesthetic simply in terms of a deceptive intervention replacing ethical or political discourse with entertaining theaters of power. Rather, fascist aestheticization describes a form of domination by means of which a postliberal state symbolically hopes to settle social and economic struggles while simultaneously promoting the charismatic image of the autonomy of the political. For Benjamin, to nurture the very idea of autonomous politics itself already evidences a precarious desire to airlift decadent aesthetic values to the realm of twentieth-century political discourse and will-formation. Significantly, however, in fascism the assault on the procedural complexity and normative substance of twentieth-century politics coincides with a peculiar way of tapping the dialectics of modern culture and mechanical reproduction. Benjamin's notion of fascist aesthetics points to a peculiar organization of sense experience under the sign of modern mass culture. Aesthetic configurations in fascism reckon with distinctly modern structures of experience: the masses' hunger for distraction and scopic pleasure. More precisely, it is by recycling within the boundaries of postauratic culture the iconography and affective registers of auratic art that fascism hopes to recenter the workings of a differentiated, secularized, and bureaucratic state and give political operations the reenchanted look of willful, decisive, and unified action. The task of the aesthetic under fascism is thus to emancipate the public image of political decision making from the putatively emasculating effects of self-sufficient economic, military, or administrative imperatives. We would misunderstand Benjamin's argument if we considered fascist aestheticization and mass aesthetics simply as stopgap measures – as cunning strategies of wrapping alluring veneers around bad realities. While the function of the aesthetic in fascism is clearly to halt a revolutionary turn of society as well as any further diffusion of political power into increasingly independent and competing agencies of domination, fascist aestheticization at the same time actively reshapes individual and collective modes of reception and channels disparate hopes for charismatic redemption into the uniform gestalt of collective mobilization. Like the dream world of nineteenth-century commodity culture, fascism appeals and gives expression to the seeds of utopian desires. It appropriates certain properties of social and cultural modernity in order to reconstruct the modern state as a phantasmagoria of power and community, as a shifting series of deceptive appearances that change the very parameters according to which people perceive the real and thus in effect change reality itself. Instead of merely targeting the preservation of past dependencies, the aesthetic moment in fascism reconfigures existing social spaces and perceptions in a way that both prefigures and culminates in warfare. For imperial warfare presents fascism's ultimate answer to the pathological elements inherent in the dialectics of capitalist modernization; only warfare can fulfill the palingenetic promise of national rebirth and racial purification. Fascism pictures violence and warfare as the climax of an alternative modernity, one in which selective components of social, cultural, and technological modernization eclipse the normative substance of political modernity; that is, any reasonable claim for equality, justice, freedom, and any concomitant acts of recognition across existing lines of ethnic, social, or gender difference.

Throughout the past three decades or so, this complex, though mostly fragmentary, analysis of fascist aestheticization and mass aesthetics has experienced a curious popularization and vulgarization both within and outside of the academy. Severed from Benjamin's materialist anthropology, from his theory of experience and sense apperception, the concept of fascist aesthetics today occupies a seemingly uncontested place within the taxonomies of popular art history. It has become a label for a distinct period of artistic articulation as much as for a peculiar mode of expression or style. Speaking about Nazi aesthetics today is like speaking about "impressionism" or "new objectivity." It involves the habitual identification of stylistic features such as the iconography of metalized bodies, the fascination with images of death and transfixation, the phobic veneration of total symmetry, and the fetishistic appeal to monumental theatricality. Leni Riefenstahl, in Ray Müller's 1993 documentary, might still maintain that the concept of fascist aesthetics makes little sense to her.[2] Yet within mainstream scholarship, and in fact the popular dimension in general, Nazi aesthetics seems to denote a fairly predictable set of signifiers and an uncontroversial array of iconographic examples. Needless to say, Hollywood itself has contributed in no small way to the fact that the aesthetic allure of Nazi Germany has become one of the most enduringly potent and successful commodities in today's mass culture, part of the inventory by means of which postmodern consumer culture replays the past forever as movie and myth.

Benjamin's epigrammatic aestheticization thesis has thus been canonized at the cost of watering down some of its most challenging and critical insights. Benjamin's enigmatic and overdetermined style of argumentation has clearly contributed to the appropriation of his theory for various agendas. The vulgarized version of Benjamin's aestheticization thesis invites a myriad of sweeping comparisons and political equations on both synchronic and diachronic scales. Once the debate about fascist aesthetics becomes a mere discussion of representation and style, one is tempted to ask whether John Russel Pope's National Gallery in Washington DC, for example, is as "fascist" as Paul Ludwig Troost's Munich House of Art. Are the ornamental bodies in Madonna's music video "Express Yourself," transmuting work into workout, direct descendants of Riefenstahl's iconography of beautiful, albeit faceless types? Is all monumental art, symmetry in architecture, or the display of fierce muscles impossible after Auschwitz? There are good reasons why one cannot immediately dismiss such questions as simply ungrounded or inherently meaningless. Any theoretical framework proposing a concept of fascist aesthetics and political aestheticization must be able to provide viable answers to such concerns, or at least identify parameters that will clarify what is wrong with their mode of interrogation. At the same time, however, it is not difficult to see that the popular understanding of fascist aesthetics as a mere mode of representation poses more questions than it can potentially answer. Truncated from the analysis of the modern state, its economical and social determinants, and a theory about the shifting topographies of modern experience and cultural consumption, the vulgarized concept of fascist aesthetics inevitably leads to a pretentious political posturing of aesthetic criticism while it simultaneously trivializes the unique role of the aesthetic during the National Socialist period. If inflationary concepts allow us to name Troost and Pope, Speer and Haussmann, Riefenstahl and Madonna in one and the same breath, then we are in danger of eradicating our awareness for the distinctive implication of fascist aesthetics in a project of imperial warfare, national purification, and genocide – and thus, of erasing our understanding of the historical uniqueness of the Shoah itself.

In the 1996 megashow "Art and Power" – sponsored by the European

Council, curated by the London Hayward Gallery, and installed in the Deutsches Historisches Museum in Berlin – these universalizing and hence normalizing itineraries of the postmodern encounter with historical fascism have found a highly instructive formulation. The exhibit recalls the interfaces between totalitarian power and modern culture between 1930 and 1945 in a broader European context. Its point of departure is the monumental mise-en-scène of the 1937 World Fair in Paris, a mega-spectacle itself, used particularly by the regimes of Germany, the Soviet Union, Italy, and Spain to showcase their respective appropriations of modern culture, to demonstrate their might by showcasing their very capacity to forge symbolic materials into impressive constellations. "Art and Power" construes its notion of fascist aesthetics – understood as part of a larger European formation of totalitarian modernism during the interwar years – against the backdrop of the desirability of an innocent and timeless realm of the beautiful. The exhibit defines fascist aesthetics via stylistic criteria such as monumentalist gesture, symmetrical indulgence, heroic posture, futuristic coolness; it maps the politics of art as a relatively coherent system of representation rather than a crucible of cultural practices, affective agendas, and contingent appropriations. Reducing the iconographic language of art to a direct expression of power, totalitarian modernism – the exhibit suggests – systematically taps the erosion of boundaries between art and life prefigured in the agendas of the historical avant-gardes; totalitarian regimes can effectively politicize art only because modern art itself seems to have lost faith in preserving its autonomy. Significantly, in all of its four major sections the exhibit also brings to view the work of artists who tried to resist the stylistic vocabulary of totalitarian modernism by insisting on antirealist and antimonumentalist, nonheroic and abstract, idioms of representation. A selection of Rodtschenkos, Fontanas, Beckmanns, Kollwitzes, and Schlemmers is meant to document the existence of an expressive inventory that defied the appropriation of art as a vehicle of totalitarian self-aggrandizement, a beleaguered island of modernist experimentation amid the violent storms of what is presented as the full and perverse unfolding of the hopes of the avant-garde.

"Art and Power" blames art for ending up as an organ of totalitarian mass deception. It is not difficult to see, however, that the exhibit's alternative between the iconographies of totalitarian modernism and enigmatic modernism oversimplifies the politics of cultural expressions during the 1930s and 1940s. "Art and Power" completely eludes the fact that the disintegration of aesthetic autonomy was not just the product of an inner-aesthetic or stylistic development, but a reflex to the comprehensive redefinition of cultural spaces ever since the middle of the nineteenth century, a response to the ever-increasing commodification of aesthetic expressions as much as to the emergence of mass cultural practices and new and technologically mediated forms of diversion. It is precisely this reductionist reading of totalitarian modernism and fascist aesthetics as merely a chapter of art history that links the exhibit to those revisionist projects of normalization enumerated above, projects that have populated the scenes of German historiography ever since the historians' debate of 1986. "The period of dictatorships," writes Christoph Stölzl, the director of the Historisches Museum, "was a European catastrophe. Our commentary on this must emerge from the spirit of a common European enlightenment."[3] Stölzl interprets fascist aesthetics as an integral expression of a broader European phenomenon. More importantly, instead of thinking through the more complex force field of art, power, and mass culture, of social and cultural modernization, of culture and genocide, his merely stylistic concept of Nazi aesthetics and totalitarian modernism invites us simply to invert – and thus reaffirm rather than explode – the very categories according to which Nazi ideology itself sought to classify the value of art: "Art and Power" grants Hitler and Goebbels a posthumous victory as it reconstructs the past according to the Nazis' self-perceptions. An integral part of a shared European catastrophe, the concept of Nazi aesthetics thus replays in reverse the taxonomies that informed Nazi ideology itself instead of yielding new insights into the sources and structures of domination during the 1930s.

Like many vulgarizing versions of Benjamin's aestheticization thesis, "Art and Power's" way of talking about Nazi aesthetics clearly relies on an aestheticist view of art itself. The exhibit revisits the Nazis' megalomaniac dreams about a total fusion of art and the political much more than it scopes the historical realities of Nazi society. While implicitly rendering all postauratic art per se responsible for authoritarian politics, and while heroizing the formal idiom of a few enigmatic modernists as sole outcries against the pan-European normality of totalitarianism, the exhibit ironically ends up reaffirming the problematic stereotype of Nazi Germany as a flawless mechanism of coordination and homogenization that left no space for resistance or opposition. Linking the concept of Nazi aesthetics to a debate over styles and iconographies, not to a theory of power, secularization, and sense perception, "Art and Power" obscures the racist system of inclusion and exclusion that was at the core of Hitler's project of social beautification. In the final analysis, on the one hand the exhibit draws sweeping comparisons between the stylistic surfaces of 1930s architecture and art, and thus both revalorizes an ahistorical notion of aesthetic autonomy and denies the peculiar function of art and culture in National Socialism as a cultural laboratory of racial rebirth through imperial warfare; by recycling the cliches of fascism as a fascinating, all-inclusive, and monumental seduction, it solicits viewing positions that arrest the visitor in a silent fascination with the aesthetic surfaces and sublime self-representations of fascism. On the other hand, "Art and Power," in rewriting the myth of Hitler Germany as a perfectly organized machine of domination and mass deception, disregards the fact that both the Nazi state and Nazi society were much more heterogenous and diverse than the Nazis themselves and many historians of the immediate postwar era believed. Captivated by the monumental choreography of Nazi politics, the exhibit ignores the actual receptivity of Hitler's subjects to this new mass aesthetics; it ignores to question the extent to which individuals actually appropriated the unprecedented surplus of spectacular signs and ritualistic symbols in order to articulate them within the fabrics of everyday life.

Given such trajectories of popularization and vulgarization, the legacy of Benjamin's definition of fascism as the aestheticization of politics today seems to obscure any deeper understanding of the interfaces of politics and culture during the National Socialist period or under Italian Fascism. Academic and cultural commodities of the first order, references to the aesthetic veneers of power enable our contemporary bricoleurs to exploit the iconographic inventories of the past in order to infuse postmodern boredom and melancholia with the rhetoric of existential danger and resolution. Benjamin's popularity thus paradoxically coincides with his oblivion. To the extent to which academic and popular culture today severs the meaning of Nazi aesthetics from its practice and historical function, it progressively eclipses what was at the core of Benjamin's original account: to define the aesthetics of politics as a peculiar strategy of domination that reckoned with distinctly modern and, hence, historically contingent structures of experience, seeing, and feeling. But we must be careful not to fault Benjamin's writings themselves for their posthumous canonization and subsequent vulgarization. If for Benjamin the history of modernity is the "history of the desire to reformulate subjectivity in a disenchanted world where the energies of reenchantment spell political disaster," then what is needed is a strategy of reading that emancipates the academic treasure Benjamin from the spell of canonization.[4] If the task of the historian – according to the "Theses on the Philosophy of History" – is indeed to brush history against the grain of dominant traditions and fixed interpretations, then Benjamin's readers, too, should resist governing narratives of canonization and expose Benjamin to the litmus test of actuality: "For every image of the past that is not recognized by the present as one of its own concerns threatens to disappear irretrievably" (ILL 255; GS I:695).

The two chapters of this second part therefore attempt to take Benjamin at his word and ask anew what our postmodern present may recognize in Benjamin's modernist critique of fascism as elements of its own concern. Chapter 7 inquires into the extent to which Benjamin's generic definition of fascism as an aestheticization of politics holds up to some more recent historical analyses of the National Socialist period, particularly those analyses that – in contrast to most postwar accounts – emphasize the considerable plurality of everyday cultural practices under Nazi rule. Does Benjamin's notion of aesthetic politics, I shall ask, help us understand the fact that in contradistinction to the Nazis' spectacular rendition of the folk and the nation as the primary signifiers of social integration and subject-formation, many of Hitler's subjects defined their relation to the Nazi state via the prospects of a privatized, American-style consumer culture – prospects the Nazis tolerated in the folds of a highly politicized public sphere? How, in other words, can we theorize, within the framework of Benjamin's (unfinished) conceptual apparatus, Nazi society as a by no means homogenous force field of propaganda and subjectivity, terror and commodity consumption, spectacle and apolitical everyday practice? Chapter 8 takes the opposite turn and interrogates the extent to which Benjamin's aestheticization thesis can help conceptualize the location of culture in our own postmodern society of the spectacle, a society based on a massive profusion of images and distractions through a multiplicity of different and often overlapping media channels. If Benjamin's notion of aesthetic politics was meant to expose fascism as a society in which simulations supplanted experience – one in which phantasmagorias of power displaced independent perceptions of reality – then how can Benjamin be of use today to evaluate contemporary attractions and simulations without advocating impetuous comparisons or belittling the historical uniqueness of Nazi terror?

Devoted to theorizing modernity and its unchained temporalities, the modernist Benjamin suggested that one should resist any impulse to fix meaning in static or totalizing representations: it was the task of the messiah, not of the cultural critic, to pronounce the end of history and the concomitant arrival of an age of universal citability and unlimited appropriation. The following two chapters hope not only to unfix Benjamin and make his aestheticization thesis speak to us across space and time, but also, thereby, to recognize that the project of modernity, in spite of all eulogies, will linger as long as we acknowledge the undeniable need to work critically through the legacy of the past and its unrealized potentials – as long as we uphold, in other words, a notion of culture and history not as a timeless collector's item or a discount store, but as a realm of struggle, dissent, and multiplicity.

7

FASCIST AESTHETICS REVISITED

Only a few months before the German capitulation, Joseph Goebbels used the premiere of the feature film *Kolberg* in January 1945 as an opportunity to hammer home the credo of his unique approach to mass politics once more: "Gentlemen, in one hundred years' time they will be showing a fine color film of the terrible days we are living through. Wouldn't you like to play a part in that film? Hold out now, so that 100 years hence the audience will not hoot and whistle when you appear on screen."[1] Informed by Benjamin's critical matrix and Susan Sontag's often-quoted essay about the fascinating aspects of fascism, generations of critics have read remarks such as these as self-explanatory testimonies to the Nazis' theatrical blurring of boundaries between reality and fiction, appearance and essence. Aesthetic resources, following such readings, transformed the Nazi state into a Wagnerian total work of art, a carefully choreographed spectacle of ethereal bodies and geometrical shapes. Accordingly, Nazi art not only helped posit a deceptive identity of art and life, image and original, but also glorified gestures of surrender and idealized figurations of death. Nazi aesthetics taught us how to hold out – heroically and manly – in the face of total destruction. This view of Nazi art and aesthetics as ferociously rhetorical is still dominant today. An integral part of a highly ritualized and operatic public sphere, Nazi art employed authoritative modes of address and triggered politically effective emotions. It reshaped common ideas of beauty in order to render aesthetic pleasure a direct extension of political terror: a form of violence in the service of future warfare.

But Nazi rule and society, as seen from the perspective of contemporary historiography, were of course much less homogenous than Benjamin's aestheticization thesis would suggest. Not all pleasures and aesthetic materials circulated under fascism took the form of masochist feasts of submission, and we therefore – as so many historians have pointed out – can no longer take for granted the fact that popular attitudes toward the Third Reich coincided with what we see in historical images of cheering crowds, images dexterously designed and mass circulated by Goebbels's media industry. Mapping the topographies of popular culture during the National Socialist period, recent research instead suggests that large sections of the population led a double life: delivering vows of political loyalty in public rituals *and* pursuing apolitical leisure activities in the niches of private life.[2] Contrary to the regime's rhetoric of political coordination and total mobilization, the Third Reich not only promised new career opportunities but also new tactics of diversion and commodity consumption. Apart from short periods of political euphoria, the allure of racing cars, radios, Coca-Cola, swing, and Hollywood-style comedies – rather than the choreography of Riefenstahl's spectacles – provided the stuff dreams were made of. Mass cultural consumer practices inhabited an important place in the era's culture. Instead of bracketing it as kitschy or trivial, we need to face and think through the fact that the popular, as Eric Rentschler argues, "played a prominent and ubiquitous role in everyday life, in cinemas, radio programs, dance halls, advertisements, tourist offerings, and the latest consumer items."[3]

In contradistinction to postwar views of Nazi Germany as a flawlessly functioning machine of domination and coordination, historians today seem to be in agreement about crucial hiatuses between ideological demands and everyday practices, between the aesthetic spectacles of Nazi propaganda and the existence of a relatively unpolitical sphere of American-style consumption, distraction, and commodity display. In an important publication of 1981, Hans Dieter Schäfer reconstructed a typical day in Berlin in September 1937:

> At the same time Mussolini [during his state visit] was driving along the "via triumphalis," it was possible to enter the world of the film *Shanghai Express* and to applaud Teddy Stauffer performing in the "Femina Bar." With his songs "Swingin' for the King"and "Goody Goody"Stauffer denied in his own ways the military-folkish ambitions of the Hitler state. During the same evening, the 20th-Century-Fox film *On the Avenue* captivated the audience of the "Marmorhaus" as it had done for the past two months already, while at the box office of the "Staatsoper"people simultaneously were standing in line for the premier of Igor Stravinsky's ballet *The Kiss of the Fairy*.[4]

For Schäfer, the contradictions between ideology and everyday practice, political aesthetics and commodity consumption, proved the pathological and psychopathic nature of Nazi society. Contrary to Schäfer, I suggest that we need to understand this split consciousness not as a symptom but a shrewd technology of power: Nazi cultural politics allowed for seemingly unpolitical spaces of mass consumption and diversion because they were useful to reinforce the workings of existing political dependencies and identities. Very well aware of the fact that overpoliticization might quickly lead to apathy, the Nazi government endorsed private spaces of commodity consumption because they provided the political system with "an input of highly diffuse mass loyalty."[5] At variance with the strict demands of ideological correctness, American-style consumerism in Nazi society thus delineated an ideal stage for what Theodor W. Adorno in his analysis of American mass culture considered pseudo-individualization – the "halo of free choice" on the basis of standardization itself.[6] Unlike the homogenizing rituals on the Nuremberg rally grounds, the commodity spectacles of Nazi mass culture entertained the individual with the utopian illusion that certain spaces remained beyond control, beyond politics, beyond the effects of coordination. In this way, consumer satisfaction became as important a vehicle of political integration and legitimation as the aestheticist rhetoric of total mobilization and of the autonomy of the political. By satisfying the popular demand for material and cultural commodity items, the agents of power were able to undermine articulations of solidarity that had the capacity to contest the legitimacy of Nazi politics. The cult of private con-sumption impaired alternative definitions of German identity and solidarity coupled to notions of individual autonomy and emancipation. While hoping to remake the Third Reich as a national family, the Nazi culture in-dustry domesticated un-German sights and sounds in order to set individuals apart against one another and thus to produce lonely crowds.[7] It allowed for private consumption, but only to deflect the formation of counterpublics, to arrest and rechannel the popular's "ineradicable drive towards collectivity."[8]

Benjamin's famous catchphrase of fascism as the aestheticization of politics has often led to definitions of the spectacular elements of Nazi politics exclusively in terms of Riefenstahl's mass rituals or Speer's architectural appeals to timeless dignity and monumental symmetry. Recent scholarship on everyday culture under Nazi rule, however, suggests that to think of the Nazi spectacle simply in political terms and to describe it solely as a technology of seamless unification misses the point. In their pursuit of a homogenous and bellicose community of the folk, the Nazis made numerous concessions to the popular demand for the warmth of private life and pleasure in a modern media society. In many cases such concessions – as David Bathrick has argued in a different context – "left the government caught in ludicrous forms of self-redress and strategic withdrawal before the commodity fetish."[9] Yet at the same time, the Nazi government clearly hoped to realign depoliticized practices of cultural consumption and the desires of restless pleasure seekers with their larger political agendas. The spectacle of modern consumer culture was meant to break the bonds of old solidarities and to prepare the atomized individual for the auratic shapes of mass politics, for mass rituals that promised a utopian unification of modern culture and drowned doubts about ideological inconsistencies in an unprecedented surplus of signs and symbols. Nazi cultural politics and spectacle, in other words, relied on both at once – on the charismatic power of public mass events and the lures of privatized consumption; on the mass-mediated staging of political rituals as much as on the appeals of a seemingly nonpolitical, American-style leisure culture; on total mobilization as much as on the atomizing pleasures of imaginary escape. Guy Debord's famous aphorism holds true of Nazi society as well: "The spectacle is nothing more than the common language of this separation. What binds the spectators together is no more than an irreversible relation at the very center which maintains their isolation. The spectacle reunites the separate, but reunites it *as separate*."[10]

To the extent to which it brings into focus the relative heterogeneity of politically domesticated pleasures in Nazi Germany, more recent historical research asks us to rethink a number of aspects of Benjamin's aestheticization thesis. Benjamin's theory is helpful to explicate the unifying powers of the Nazi spectacle, but it seems to ignore cultural technologies of atomization as well as the nexus of domination and private commodity consumption during the National Socialist period. Explaining fascist aesthetics as a monolithic space of false reconciliation, as a postauratic renewal of aura, Benjamin did not yet address the ways in which mass culture and the popular in Nazi Germany openly avowed postauratic diversions, shaped new attitudes toward beauty and pleasure, and in so doing provided a government with diffuse forms of loyalty. Furthermore, in spite of Benjamin's emphatic notion of individual and collective experience, what remained absent from his analysis of fascist aestheticization is any sense of how Hitler's subjects explored the landscapes of political culture and transformed them into their lifescapes. Although it would be foolish to tax Benjamin's fragmentary remarks on fascism with all of these omissions, it is equally important to understand that Benjamin – confined to the condition of exile – primarily deciphered the politics of fascist culture from "above." With highly limited data at his disposal, he was unable to examine in further detail how Hitler's subjects inhabited both the political spectacle and the symbolic materials of a modern leisure and media society in order to take position and construct however precarious and inconsistent identities.

Yet to thus point with historical hindsight toward some of these understandable blind spots in Benjamin's critique of German National Socialism and Italian Fascism once again falsely considers the epilogue of the artwork essay as Benjamin's only word about the aestheticization of politics. Benjamin's *Arcades Project* in fact provides a much broader framework to theorize the nexus of domination *and* commodity consumption, power *and* leisure, homogenization *and* fragmentation, and thus may help supplement what had to remain absent from the artwork essay. The following chapter suggests that the aestheticization thesis should be considered together with certain observations from Benjamin's unfinished magnum opus. When commenting on Benjamin's materialist anthropology and the *Arcades Project*, chapter 5 implied that nineteenth-century phantasmagorias prefigured the operations of the fascist mass ritual. Following Benjamin's own lead, I argued that nineteenth-century culture, like fascism, played on peculiarly modern modes of experience and diversion: the flâneur's voyeuristic pleasure anticipated the mesmerized gaze of, and at, Riefenstahl's men in the ornamental crowd. In order to probe the compatibility of Benjamin's aestheticization thesis with the results of contemporary research, the following pages will more emphatically state the relation of the artwork essay and the *Arcades Project*, of fascist spectacle and nineteenth-century modernization. If chapter 5 conceptualized the fascist mass ornament, seen as analogous to the nineteenth-century phantasmagoria, as a *seductive feast of symbolic homogenization*, the present chapter reconstructs Benjamin's notion of aestheticization so as to emphasize the role of private consumption under fascism, of *spectacular atomization rather than all-inclusive coordination*. According to this third version of Benjamin's aestheticization thesis, fascism constitutes a phase of capitalist modernization in which the political dimension itself becomes a market item, a target of the kind of commodification and mass consumption Benjamin so intriguingly analyzed in the *Arcades Project*. As it embraces the mechanisms of an American-style culture industry, fascism not only accelerates the fragmentation of traditional environments, it also grafts onto acts of political representation the logic of nineteenth-century commodity fetishism. Politics, I conclude, becomes aesthetic in fascism because fascism explicitly utilizes the charismatic promise of autonomous politics as a viable consumer good, a carefully designed and marketed product that appeals to dormant desires of modern consumers and window-shoppers.

Peter Labanyi has argued that Nazism – as a highly incoherent political ideology – relied on advanced marketing strategies to sell itself as "a multipurpose ideological commodity."[11] It put principles of modern advertising in the service of the production of mass loyalty and political consumer satisfaction. It was only because Nazism managed to package itself as offering something to everyone that it was able to gain mass support. German fascism confiscated the aesthetic dimension, the domains of pleasure, desire, and representation, in order to massage the masses and bridge the gap between ideological use-values and exchange-values, between real and imaginary needs. Circulated as one of many other objects of popular desire, the politics of fascism should thus ultimately be understood as a form of commodity aesthetics: "An ideological product – the Führer, folk community, or whatever – is supplied with a brand name and a trade-mark – the swastika – and a product-image is carefully designed."[12]

Reread in light of the *Arcades Project*, Benjamin's aestheticization thesis helps elucidate this broader understanding of the Nazi interfaces between power, pleasure, and the popular. It allows us to interpret fascism as the incorporation of militant and ultranationalist agendas into the operations of a modern culture industry, and to define fascist aesthetics as a historically unique endeavor of breaking older bonds of solidarity while simultaneously rendering modern consumerism, including the consumption of charismatic politics, a privileged ticket to national rebirth.

Ever since the 1930s, German intellectuals have mostly seen the role of National Socialist ideology as a substitute for authentic meaning. Nazi ideology, according to this view, fabricated fake dreams in the service of disabling a critical understanding of social realities; it disseminated powerful delusions that sweetened political and economic domination. But National Socialist ideology, as Michael Geyer has argued correctly, did not simply aim at a change of discourse or a remaking of symbolic expression; rather, its specific character consisted in what might be understood as its progressive concreteness. "This is what the German intelligentsia disliked about it. It was not words, symbols, and discourses. Ideology was contained in the material practice of politics in the Third Reich. In fact, it increasingly became politics."[13] National Socialist ideology was not dedicated merely to transfiguring social realities; it radically altered and restructured existing social relations. If National Socialism was able to muster mass support, it did so mostly because it responded to real needs and desires, because it understood how to build individual wish-fantasies and diffuse utopias of collective rebirth into the material architectures of public and private life. Not sex, romance, glamour, or exotic lures, but the political itself became the stuff of the popular imagination. As a material practice, Nazi ideology crystallized in the very gestalt of everyday life, in the mass ornaments as much as in the products of Goebbels's distraction factories. Ideological politics provided the masses with the powerful experience of a new national family, yet at the same time – in pursuing its core agendas – it "broke families apart, alienated young women from older ones, children from parents, and reshaped the relation between men and women – as far as it could. It poisoned the life in villages and houses, broke apart friendships and associates."[14] To the extent that it rebuilt reality as dream (and nightmare), ideological politics in Nazi Germany became an exercise in a kind of radical materialism: it changed the world by reinterpreting it. National Socialist ideology "spoke" to sentient bodies rather than minds. Shrewdly reckoning with and reorganizing the people's mimetic faculty – their ability to imitate the other, to bridge rather than collapse differences between subject and object, and to produce resemblances; their desire to connect with or be transformed by the other so as to develop sympathetic, noncoercive relationships between nonidentical particulars – Nazi cultural politics engineered emotions and domesticated perception in order to recast the nation's political body.[15]

As I have suggested in chapter 5, Benjamin's nineteenth-century Paris – the capital of high capitalism – anticipates the cunning ways in which Nazi politics embodied ideology in plastic forms. As a heaven of consumption, fashion, and conspicuous luxury, the Paris of the *Arcades Project* signifies a modern-day Babylon where people – unable to structure their social relationships – happily surrender to the magic of objects-turned-commodities. Like Nazi Germany, Baudelaire's Paris is a dreamed one: everyday phenomena bear the signatures of collective wish-fantasies and age-old utopias. As they constitute themselves as modern mass in front of the spectacular displays of new department stores, shopping arcades, and world fairs, customers and window-shoppers find ancient myths embodied in the very gestalt of the latest lures and inventions. As importantly, however, nineteenth-century commodity culture also prefigures the logic of fragmentation that is at the core of Nazi ideological politics. The progressive commodification of objects and human relationships makes Paris into a latter-day Babel. The commodity form destroys traditional notions of unity and organic totality; it devalues objects and meanings, strikes experience with a Medusian shock of petrification, and thus separates from one another the speechless individuals of the crowd. Far from solely yielding a totalizing spectacle of frenzied but coordinated mass desires, nineteenth-century commodity culture recycles the allegorical regimes of the seventeenth century, including the baroque's melancholia, forlornness, and mortifying secularization: "The emblems recur as commodities" (CP 49; GS 1:681). "The devaluation of the world of objects in allegory is outdone within the world of objects itself by the commodity" (CP 34; GS 1:660).

These strange and subterraneous links between high capitalism and National Socialism, on the one hand, and between the seventeenth and the nineteenth century, on the other, between allegory, commodity form, and social fragmentation, clearly beg for further explanation as Benjamin seems to amalgamate his no doubt unconventional reading of Marx with his no less idiosyncratic baroque studies of the 1920s. Babel and Babylon alike, nineteenth-century commodity culture – so much seems clear at the outset – casts into embodied form what in the context of *The Origin of German Tragic Drama* was understood as a reflex and refraction of a melancholic gaze, as a figure of the poet's artistic inventory. Far from simply rejecting nineteenth-century commodification and reification, Benjamin embraces it as part of the progressive deauraticization of the world. The emergence of the commodity form represents a historical phase in which objects are yanked out of their habitual contexts and delivered to the demands of distracted consumers. Like seventeenth-century allegory or twentieth-century montage cinema, the commodity destroys both the representation and the experience of organic totality and meaningful unity; it shatters an object's aura, transforms the world of objects into a petrified landscape that may cater to the specifically modern urge to get hold of objects at very close range. Nineteenth-century capitalist modernization, therefore, administers within the sphere of economic production and circulation what mechanical reproducibility does to cultural artifacts: it obliterates an object's here and now by transforming this object into a commodity wandering across traditional boundaries between private and public spaces, the local and the global; it empowers the human collective to appropriate things according to their always peculiar needs, desires, and experiences. In contrast to the falsifying transfiguration of classical symbolism and auratic art, the commodity – like the baroque's allegorical gaze or Eisenstein's art of cutting and editing – potentially undermines any cult of beauty and figurative transcendence as it extinguishes all appearances of harmonious, timeless perfection. The commodity form is both vehicle and expression of the disintegrated character of modern life. It bears testimony to the fundamental untruth of a society struck by the logic of alienation and fragmentation.

And yet this testimony is far from complete or successful, for capitalism is at pains to mask the very fact that objects are commodities. Capitalism hides what is allegorical about the commodity form under the veil of spectacular displays and symbolic arrangements; it grafts onto the commodity's postauratic character the autographs of auratic art. "Ever more callously," Benjamin argues in an aphorism of "Central Park," "the object world of man assumes the expression of the commodity. At the same time advertising seeks to veil the commodity character of things. . . . This attempt has its equivalent in the simultaneous attempt of the bourgeoisie to personify the commodity *(vermenschlichen)*: to give the commodity, like a person, housing. This then was the promise of the *etuis* (small box), the covers, the sheaths with which the bourgeois household effects of the time were being covered" (CP 42; GS 1:671). Nineteenth-century capitalism cannot admit its own truth. In the context of the arcades, the department stores, and the world fairs, capitalist culture recodes the petrified outlook of commodities as phantasmagorias, as animated, self-sustaining entities. It glorifies the exhibition values of marketable goods in order to undermine their allegorical thrust, their potential to introduce a new chapter within the development of the human senses and the relation of the human collective to the world of objects. Nineteenth-century capitalism, in sum, sells allegories as symbols, disempowerment as empowerment, and in so doing it cunningly engenders a state of fragmentation and separation underneath a magic label of unified meaning and symbolic totality.

Benjamin's remarks about the enigmas of the commodity form have continuously provided material for heated discussions. Not surprisingly, the question as to the relation between Benjamin's critique of capitalism and Marx's notion of commodity fetishism, between Benjamin's and Marx's different conceptions of use-value and exchange-value, has figured prominently in these debates. In the final analysis, however, as Heinz-Dieter Kittsteiner rightly argues, Benjamin's assumptions about the extinction of use-values and the concomitant concealment of the commodity form in high capitalism has very little to do with Marx. Unlike Benjamin, Marx "never simply extinguished 'use value'; rather, he always, and for good reason, held fast to the unity of use value and exchange value."[16] From the perspective of a classical Marxist, Benjamin's postulates about the commodity form and the eclipse of use-value remain undialectical: "To the extent that such allusions appear in Benjamin, they are based not on a well-grounded knowledge of Marx, but on the widespread schematics of a rather conservative critique of civilization which was amalgamated in the 1920s and 1930s with the position of the 'Left.' "[17] Be that as it may, rather than once again pondering the authenticity of Benjamin's Marxism, it will prove much more fruitful to follow the links Benjamin's work indicates between the aborted allegories of capitalist modernization and the emergence of what one might call with Andreas Huyssen the great divide of modern culture, the split between the commodified realms of mass culture and diversion on the one hand, and the terrains of enigmatic modernism on the other.[18]

Whether he misunderstands Marx or not, Benjamin's phantasmagorias of capitalist modernization in his analysis provide the cultural material around which the modern mass constitutes and experiences itself as mass: "With the establishment of the department stores, consumers began for the first time in history to feel like a mass. (Previously, only privation had taught them to feel this way.) Thus the circus-like or exhibitory aspect of trade increased to a quite extraordinary extent" (GS 5:93). What Benjamin understands as the glorification of exchange-values in capitalism coincides with the emergence of cultural practices that are deeply enmeshed in commodity consumption and industrial standardization, practices that no longer have anything in common with older forms of popular or folk art. Popular culture in the strict sense originated as the quasi-organic expression of distinct social communities. Existing in the plural alone, it reflected the always particular and contingent values, traditions, institutions, and lifeworlds of well-defined social bodies. As remystified disenchantment, Benjamin's fetishized commodities, by way of contrast, appeal to each and every cultural constituency regardless of their social and historical specificity. Nineteenth-century capitalism on the one hand atomizes traditional communities and lifeworlds into isolated private individuals and market competitors. On the other hand, however, it wraps commodities into a magic aura in order to appeal to archaic utopias of homogenous meaning and collectivity amid the heteronomy of the market. Phantasmagorias embody collective wish- and power-fantasies. They soothe the minds of lonely crowds while entertaining the amorphous mass with the illusion that meaningful experiences are still possible in spite of the fragmenting force of capitalist modernization. Instead of understanding Benjamin's phantasmagorias solely in terms of manipulation, diversion, or degradation, as empty distraction or mere false consciousness, we must therefore conceive of them as predecessors of the works of twentieth-century mass culture: as transformational works on social anxieties and political fantasies that – in Fredric Jameson's words – "have as their underlying impulse – albeit in what is often distorted and repressed unconscious form – our deepest fantasies about the nature of social life, both as we live now, and as we feel in our bones it ought rather to be lived."[19] Nineteenth-century phantasmagorias, like the products of the twentieth-century culture industries, entertain relations of repression with fundamental anxieties, concerns, and hopes, even if in most cases such fissures are resolved into imaginary resolutions and illusions of existing social harmony. As it conceals the allegorical thrust of the commodity form, modern consumer society engenders modes of mass cultural entertainment in which repression and wish-fulfillment, fantasy and symbolic containment, join together in the unity of a single mechanism.

If nineteenth-century commodity capitalism, by simultaneously producing and concealing allegorical experiences, designates the origin of modern mass culture, it is at same time also the hidden force behind the emergence of aesthetic modernism in the works of Charles Baudelaire. Baudelaire revalorizes the baroque's allegorical gaze – the "armature of the modern" (CP 49; GS 1:681) – because it allows him to outfetishize the fetishes of consumer capitalism. "The allegorical mode of seeing which shaped style in the 17th Century no longer did so in the 19th. Baudelaire was isolated; as an allegorist his isolation was in certain respects that of a straggler" (CP 55; GS 1:690). With the help of allegory, the "antidote to myth" (CP 46; GS 1:677), Baudelaire lays bare the allegorical reason behind the shining wrappers of commodity displays. He makes the commodity's spectacular aura the object of allegorical devaluation and reveals the commodity as commodity, reveals what is allegorical about the commodity form itself. Writing poetry for an age no longer concentrated enough to read poetry, Baudelaire's modernism responds to similar experiences, anxieties, and concerns that structure the outlook of the nineteenth-century popular dimension. In contrast to mass culture's imaginary resolutions, however, Baudelaire invents compensatory structures that are meant to speak the truth about the commodity and work through the loss of organic totality under the reign of capitalist modernization. Baudelaire's aesthetic modernism is modern mass culture's other side. Both emerge against the background of one and the same condition – namely, capitalism's need to conceal the allegorical thrust of the commodity form – but both suggest mutually exclusive strategies of translating the experience of modernity into symbolic expressions. Whereas industrial mass culture casts anxiety into exhilarating fantasies of harmony, Baudelaire's modernism maps modern life as fundamentally fragmented and petrified, and in so doing, uncovers the melancholy, boredom, and isolation that prevails behind the scenes of enthused consumerism. Deeply connected to the poet's allegorical intention, Baudelaire's spleen "is that feeling which corresponds to catastrophe in permanence" (CP 34; GS 1:660).

But what, then, does Nazi aestheticization and consumer culture have to do with Baudelaire's modernism, the allegory of the commodity form, and the dialectics of modernism and mass culture? How does fascism inherit what Benjamin considers the legacy of the nineteenth century?

In order to answer these questions, let me recount the argument thus far. Benjamin suggests that the formation of the modern masses vis-à-vis nineteenth-century commodity fetishism not only coincides with a progressive mechanism of atomization and privatization, it also results in the division of modern culture into two dialectically opposed tracks of cultural and aesthetic modernization: high modernism and popular mass diversion. High modernism articulates what is glossed over in commodified mass culture; it reminds us of the melancholy, despair, and fragmentation that is at the bottom of the experience of capitalist modernity. Adorno and Horkheimer, we remember, believed that the American culture industry sought to paper over the peculiar dialectics of modern culture. Hollywood during the classical studio era did not eclipse Schoenberg or Beckett, but it tried to adorn mass cultural products with the charm of high art and thus forge into a false and ruthless unity what no longer could add up to a whole. If we continue Benjamin's unfinished line of argumentation, we will come to the conclusion that Nazi culture in fact itself by far outdid Hollywood's technologies of power not only in its mass spectacles at Nuremberg but also in the context of its own American-style culture industry. National Socialism curtailed the expressive registers of aesthetic modernism and autonomous art, while it at the same time – domesticating the popular imagination – sought to engender mass culture from above, to ensure that something was provided for everyone and that none could escape.

What Benjamin calls the aestheticization of politics, then, signifies fascism's peculiar way of resolving the antinomies of modern culture. Not only did German fascism reckon with the fact that a full-fledged politicization of public life would render this empty and provoke the retreat into nonpolitical privacy and consumerism. Nazi Germany in fact transformed the political itself into an item of mass consumption, a commodity concealing its status as a commodity (and allegory), a symbolic spectacle meant to produce lonely crowds and unite the masses as separate. Detlev Peuckert has argued that even the regime's own symbols such as the wireless set and the Volkswagen "served in practice to promote individualism in leisure and transport, albeit in the standardised form determined by the needs of mass consumption in a modern industrial society."[20] Understood in light of Benjamin's account of modern consumer capitalism, such strategies of aestheticization – far from simply signifying seductive mechanisms of social homogenization – must be conceptualized as techniques of power that sought to confiscate the popular imagination within the domains of a homemade culture industry in order to unbind traditional bonds of solidarity, to engender isolation, to entertain relations of repressions with fundamental anxieties and utopias, and to provide compensatory structures of symbolic integration. Though Benjamin himself did not explicitly fuse his remarks about commodity capitalism with his theory of fascism, his work suggests that perhaps not Hollywood – which even during the studio era was much more heterogenous than Adorno and Horkheimer believed – but the union of politics and commodity consumption in Nazi Germany was the most pertinent historical manifestation of the system of the culture industry as well as its various mechanisms of producing loneliness and mass consent through pseudo-individualization.

"The purpose of the Fascist formula, the ritual discipline, the uniforms, and the whole apparatus, which is at first sight irrational, is to allow mimetic behavior. The carefully thought out symbols (which are proper to every counterrevolutionary movement), the skulls and disguises, the barbaric drum beats, the monotonous repetitions of words and gestures, are simply the organized imitation of magic practices, the mimesis of mimesis."[21] According to Benjamin's confrères Adorno and Horkheimer, fascist aestheticization mimics mimetic behavior because fascism wants to enlist a rebellion against domination as a useful tool of domination itself. Fascism opens up symbolic spaces in which suppressed nature – sentience, spontaneity, and the desire to imitate and connect with the other – may articulate itself only to succumb even more effectively to the mechanisms of disciplining and suppression. Benjamin's valorization of allegory as an armature of modernity results from his hope not to do away with the magic of mimesis altogether but to find antidotes to this political organization and manipulation of "primitivist" residues. In Benjamin's view, allegory undercuts the possibility to seize nature and what seems forbidden or repressed in actual life for projects of domination. Antimimetic in character, allegory allows us to experience the world as one in which the realms of nature and of human affairs are radically separate. As a discontinuous structure of representation, allegory sharpens our awareness for the constructedness of meanings, institutions, and values; it disrupts symbolic totalizations within the public sphere that try to imitate and organize mimetic urges, to naturalize meaning and history, and thus to engage in a fateful mimesis of mimesis.

Benjamin's theory about the imbrication of allegory and commodity form urges us to reconsider what is often seen as a striking gap between ideology and practice during the Nazi period. Read in light of the *Arcades Project*, Benjamin's remarks about the aestheticization of politics in fascism suggest that the spectacular stage management of Nazi ideology and the vicissitudes of Nazi leisure culture form two sides of the same sign of capitalist modernization. Instead of seeing Riefenstahl's political choreography and Nazi consumerism as signs of a split consciousness of Nazi society, Benjamin's formula of aestheticization emphasizes that both aspects are implicated in larger processes of commodification, processes that increasingly render consumerism the primary tool and ideology of social integration. The public spectacle and the cult of private consumption alike eclipse what is potentially emancipatory about the deauraticization and disenchantment of the world in modernity. Both result in a regressive mimesis of mimesis. Both remystify and retotalize the world while turning individuals into atomized consumers and pleasure-seeking monads.

What makes fascism so abominable, then, is the fact that it aspired to subsume everything under the logic of a modern culture industry, hoping to crush the emancipatory substance of modern life through modern technologies themselves. Fascism constituted a dictatorship *over* the new media and a dictatorship *of* the new media, an Orwellian and a Huxleyian dystopia alike.[22] While it transformed even its charismatic ideology of strong, autonomous politics into a marketable good of diversion, it sought to conceal the commodity form of this good behind a symbolic cocoon of auratic appearance. Through styling, packaging, and advertising, Nazi power invested its products – its political promises as much as its material goods – with a universal aura that was meant to appeal to the masses' mimetic desires. Nazism – much more effectively than the American culture industry in Adorno and Horkheimer's description – "gained mass appeal because it managed to offer something to almost everyone."[23] Urging us to reconsider Dimitroff's famous and hopelessly one-dimensional formula, Benjamin defines fascism as that final state of capitalism in which the political itself becomes a commodity. Not the department store, but the commodification of politics in fascism is "the *flâneur*'s last practical joke" (REF 156; GS 5:54). Under the condition of fascism, even the politician needs to go to the market, not simply in order to find customers but in order to sell himself.

Ian Kershaw, in a series of books and articles, has recently demonstrated the extent to which this logic of Nazi commodity aesthetics was projected even onto the person of Adolf Hitler himself.[24] Often at odds with the rising disdain for the Nazi party, Hitler's undeniable popularity particularly during the prewar years resulted mostly from a masterly achievement of image building. The making of Hitler skillfully catered to anxieties, desires, and values that "conditioned the acceptance of a 'Superman' image of political leadership."[25] Constantly refashioned according to the shifting needs and fortunes of the Nazi movement and state, Hitler's image was to promote the highly desirable commodity of autonomous politics. It was mass circulated as panacea for diffuse hopes to recenter the state, to reassert the sovereignty of the political vis-à-vis the progressive pluralization of power in modernity, and to replace the putatively effeminate structures of procedural politics with resolute, manly action. Accordingly, Hitler was stylized into symbol of the nation. Goebbels's ministries of illusion manufactured Hitler into a ruthless, resolute, and uncompromising yet simultaneously self-sacrificial, modest, and righteous individual in whose appearance the people and the nation could find their identity. Hitler's star persona incarnated a triumph of Germanic male virtues over the feminized order of the Weimar period and its parliamentary order. Similar to the dreams of nineteenth-century political romanticism, Nazi propaganda marketed Hitler as a site at which the existential affairs of the German nation and its individuals were at stake. But unlike the romantic theory of the state, the body of the leader was not solely designed for the purpose of giving a metaphorical expression to transcendental values, for making the unspeakable visible.[26] Instead, though Nazi propaganda advertised Hitler as an extraordinary intervention into the weary domains of everyday routines, it at the same time surrounded his appearance with a pathos of human, "earthly" qualities. The remarkable catalog of human virtues – Hitler's toughness, severity, determination, loneliness, sadness, and care for the nation – "was set alongside the political genius of the Führer as a human counterpart to the image of the lofty, distant statesman. It amounted to almost a mirror of contemporary bourgeois values – characteristics with which almost everyone could find some point of association."[27] Making Hitler human by packaging the commodity into an affective coat, Nazi politics and mass culture sought to ensure that something was provided for everyone's peculiar needs.

Once established as a mass cultural icon, the image of Hitler catered to popular desires for a strong and uncompromising state authority, for a ruthless reconstruction and preservation of law and order. Hitler's star image suggested the posture of a magnetic leader resolutely upholding the autonomy of the political and in fact advancing resoluteness to the primary value of political action. In Hitler's image, the kind of legal decisionism and political existentialism I discussed in various chapters of part I reached full public fruition. With the Hitler myth as its flagship, Nazi politics was dressed as a self-referential realm beyond fact and value in which – in Alfred Baeumler's words – "action means 'setting off in a direction,' 'taking sides,' by virtue of a mandate of destiny, by virtue of 'one's own right.'"[28] Increasingly isolating Hitler from the growing unpopularity of the NSDAP party, the Hitler myth thus packaged the führer as the prime architect of national reassertion and economic recovery: a leader who was remorselessly devoted to act against the nation's inner and outer enemies; a military genius who outwitted the foe with brilliant strategies; a humble servant of the folk putting aside all particular, material, and private interest for the sake of the nation – in sum, an alluring alternative to the allegedly monotonous, sterile, self-centered, and unsensual routines of procedural politics and liberal-democratic will-formation.

It has often been noted that, in couching Hitler's persona in an aura of heroic leadership and political redemption, Nazi propaganda established Hitler as a representative of what Max Weber only a few decades earlier had theorized under the rubric of charismatic authority.[29] A term borrowed from the Strasbourg church historian and legal scholar Rudolf Sohm, charisma in Weber's conceptual framework was to denote the aura of self-appointed leaders who appeal to their followers by virtue of their "supernatural, superhuman, or at least specifically exceptional powers."[30] Charisma, literally meaning the "gift of grace," interrupts the profane continuum of history; it discontinues exhausted value orders and habitual modes of thinking, fleshes out pristine semantic reference points, and thus restores authentic creativity, sensual pleasure, and intellectual integrity.[31] According to Weber, charismatic authority results as much from the actual qualities of a political leader as from the peculiar ways in which his followers perceive his performance. Charisma is a social product.[32] Like Benjamin's category of aura, Weber's charisma describes a relation of subject and object, a mode of experience rather than an empirical fact.

Nazi propaganda elevated charisma to Hitler's universally recognizable trademark. It advertised charismatic experiences as the most captivating appeal of the product "Hitler." To the extent to which the Nazi movement lost momentum, the Nazi culture industry was therefore forced ever more aggressively to fend off what – according to Weber – constitutes the dialectics of charismatic authority: charisma's ineluctable routinization and self-consumption. In order to warrant Hitler's aura of exceptionality, mass cultural representations progressively severed Hitler's persona from reality and the orders of the day. Ironically, however, the myth of Hitler thus experienced a curious return of the repressed: the spiraling idolization removed him from any possible enactment of what his image was meant to promote; namely, existential resolution and manly action. Like the Hollywood star cult, the Hitler myth instead "surrounded Hitler with toadies, flatterers, and sycophants, shielding him from rational criticism and genuine debate, and bolstered increasing detachment from reality. . . . His own person gradually became inseparable from the myth."[33]

Hitler's charisma and the popularity of the Hitler myth were surely by no means complete or unified. Hitler's image required continuous realignment in order to maintain its impact on a progressively disillusioned population. But what is striking are the parallels between the making of Hitler into a multipurpose vehicle of symbolic integration, on the one hand, and Benjamin's analysis of the integrative appeal and power of commodity fetishism, on the other. Benjamin invites us to understand the fabrication of the Hitler myth as the most extreme chapter within modernity's transmogrification of commodities into phantasmagorias. Accordingly, fascism surrounded its ideological good – namely, autonomous politics and the promise of a resolute rebirth of the nation – with the affective wrapping of "Hitler," thereby hoping to appeal to diverse consumer desires and to constitute the masses as masses. Pumping Hitler's far from monosemic image through the circuits of a state-controlled culture industry, fascism furthermore constantly tried to humanize and sentimentalize its ideological commodity, transform it into a spectacular symbol of national and individual rejuvenation, and thus eclipse the supreme commodity's allegorical commodity form. "Hitler," then, like the texts of modern mass culture, was a transformational work on social anxieties and diffuse utopias of successful collectivity. His image allowed for a playing out of fantasies as much as for their symbolic containment. To understand Hitler solely as an agent of ideological mobilization and mass politicization, therefore, would clearly underestimate his role and effectiveness. Understood as a multivalent object of consumption, "Hitler" inhabited a key position within the popular imagination. Like the Hollywood movie star, the image of the führer represented "the focal point at which identical reactions of countless citizens intersect"; Hitler was a function of the Nazi propaganda machine, "not so much a father-figure as a collective and overexaggerated projection of the powerless ego of each individual."[34] In conjunction with countless other and often conspicuously unpolitical products delivered by the Nazi leisure industry, the charismatic commodity "Hitler" helped atomize consumers into self-entertaining monads while simultaneously elevating consumerism to the most effective engine of mass loyalty and social integration. Nazi aesthetics designed "Hitler" as a cultural icon that could be read and appropriated in many ways. Similar to the standardized texts and objects of modern mass culture, the unique brand name "Hitler" appealed to disperse needs, desires, and wish-fantasies; its success resulted from the fact that consumers were able to incorporate the fetish "Hitler" in far from univocal ways into the realm of everyday practices.

Contemporary cultural criticism, informed by the British culturalists, is quick to assign subversive meanings to such heterogenous appropriations of mass cultural symbols. Polemically challenging older accounts of the culture industry as a crucible of conformity, this new generation of cultural critics emphasizes how the consumers of mass culture creatively reshape popular artifacts and images according to their own needs. John Fiske does not hesitate to understand the mass cultural consumer and reader as a "poacher, encroaching on the terrain of the cultural landowner (or textowner) and 'stealing' what he or she wants without being caught and subjected to the laws of the land (rule of the text)."[35] Nazi mass culture and the fetishism surrounding the commodity of autonomous, resolute politics reveal some crucial blind spots built into such positive notions of cultural poaching. For, as I argue, Nazi Germany clearly anticipated what contemporary audiences might have seen and today's revisionists celebrate as enactments of plurality and resistance. A counterpart to a highly politicized public sphere, the Nazi culture industry and its circuits of commodity consumption reckoned with cultural poachers. Whether it delivered Volkswagen, Hollywood-style comedies, or the image of Hitler, Nazi mass culture invited people to appropriate according to desire, to consume the illusion that within Nazi Germany certain spaces could remain free of politics and ideological imperatives. It enticed poachers to poach and provided local sources of individualization and empowerment, only to strengthen – to extend Fiske's metaphor – the laws that regulated the distribution of land outside the distraction factories. The cultural poachers of the Nazi era transformed cultural poaching into a pleasurable experience of consumption itself – a commodity. Instead of consuming illegitimate meanings, they ended up being consumed by the very objects of their pleasure.

The dreams dreamed within the realms of modern consumer culture, as Benjamin himself has aptly pointed out, in strange and often unpredictable ways outlast the very reality that gives birth to them. The iconographies of mass consumption not only transform historical realities into dreamed ones, their perseverance also recast the past as myth. It is perhaps no coincidence, then, that the commodity "Hitler"has long outlived Adolf Hitler. An object of mass consumption already during the Third Reich, the image of Hitler became one of the most enduringly potent and successful commodities in postwar mass culture, part of the inventory by means of which German (or American) consumer culture continuously replays the past forever as myth. Unremittingly spellbound by Goebbels's masterful commodity aesthetics, 48 percent of the West German population in 1955 believed that Hitler could have been one of the greatest German statesmen had he not started the war.[36] Perverse though it may seem, this persistence of the Hitler myth coincided with the postwar triumph of another commodity that had aroused frenzied dreams of consumption already during the Third Reich. When reintroduced a few years after the end of World War II, Coca-Cola – the single most popular soft drink in Germany during the 1930s – was simply marketed with the slogan that, finally, it was back. So deeply had this icon of American mass culture penetrated the popular imagination during the Third Reich that it was directly able to resume its former prominence in spite of postwar suffering and introversion. Once an integral element of Nazi leisure culture and the state-controlled modes of generating diffuse mass loyalty, the youthful appeal of Coca-Cola – similar to the fetish "Hitler" – subterraneously survived a war that Nazism had advertised as a conclusive rejuvenation of the German nation.

Realigned, then, in light of both recent research on Nazi everyday culture and Benjamin's own studies of modern consumer capitalism, the third version of the aestheticization thesis seems quite different from what generations of Benjamin scholars have suggested. Neither does Benjamin's catchword of fascist aestheticization simply signify the ornamentalization of the masses à la Riefenstahl; that is, a choreography of public life meant to provide phony scenarios of affective integration within a highly conflict-ridden society. Nor does it solely denote a quasi-romantic reduction of procedural politics to aspects of sensual perception, to a stimulation of the imagination, to sights and sounds that at once entertain and discipline the masses' desire for distraction. Rather, Benjamin defines fascism as a catastrophic phase of capitalist modernization in which the logic of political action and representation themselves become subsumed under the laws of commodification and commodity fetishism. Fascism aestheticizes politics because it transforms its ideological core – the promise of a strong, autonomous, and resolute state – into an eminently marketable object of mass consumption, a multipurpose commodity circulated by a peculiarly modern and Fordist culture industry.

Benjamin's expanded formula has the advantage of calling into question popular myths of Hitler Germany as a fully coordinated spectacle of seduction and manipulation. Addressing the conflicting vectors of public and private, homogenization and atomization, Benjamin underlines how the role of the aesthetic under fascism was not simply to offer symbolic placentas, deceive the masses, and freeze possible unrest, but rather that it was a sinister means of resolving in a unique fashion the dialectics of modern culture. Aesthetic politics shaped fundamentally new social realities; it reconstructed the nation through imperial and genocidal warfare.

But in understanding fascist aestheticization in the above terms as an integral step within a process of capitalist modernization that links the Wilhelminian Reich, the Weimar Republic, the Third Reich, and in fact postwar Germany, the Benjaminian concept also seems to support a normalizing or trivializing view of the National Socialist period. While it may appear already perverse to interpret Hitler's role in recourse to a larger theory of commodity fetishism, it may be seen as even more troublesome to reconstruct arenas of (consumer) agency and multiplicity in Nazi everyday culture and to understand fascism as only one among several paths of social modernization. How modern, then, we should ask ourselves, is Nazi consumer culture, and in what ways does fascism's modernity compromise the entire project of modernity? To what degree does the expanded notion of fascist aestheticization propose a universalizing model that levels necessary historical distinctions and substantive meanings? And how can we argue with or beyond Benjamin for an interpretation of fascist aestheticization in the above sense that recognizes the historical uniqueness of fascism and resists contemporary hopes to normalize the most gruesome chapter of German history?

Any attempt to answer these questions constructively requires a preliminary clarification of what entrenched concepts such as normalization, historicization, and trivialization actually mean. Products of the 1986 historians' debate on the one hand and of postunification battles over the putative need to repunctuate German national history on the other, catchwords such as normalization and historicization have more often clouded than illuminated the task of contemporary German historiography and the critical recognition of the legacy of fascism.[37] Launched as a debate over the putative need to reevaluate the meaning of the fascist past and to redefine the parameters of German national identity, the historians' debate and its postunification follow-ups provided a variety of conservative historians with a platform to reconsider the National Socialist period within the context of European totalitarianism; that is, to understand the Holocaust as one among other comparable expressions of barbarism during the 1930s and 1940s. For historians related to the so-called Bavaria Project and dedicated to researching everyday practices during the Third Reich, the notion of historicization primarily entailed the suggestion to subject Nazism to the same methods of scholarly rigor as any other period – even if it implied that in portraying the patterns of normality and continuity underneath Nazi barbarism, Nazism itself might fade away from the picture.[38] Although fundamentally different in intent and nature, both strategies of historicization often resulted in a similar normalization of the German past – in an effort, deliberate or not, to consolidate things German after unification, to reinterpret Nazi culture as an integral chapter within the larger narratives of European modernization, and to excise the memory of Auschwitz from the inventories of collective identity today.

It is important to note that this contemporary drive to reevaluate the Third Reich and free German nationalism from the shadows of fascism coincides with belated German struggles over the meaning of postmodernity and a vociferous critique of the overall project of modernity. Although it is important to explore patterns of social change that form a continuum from the Weimar period to the Federal Republic, it is disturbing to see that scholarly research about the ways in which Nazi culture continued or even accelerated various trajectories of modernization often serves as a screen for undifferentiated attacks on the entire modern condition. The right-wing position of the Berlin historian Rainer Zitelmann, arguing that Hitler Germany demonstrated "the other, the totalitarian side of modernity," is a good case in point here.[39] While he rightly draws our attention to the modernizing function of Nazi Germany within the arenas of technology, mass culture, welfare policy, and social mobility, Zitelmann at the same time wants to blame all ills of Nazism on modernity. In order to do so, he categorically purges the notion of modernity from any reference to the normative substance of post-Enlightenment politics – the ideals of emancipation, equality, and justice. Firmly standing on his postmodern vista, Zitelmann vigorously denies that the concept of modernity should or could include any consideration of peculiarly modern political achievements such as the practice of a participatory and constitutional democracy or the vision of unconstrained collective will-formation. Rather, what Zitelmann understands as modernity amounts to a regime of symbolic totalizations, a theology of progress: modernization aims at an ever-increasing annihilation of difference and a formal rationalization of power and social management. It therefore does not come as a surprise that his analysis of the modernizing functions of Nazism collapses into a fundamental critique of modernity – one that in some respects repeats the conceptual pitfalls of Horkheimer and Adorno's universalizing critique of reason. To the extent to which he renders fascism as one among other equally possible concretizations of modernity, Zitelmann ends up leveling all meaningful political distinctions. Arguing with postmodern hindsight that emancipation, humanity, and democracy can be just as modern as terror, dictatorship, and inhumanity, Zitelmann resorts to the very kind of totalization that he denounces as the alleged core of modernity.

Any examination of Nazi aesthetics and everyday practice today must face the fact that the acts and consequences of Nazi culture have to be critically integrated into the cultural history, collective memory, and any formulation of postunification German identity. "The discrete treatment of Nazi culture as separate from Weimar on the one hand and postwar culture on the other will no longer do."[40] The decisive challenge, however, is to accomplish this integration of the Nazi past without trivializing the Holocaust – critically to recognize the kind of continuities that link the Third Reich to nineteenth- and twentieth-century developments without normalizing the darkest chapter of German history. In mapping the question of fascism directly onto larger debates about the configuration of modernity and postmodernity, Zitelmann simultaneously solicits and undercuts a critical reevaluation of the modernizing effects of Nazi culture: already safely displaced by Zitelmann's own regime of postmodern reason, the actual culprit behind Nazi terror – modernity – emerges as an inhabitant of a galaxy far, far away.

Detlev Peuckert's calibration of Nazi culture, everyday practices, and social modernization suggests a much more viable model. For Peuckert, the normality of cultural practices during the Third Reich – that is, what ties fascism to the Weimar or postwar era respectively – is rooted in a theory of an asymmetrical, pathological, and hence *fundamentally unfinished* unfold-

ing of the diverse tracks of nineteenth- and twentieth-century modernization. Similar to Zitelmann, Peuckert argues that the modernity of Nazi
everyday culture – leisure activity, private consumption, and nonpolitical
pleasure – does not constitute a counterpoint to the barbarism of Nazism
but a framework within which criminality became possible. Unlike Zitelmann, however, Peuckert points out that this barbarism was not one normal outcome of modernization per se, but rather the unique result from a
strategic prioritization of technological, social, and economic over political,
legal, and moral modernity. What links Nazi culture to both the Weimar
and the postwar eras is not individual achievements within the arenas of social policy, technological progress, or social mobility so much as the ways in
which Nazi Germany succeeded in destroying prevalent bonds of solidarity
and produced coherence primarily through bureaucratic procedures, institutions of incorporation, and the charms of modern mass consumption.
Nazi culture sold images of homogenization and communality, yet in fact
produced lonely, separated individuals. "If the Third Reich could boast any
achievement, it was the destruction of public contexts and responsibilities
and the dislocation of social forms of life, even in traditional environments
which provided some measure of refuge and scope for resistance. Private
spheres of behaviour were impoverished and isolated, relapsing into a self-
serving individualism devoid of all potentially dangerous social connections and meanings. The *Volksgemeinschaft* that had been so noisily
trumpeted and so harshly enforced became, in the end, an atomised society."[41] Culture under fascism, then, constitutes an extreme case within a
twisted process of modernization. It evidences the extent to which normal
daily obsessions, leisure activities, and commodity consumption can consume such energy that they result in fundamental indifference to barbarism,
and thereby provide indirect, but highly effective, sources of political support. It is for this reason, also, that we cannot file away the legacy of Nazi
culture today. For not only did the mood and dynamism of the postwar
"economic miracle" directly profit from the isolating and depoliticizing effects of Nazi politics; atomization, the destruction of community, and indifference continuously inform postunification Germany as well, whether
it understands itself as postmodern or not.

Even in his most pessimistic moments, Benjamin lends powerful arguments to support a view of the "modernity" of fascist culture as differentiated as Peuckert's. Surely, Benjamin's account about the location of culture
in fascism, like Zitelmann's, at first seems to level all meaningful distinctions between prefascist and fascist modernity. What Benjamin calls the aes-

theticization of politics – the interlocked aesthetics of stage-managed political action and American-style mass consumption – directly appropriates elements pertinent to the overall process of capitalist modernization ever
since the middle of the nineteenth century. Yet Benjamin's apocalyptic epi-
thet about Baudelaire's Paris and the logic of commodity consumption
equally holds true for the examination of fascist culture as well: "That
things 'just go on' *is* the catastrophe. It is not that which is approaching but
that which is. Strindberg's thought: Hell is not something which lies ahead
of us, – but *this life here*" (CP 50; GS 1:683). A closer inspection reveals that
in the context of what I have suggested above as Benjamin's expanded formula of fascist aestheticization, catastrophic modernism in fact undergoes
an additional turn toward a qualitatively different stage, a turn that constitutes the diabolical uniqueness of fascist culture. For fascist aesthetics according to Benjamin secretly seeks to transform hell itself into a
commodity, an item of pleasurable, albeit self-destructive mass consumption. Although the Nazis in 1939 clearly failed to repeat the spontaneous en-
thusiasm of 1914, imperial warfare in Benjamin's analysis figures as the
logical outcome of the prewar spectacles; only war can finally uphold the
kind of repression that is at the heart of the aestheticizing celebration of
order, dynamism, power, and community. If nineteenth-century capitalism
entertained the masses with phantasmagorias of utopian collectivity and
mythic totality, fascism, in contrast, captures the minds and emotions of the
masses by appealing to diffuse popular desires for resolute politics and national rebirth. In order to do so, fascist ideologues do not even hesitate to
sell warfare as a utopian panacea for all ills of modern culture, a most entic-
ing commodity powerful enough to suture atomized individuals into a virtual community of seemingly equal window-shoppers and consumers.

However "theological"and overdetermined in character, Benjamin's thesis about the roots of fascism in fundamental pathologies of capitalist modernization ought to remind us that contrary to what historians such as
Zitelmann suggest, there is nothing genuinely "normal"about Nazi culture
after all. Fascism does not simply do what the allegedly totalitarian dimension of modernity wanted all along. Rather, fascism brings to a climactic
conclusion progressively radical attempts to contain the liberating aspects
of modern disenchantment and deauraticization, their power to disrupt
symbolic totalization and impede any regressive mimesis of mimesis. In
doing so, fascism ironically allows us to distinguish for the first time between what was utopian and what catastrophic about the overall process of
modernization. Though rightly arguing against a discrete treatment of fas-

cism, Benjamin's remarks about the nexus of fascism and modern experience therefore do not yield a universalizing conception void of any historical specificity. Nor do they allow us retrospectively to normalize the National Socialist period within the history of the German nation or the larger European or Anglo-American context of modernization. What to many of today's historians appears "normal" in Nazi culture, in the eyes of Benjamin in fact participates intimately in technologies of power and legitimation that make strategic use of distinct pathologies of modernization. Even if we consider the fact that Nazi cinema, for instance, directly adopted the grammar of contemporary Hollywood films, Hollywood's generic conventions, modes of spectatorship, and the star system, we were to misjudge the function of Nazi mass culture if we rendered it compatible with other nationally specific crystallizations of nonpolitical diversion. Nazi leisure culture, in other words, does not form an odd counterpoint to the politicization of the public sphere and the stage managing of the political. Rather, both the political spectacle and the private cult of pleasure-seeking formulate fascism's peculiar and combined answer to the dialectics of modern culture. Instead of theorizing the relation of ideology and leisure in Nazism in terms of a split consciousness, as a hiatus between ideological imperatives and everyday practices, Benjamin suggests that political spectacle and everyday consumption are integral moments of an attempt to enlist the auratic logic of commodity fetishism for the projects of ideological politics and thus to restrain modernity's sparks of liberation. Fascism, for Benjamin, plays out all relevant political questions within the field of commodity consumption while it at the same time masks the respective commodities' commodity form, reenchants the disenchanted, and thus wraps capitalism, modernity, and alienated labor in the iconographic cocoon of an organic, anticapitalist community. What Benjamin calls fascist aestheticization denotes a historically specific regime of production, representation, and cultural consumption in which political leadership and war can be advertised, packaged, and consumed like mass-produced Volkswagen cars.

But what, one might ask from today's perspective, is so singular about this nexus of politics, commodity production, and mass consumption in fascism? What makes Nazi cultural politics so different from contemporary media societies eager even to cast events such as the Gulf War into conventions drawn from the commodified arenas of popular culture? Hasn't Benjamin's catastrophic account of aestheticization in fact become the order of the day under the rule of postmodern simulation and simulacra? In an age that not only considers the televised image a material force shaping history and making the world, but also renders viewer rating and screen presence the primary catalysts for political success and legitimation, Benjamin's concerns about the commodification of the political seem still to apply. It is in the following, final chapter that I will now finally pose the ineluctable question as to whether or not Benjamin's aestheticization thesis suggests that the Third Reich grants a preview of coming postmodern attractions – the question as to whether or not Benjamin's aestheticization thesis might still help us to understand our own present.

8
Benjamin's Actuality

In our present era of global media networks and ever more inclusive technologies of space contraction, visual culture seems to have gone far beyond the task Walter Benjamin envisaged as the utopian charge of film and photography. In a famous and literally explosive passage of the artwork essay, Benjamin wrote in 1936: "Our taverns and our metropolitan streets, our offices and furnished rooms, our railroad stations and our factories appeared to have us locked up hopelessly. Then came the film and burst this prison-world asunder by the dynamite of the tenth of a second, so that now, in the midst of its far-flung ruins and debris, we calmly and adventurously go traveling" (ILL 236; GS 1:499–500). More than half a century later, film's once astonishing displacement of time and place has become the order of the day. What Benjamin analyzed in terms of the figure of shock – namely, the image-based clash of different temporalities and incompatible social topographies – for contemporary couch potatoes constitutes a daily living-room routine. Individuals as much as nations today formulate their agendas, memories, and identities in response to values and passions that are increasingly formed through mechanically reproduced images: images from TV and advertising to cinema and the Internet.

Anne Friedberg has introduced the concept of a "mobilized virtual gaze" in order to theorize the effects of postmodern media and consumer culture on our modes of perception, our sense of history, our strategies of cultural consumption, and our construction of individual and collective identities. Rooted in precinematic cultural activities such as walking and traveling, on the one hand, and in all forms of visual representation – including cave painting – on the other, the compound term is meant to describe forms of scopic pleasure that travel "in an imaginary *flânerie* through an imaginary elsewhere and an imaginary 'elsewhen.'"[1] According to Friedberg, virtual mobility today is inseparable from transnational commodity display and commodity consumption. Its logic of spatiotemporal displacement may be found in the increasingly unstable spheres of public and private interaction – in shopping malls, multiplex cinemas, or in front of the home multimedia station. Driven by the imperatives of global capital, such practices of virtual traveling seem to bring to full fruition what Benjamin described as the explosive thrust of mechanical reproduction. To the extent to which postmodern visual culture ever more aggressively supplants us into imaginary elsewheres and elsewhens, it caters with unprecedented means to the urge to pry an object from its auratic shell, its unique location in space and time. A kaleidoscope of instant global links and discontinuous image bits, the World Wide Web clearly outstrips film's power to enable the individual "to get a hold of an object at very close range by way of its likeness, its reproduction" (ILL 223; GS 1:479). The irony of Benjamin's 1936 argument, then, as seen from today's perspective, is that the mode of experience Benjamin associated with emancipatory and communist cultural practices has transformed into standard fare for audiences bound up in scenarios of globalized commodity consumption.[2]

The centrality of visual experiences and virtual gazes in contemporary culture indicates that images can no longer be seen as simply reflecting the world in which we live. Instead, images, displays, and scopic experiences are now as much a material force of shaping history as social or economic forces; they intimately contribute to the making of the world. What is important to emphasize, however, is that postmodern culture produces not only despatialized and detemporalized viewing subjects, but also a field of visual images that appears intrinsically heterogenous and hybrid. No longer do we simply experience a film at the movie theater, but also as video, through posters and advertisements, trailers and TV clips, newspaper reviews, and official or unofficial Internet sites. Indicative of a profound change in the ways we make use of cultural materials in order to negotiate meanings and construct identities, visual culture today issues an ever more accelerated multiplication of hardly ever consistent viewing positions. In doing so, it progressively undermines what Victor Burgin calls the integrity of the semantic object.[3] Under the aegis of remote controls, fast-forward buttons, and other technologically mediated modes of cultural access and consumption, traditional models of hermeneutic understanding – models that locate meaning primarily in an artifact's peculiar registers of representation or its modes of spectatorial address – no longer will do. Seemingly stripped of all auratic authority, contemporary technoculture takes the expression of a construction site, one at which meaning is produced in competing, highly selective, and often unpredictable gestures of post-hermeneutic appropriation, in the kind of cultural practices that map and incorporate symbolic material through various media channels – practices steeped in different affective, intellectual, and temporal registers at once.

But does this kaleidoscopic gestalt of our postmodern age of digital re-production, a terrain of distracted virtual travelers in Benjamin's sense in-deed, really conclude the elimination of aura that Benjamin attributed already to film and photography? Don't we observe ubiquitous attempts to resurrect auratic sentiments, to resurrect – in Hans Jürgen Syberberg's words – "with the means of contemporary technology a new aura, in par-ticular in film and photography?"[4] Can we continuously rely on Benjamin's dichotomy of auratic and postauratic art if postmodern culture, while em-phatically endorsing technologies of temporal fragmentation and spatial stretching, is obsessed with cultural airlifting, with a de- and recontextual-ization of auratic art in mega-exhibitions and digitally remastered CD col-lections? Does the popular success of events such as the "Three Tenors" concerts, the mythic temptations of an Anselm Kiefer, or the orchestrated proliferation of aura as special effect in contemporary Hollywood block-buster films represent yet another variety of aesthetic politics, or do they in-dicate an ironic and belated triumph of aura over distraction that relegates Benjamin's modernist critique of auratic revivals to the dustbins of intellec-tual history?

It is not difficult to see that these questions address issues much more complex than the academic concern with proper classification and peri-odization. For according to Benjamin, the unsurpassed theorist of aura, the resuscitation of auratic values through postauratic means of reproduction would result in the aestheticization of politics – that is to say, fascism. As I have detailed in the preceding chapters, Benjamin in fact tends to define fas-cism generically as the attempt to recycle auratic modes of perception in the context of a postauratic culture: fascism reinscribes aura in order to mas-querade a society of commodity production and consumption as an organic and racially homogenous community. How useful, then, we must ask, is Benjamin's conceptual apparatus when discussing the spectacular elements of contemporary media societies and their massive reproduction of auratic values? What seems clear at the outset is that given the ubiquitous perse-verance of auratic elements in contemporary art *and* popular culture, any political evaluation of the postmodern imaginary in mutually exclusive, normative concepts of auratic and postauratic art, of contemplation and di-version, of originality and mechanical reproduction, appears off the mark.

Christo's controversial 1995 wrapping of the Berlin Reichstag building, a supreme exercise in mingling auratic and postauratic elements, is a good case in point.[5] In contrast to the spatial politics of nineteenth-century monuments and their function to shape a homogeneous national community, Christo's spectacle constituted the focal point of eminently decentered cultural practices and gestures of consumption.[6] While emerging as the object of Christo's own sketches, as the source of abundant allusion within the domain of advertising, as the center of discussion groups on the World Wide Web, or as the point of contention in the ardent debates in the German Parliament, *Wrapped Reichstag* ended up inviting multidiscursive and highly unstable strategies of appropriation. Significantly, the speechless awe in front of the final product and its unique appearance in space and time was as much a part of what must be considered the spectatorial response to *Wrapped Reichstag* as the nervous distraction of those who waited for the latest reproduction on the various websites. Auratic through and through, Christo's shiny propylene fabric, one might therefore argue, literally served as a silver screen on which to project competing agendas, ideologies, and tactics of diversion. Auratic elements in the context of *Wrapped Reichstag* allowed for the temporary emergence of a multilingual vernacular whose specific manifestations were highly dependent on the materiality of the viewing situation – that is to say, the ways in which situated viewers made use of the various and overlapping interfaces that mark cultural exchange and consumption today.

It is important to note that in spite of this decentering and polysemic force built into Christo's renegotiation of aura, many of Christo's opponents directly applied Benjamin's critical apparatus in order to debunk the project as a monumental seduction of the masses. Accordingly, *Wrapped Reichstag* was understood as a refeudalization of the public sphere reproducing the introduction of aesthetics to politics so prominent in Nazi Germany. Like the Nazi spectacle, Christo's project, it was argued, replaces rational communication with scopic politics: *Wrapped Reichstag* – in the tradition of the ornamental politics of German fascism – endorses empathy, identification, and auratic contemplation in order to arrest the individual in gestures of collective emotional subordination, and thus to obscure the complexity and ethical dimension of contemporary politics.[7] But to consider Christo's viewers as duped by the auratic power of the project not only underestimates the cultural authority of today's consumers – the ways in which the popular dimension fosters forms of visual literacy that in many respects may be more critical than the traditional guardians of cultural taste and meaning might assume; as importantly, it also fails to recognize what must be understood as the altered role of auratic elements in a post-Fordist information society. The aura of Christo's *Wrapped Reichstag* was at the core of cultural practices that in often seemingly contradictory ways could have it both ways at once, depending on the viewers' ability to surf the various channels of reception offered by our contemporary media society. Similar to the ways in which Caruso enjoys a curious rebirth today as a digitally re-mastered CD recording, the event *Wrapped Reichstag* did not situate its viewers – whether they gathered in front of the "real thing," confronted its iconography in the news media, or checked it out on the Internet – solely on only one side of the faultline between the auratic and postauratic. In-stead, contradicting Benjamin's account of the elimination of aura in the modern age, Christo's project points to the fact that aura not only outlived mechanical reproduction but also, as Jim Collins has argued in a different context, no longer designates a mode of textual address and enunciation. Rather, aura becomes a matter of personal projection and appropriation that ironically cannot be realized *without* technological mediation and exists as one tactic aside many others that make use of cultural material. Repre-sentative of an age in which bourgeois high art has been thoroughly incor-porated into the circuits of commodified culture, Christo's project belies any attempt to ground accounts of the politics of today's culture in facile juxtapositions of aura and mechanical reproduction, high art and popular entertainment. If the spectacle *Wrapped Reichstag* has one dominant mean-ing at all, then it is to convey to us that "rather than being *eliminated* by ever more sophisticated forms of distribution and access, the production of 'aura' has only *proliferated* as it has been dispersed through the multiplica-tion of information technologies and agents responsible for determining value."[8]

Systematically blurring the lines between the idioms of high art and the expressions of popular culture, *Wrapped Reichstag* neither resulted in a mere Hollywoodization of avant-gardist practices nor did it reproduce the postauratic aura and monumentalism of fascist strategies of aestheticiza-tion. As Andreas Huyssen has argued, *Wrapped Reichstag*, to the extent to which it rearticulated aura as a process, product, and catalyst of historical memory in postauratic times, "stood as a monument to a democratic cul-ture rather than a demonstration of state power."[9] The event thus urges us to rethink Benjamin's theory of experience and the dialectics of aura in twentieth-century culture and politics. Does the present resurgence of aura as a critical and intrinsically heterogenous corrective to accelerated global stretching and amnesia render Benjamin's critique of technological aura as insufficient? To what extent does Christo's public rearticulation of aura render Benjamin's aestheticization thesis a typical expression of a modernist and Fordist discourse – a discourse that neither provides adequate answers to nor asks the right questions about the cultural politics of postmodernity? Is it possible at all continuously to identify with the help of Benjamin strategies of aestheticization today without classifying them as "fascist"?

The following chapter seeks to give some answers to these questions, thereby thinking through what the veritable industry surrounding Benjamin today mostly takes for granted: the actuality of the aestheticization thesis for the analysis of postmodern consumer culture. In order to do so, I first recapitulate Benjamin's theory of auratic and postauratic experience in light of the arguments of some of his most insightful critics, in particular Theodor W. Adorno and Miriam Hansen. Second, I examine postmodern interfaces between technology, identity, memory, and the popular dimension in order to better understand not only the resurfacing of auratic sentiments today but also their altered function in contemporary public and private spheres. And in a third step, I rephrase the question of Benjamin's actuality, arguing emphatically that contemporary criticism can still learn from the aestheticization thesis, even if the imbrication of politics, perception, and culture in the late twentieth century fundamentally differs from the peculiar configuration Benjamin sought to identify during the 1930s.

A term only inappropriately captured by the English term "experience," the category of *Erfahrung* is at the heart of Benjamin's entire critical program. It unifies in various configurations his overall work from the 1910s to his final theology of history of 1940. Explicitly opposed to instrumentalist, scientific, or positivistic definitions of experience, Benjamin unfolds his concept along spatial and temporal vectors at once. Experience mediates individual modes of perception with collective patterns of cognition and material modalities of production, transportation, and information; experience articulates conflicting temporalities, including those of utopian promises and historical memory, of conscious and unconscious acts of recollection and remembrance. In his early metaphysical phase prior to 1920, Benjamin at certain points seemed to imply that humanity's postlapsarian embrace of history, reflection, and language itself already marked the end of experience proper.[10] Only children retain something of the paradisiacal plentitude of experience because only children can see the world without imposing distinctions and intellectual cross-references; only children according to the early Benjamin possess that kind of uncorrupted imaginative activity that sees objects with "a pure mood, without thereby sacrificing the world."[11] In the course of the 1930s, in particular in the artwork essay and the study on Baudelaire, Benjamin will crucially rethink and historicize his earlier metaphysics of experience and claim that the fundamental restructuring of temporal and spatial relations in modernity – that is, the adaption of the human senses to urban traffic and industrial modes of production, to acceleration and sensation – undermines the condition for the possibility of what he now calls auratic experience. Defined as a quasi-magic perception of an object invested "with the capability of returning the gaze" (ILL 188; GS 1:646), aura withers in modernity. Taylorism, industrial mass production, and urbanization render obsolete any spatiotemporal enchantment with a unique phenomenon however close it may be; they displace auratic experience with the modern regimes of distraction. Film, for Benjamin, is both symptom and agent of this transformation. It extends the thrust of social changes to the arenas of cultural exchange and aesthetic expression. Accordingly, the shock of cinematic montage emancipates cultural practices not only from auratic sentiments but from aesthetic experience altogether; it links cultural formulations – for better (communism) or worse (fascism) – directly to political projects. As a postaesthetic counterpart to the shifting grounds of collective perception, Benjamin's cinema no longer seems to allow for moments of profane illumination, for the magic spell of the mimetic faculty, or for a reciprocal interaction between humanity and nature. Unless it subscribes to a politically regressive and false resurrection of aura, cinema – as conceived in the artwork essay – does not return the viewer's gaze. Instead, as I have detailed in chapter 4, it circumscribes a site of rational insight and critical debate, of scientific examination and egalitarian self-representation. A training ground for distracted modes of reception and cultural appropriation, mechanical reproduction thus emancipates modern society from ritual, tradition, and the bourgeois cult of art at the cost of severing the individual from the resources of memory, nonintentionality, and playful mimesis, of the ecstasy of retrieving an unknown past, of bridging the difference between subject and object in order to establish spontaneous and noncoercive relations to the world.

It has often been pointed out not only that Benjamin overestimated the liberatory potential of postauratic visuality but also that his political appropriation of cinema remained pseudoradical in that it assumed all too close affinities between the modes of rationalized industrial production and the peculiar principles of mass cultural reception and experience.[12] A modality of experience after the end of experience proper, Benjamin's category of distraction, as a consequence, "elides – and all too readily surrenders – the regressive aspects of the cinema, its mobilizing of pre-rational mental processes, and thus unwittingly joins the long tradition of bourgeois rationality that asserts itself in the containment and exclusion of the other, of sensuality and femininity."[13] Benjamin's theory of modern disenchantment and visuality undermines the very position it seeks to emphasize. To the extent to which the category of distraction glosses over potential gaps between ideological uses of cinema and the often unpredictable ways in which actual viewers make use of the specific viewing event, Benjamin inhibits any thorough understanding of how a film makes its entry into the spectator's head, and how cinema's symbolic materials might be consumed according to very different needs and agendas. Benjamin's celebratory and deterministic use of the category of distraction, in other words, obstructs the possibility to understand cinema as a trading place of insight and articulation, as a proletarian public sphere that negotiates the concreteness of human experience across dominant demarcations of public and private. Though meant to offer a site of critical exchange and cultural empowerment, Benjamin's postauratic auditorium is populated by spectators who have nothing left to see or say anymore. Denying the masses' auratic experience, aesthetic play, and sensual pleasure, Benjamin, in fact, risks leaving the individual's emotional needs to be used and abused by the political enemies, a position paramount within the German Left circa 1930 and critiqued most forcefully by Benjamin's contemporary Ernst Bloch.

Given such critical blind spots in Benjamin's expulsion of aura from the topographies of mechanical reproduction, it should come as no surprise that even some of Benjamin's closest intellectual allies saw reason enough to challenge the conceptual centerpiece of Benjamin's interlaced theory of film and the aestheticization of politics. Rigorously questioning Benjamin's radical dismissal of aura and aesthetic experience, Theodor W. Adorno painstakingly insisted that auratic and contemplative elements clearly survived the arrival of a full-fledged culture of mechanical reproduction in the twentieth century. According to Adorno, aura not only persisted in the riddles of enigmatic modernism but also – in however perverted form – in mass culture's ruthless unity of high and low; that is to say, in the culture industry's attempt to reconcile the fault lines of modern culture "by absorbing light into serious art, or vice versa."[14] Adorno and Benjamin clearly agreed that modern technology had moved art beyond its former magic and aura, but contrary to Benjamin, Adorno insisted that modernist art in spite of its antiauratic impulses remained aesthetic.[15] Challenging the ever-increasing standardization of cultural expressions under organized capitalism, the best works of aesthetic modernism in Adorno's view evidenced a dialectical relationship to both bourgeois art and industrial culture and therefore retained aspects of the very magical aura they sought to supersede. For Adorno, Benjamin's category of postauratic distraction, on the other hand, falsely and undialectically heroized fragmentation and commodity fetishism as strategies of cultural empowerment and subversion. Benjamin's distracted poachers of modern culture, Adorno believed, simply reproduce the culture industry's ideology of pseudo-individualization, defined as the "halo of free choice" on the basis of standardization itself.[16] Read against the backdrop of what is missing in Benjamin's account of film – namely, a critical theory of the commodification of cultural practices – postauratic inattentiveness in Adorno's view disintegrates the ability to conceive of semantic unity as a repository of determined negation and resistance. Far from liberating humankind from the authority of tradition and ritual, distraction transforms disconnected parts into fetishes in front of which "consumers become temple slaves."[17] Even during the last years of his life, when cautiously applauding the emerging New German Cinema for its disruption of hegemonic meaning, Adorno remained highly skeptical about Benjamin's denigration of auratic images and experiences. Experimental auteur directors such as Alexander Kluge, Adorno argued, might capitalize on the fact that the culture industry may itself contain antidotes to its own ideology, but they at the same time bring into focus the fact that Benjamin failed "to elaborate on how deeply some of the categories he postulated for film – exhibition, test – are imbricated with the commodity character which his theory opposes."[18] Benjamin's disenchanted realism, though dedicated to the enterprise of scientifically penetrating the phenomenal surface of the object world, remains a romantic endeavor. In contrast to modernist art's protest against universal commodification, postauratic forms of representation fail to expose the reification that reigns at the bottom of reality and its mass cultural reproduction. "Every meaning – including critical meaning – which the camera eye imparts to the film would already invalidate the law of the camera and thus violate Benjamin's taboo, conceived as it was with the explicit purpose of outdoing the provocative Brecht and thereby – this may have been its secret purpose – gaining freedom from him."[19]

Adorno, in a sense, defended auratic residues against Benjamin's artwork essay because he rightly resisted Benjamin's undialectical equation of au-

ratic and autonomous art, of technological progress and the end of experience. Unlike Benjamin, Adorno in fact sensed a precarious complicity between the philosophical denigration of auratic experience on the one hand
and the industrial transformation of perception as well as the logic of commodity fetishism on the other. Played out in the hermetic realm of autonomous art, mimetic experience and art's semblance of subjectivity were
to voice Adorno's desperate protest against the leveling of critical meaning
and the disciplining of pleasure administered by twentieth-century mass
culture. In her recent *Joyless Streets*, Patrice Petro has added provocatively to
this critique of Benjamin's account of postauratic visuality, suggesting that
we understand the demolition of aura through cinema not as an effect of
cinematic technology per se, but of the peculiar and historically contingent
formation of dominant film practices and the systematic marginalization of
alternative forms of spectatorship.[20] Petro argues that by reconstructing the
course of modern experience and spectatorship in terms of a general paradigm shift from aura to distraction, Benjamin explains away the factual heterogeneity and diversity of spectatorial practices in particular in early
cinema. Most importantly, he completely elides the gender-specificity of
early cinematic forms of address and consumption, the parallel existence
of distracted and concentrated, industrialized and emotionally attentive
modes of looking. While Benjamin's category of distraction might indeed
encode the experience of those permitted to participate in the processes of
social and cultural modernization since the middle of the nineteenth century, it obscures the structures of experience of those who, owing to given
landscapes of power, remained at the margins of these processes – in particular, women. Female spectatorship, particularly during the 1920s, was often
at odds with the kind of principles Benjamin presented as a universal ontology of cinematic communication. Highly popular in Weimar cinema as
a "female" genre, the melodrama, according to Petro, bears testimony to
the existence of modes of spectatorship different from those described by
Benjamin under the rubric of distraction and inattentive, detached appropriation. "For male intellectuals," she adds, "who experienced the demise of
poetic forms with the advent of cinema, the film melodrama may have in
fact entailed disinterestedness and detachment, but for female audiences,
who were only just beginning to be addressed as spectators, the film melodrama almost certainly provoked an intensely interested and emotional in-
volvement, particularly since melodramatic representation often gave
heightened expression to women's experience of modernity."[21] In the context of the 1920s melodrama, then, mechanical reproduction addresses

those for whom distraction has not become the norm, those whose "concentrated gaze involves a perceptual activity that is neither passive nor entirely distracted."[22] Though increasingly obliterated by the industry's attempt to shape a unified spectatorial subject, the "woman's film" evidences the historical possibility of an empowering survival of aura on the grounds of mass culture itself, a nonantagonistic coexistence of mechanical reproduction and auratic perception.

Both Adorno and Petro agree that Benjamin's theory of experiential exhaustion in modernity cannot account for or evaluate the survival or discontinuous return of aura in twentieth-century art and mass culture. Understanding cinema's role primarily as a functional agent and symptom of modern disenchantment, Benjamin not only undermines the very kind of categories that energize his overall criticism of modern culture, including his studies of surrealism, nineteenth-century flânerie, Baudelaire, and Kafka. As he inseparably mixes theoretical, historical, and normative lines of argumentation, Benjamin also implies all too facile and misleading links between the persistence of aura and the aestheticization of politics, between fascism and the resurgence of aesthetic experience in mass culture. Instead of understanding modernity in terms of a differentiation of competing modes of looking and cultural consumption, Benjamin – understandably eager to denounce the ways in which fascism musters aura and the irrational to engineer political homogeneity – forges the complexity of modern spectatorship into a rather monolithic cast himself. In doing so, the artwork essay renders the effects of historical contingencies as "natural"facts; it mistakes a peculiar formation of visual culture and spectatorship for the ontology of the media.

Given these blind spots in Benjamin's reasoning on film and the politics of scopic pleasure, it appears timely to recapitulate once more the argument of the artwork essay and search for alternative or less monolithic accounts of auratic and postauratic visuality. After all, it is unlikely that Benjamin could have so drastically forfeited his self-proclaimed aim of dialectical thought without leaving behind numerous traces of containment or repression. Reading Benjamin against the grain of his iconoclastic posture, Miriam Hansen has shown that the artwork essay indeed contains a number of allusions to mimetic experience and auratic figuration "suggesting that the cinema's role in relation to experiential impoverishment could go beyond merely promoting and consummating the historical process."[23] Hansen proposes that what are often seen as the essay's most pseudoscientific pronouncements contain building blocks for an alternative theory of vision in the age of mechanical reproduction. Particularly Benjamin's comments about the tactile, ballistic, and, hence, anti-illusionary thrust of film, on the one hand, and about the photographic image's quasi-Freudian "optical unconscious," on the other, allow Hansen to reconsider Benjamin's wholesale denigration of aura. Hansen's formula will allow us to disentangle Benjamin's sweeping conceptual equation of postauratic aura and fascist aesthetics.

First of all, there is good reason to conceive of what Benjamin calls the tactile dimension of film as a mimetic figuration of the fragmented and atomized structure of modern existence and not simply as a catalyst of discursive insight and truth. "Being based on changes of place and focus which periodically assail the spectator" (ILL 238; GS 1:502), cinematic cutting and editing administer visceral shocks to the viewer and thus allow for a sensuous, somatic relationship to what is seen on screen. A source of visual attractions and visceral astonishments, film results in a radical displacement of self in sentience; it takes us outside of ourselves in likeness to the ways in which a child "not only plays at being a grocer or teacher, but also at being a windmill or a train" (GS 2:205). In the same way that Kracauer endorses distraction as a sensuous "reflection of the uncontrolled anarchy of our world,"[24] Benjamin valorizes the ballistic qualities of film because they involve a mimetic component that clearly exceeds the bounds of a Brechtian aesthetics of cognitive distanciation and discursive truth. Though hostile to the spatial dimension of auratic distance, Benjamin's cinematic image retains something of aura's temporality; it is powerful enough to actualize a prehistoric stratum of human practice. Film bestows upon the viewer the experience of quasi-magic, "primitivist" contact, a preconceptual and sensory form of knowing that resembles the infant's attempt to know an object by eating it.

Secondly, residues of auratic experience may also legitimately enter into postauratic film practice through the backdoor of what Benjamin calls the optical unconscious and the equipment-free aspect of the cinematic image. With the help of the optical unconscious, Benjamin admits dimensions into his theory of postauratic representation and spectatorship that clearly contradict his overall emphasis on presence, tracelessness, expertdom, and radical distraction. Far from solely indicating an utterly disenchanting rationalization of vision, Benjamin's equation of camera work and Freudian psychoanalysis hints at film's capacity to authorize an unprecedented mimesis of technology and nature, "a thoroughgoing permeation of reality with mechanical equipment" (ILL 234; GS 1:496). In that the camera on the one hand pierces quotidian surfaces with its peculiar technologies of representation, yet on the other tends to make its own work invisible, film is capable of ushering the spectator into the realms of profane illumination, into an arena of flash-like, nonintentional, and sensuous cognition similar to the one Benjamin unearthed in the works of the surrealists, of Baudelaire, and in the context of his own experiments with drugs and intoxication. Cinema may after all allow for forms of reciprocity reminiscent of the experience of auratic phenomena: the optical unconscious rearticulates for the era of mechanical reproduction what in romantic philosophy empowered nature to return the gaze.

All things considered, then, Benjamin's thesis about the visceral wonders of modern vision is more ambiguous and "dialectical" than it may seem at first. Not only does the advent and popular success of the filmic image far from condemn *all* auratic experience as complicit with authority and traditionalism; understood as an unsettling counterpoint to dominant film practices, a cinema that returns the gaze could also provide an antidote to the very kind of instrumental rationality and temporal fragmentation Benjamin's endorses all too quickly and homogeneously as the signatures of modern life. While the surgical devices of film and the spatiotemporal displacements of mechanical reproduction clearly participate in the destruction of the aura of first nature, of the halo that surrounds natural presences and wonders, film's mimetic powers, its physiognomical mode of signification, and its indebtedness to what Tom Gunning calls the cinema of attraction,[25] may at the same time map second nature as a dimension of profane illumination and, in so doing, empower modes of spectatorship that escape the grasp of reification Adorno saw at the bottom of Benjamin's theory of film. "If the mimetic capacities of film were put to such use, it would not only fulfill a critical function but also a redemptive one, registering sediments of experience that are no longer or not yet claimed by social and economic rationality, making them readable as emblems of a 'forgotten future.'"[26]

To thus bring into focus the artwork essay's discontinuous reinscription of aura and mimesis in and through film allows us to link Benjamin's account of postauratic visuality to critical concepts of modern mass culture – that is, theories that map the popular dimension as an ambiguous domain circulating often archaic utopias of meaningful collectivity while simultaneously perpetuating the opposite. Moreover, rectifying what both Adorno and Petro, from different perspectives indeed, vehemently oppose in Benjamin, the revised notion of auratic experience makes it possible to demystify Benjamin's mysterious concept of aura itself and free it from the suspicion that any return of auratic moments necessarily results in a political coordination of perception and a concomitant mystification of power. If even Benjamin himself observes the survival of mimetic elements within postauratic visual practices, then it would be more than foolish to construe all rearticulations of aura and mimesis in the twentieth century as a replay of fascist media politics. Surely, fascism elicits auratic experiences through postauratic means in order to relocate decadent aesthetic values to the arena of political action, to entertain the masses with the imagery of autonomous politics, and to provide a unifying product image for a heterogenous ideological commodity; fascist mass culture appeals to utopian elements in auratic experiences in order to bond the individual to a charismatic project of national rebirth and pure politics. But inasmuch as that which Benjamin calls the optical unconscious of mechanical reproduction itself offers valuable residues of auratic experiences, there is no conceptual reason why aura could not play a role in critical visual practices as well – practices that challenge fascism's politicization of the bourgeois cult of art or the ever-increasing fragmentation of lifeworlds in modernity. Aura, its decay and its return, are fundamentally ambivalent categories even in Benjamin's highly overdetermined philosophy of history and media aesthetics. Their political value is a matter of historical contingencies; it cannot be understood by means of universalizing theoretical arguments.

It has become commonplace to claim that our era of global diversified consumption uncannily reproduces the nexus of (post)auratic visuality and power in fascism. As John Thompson puts it, politics today has become "inseparable from the art of managing visibility."[27] Like fascism, postmodern politics relies heavily on a massive proliferation of images and visual appeals to affective investments, on the imagery of simulated events and mediated pseudorealities. Additionally, there is ample evidence that postmodern culture – as if to mock vulgar versions of Benjamin's critique of fascism – revels in mechanically reproduced remnants of auratic experiences and mimetic desires. To suspect, however, that any such postauratic return of aura today may yield directly regressive political effects is clearly off the mark. It would fall prey to the same kind of formalism and aestheticism Benjamin was so eager to overthrow, and at the same time also overlook the fact that postmodern culture involves circuits of cultural dissemination and strategies of consumption fundamentally different from the one at the core of fascist mass culture. Neither today's politics of commodification nor today's commodification of politics directly duplicate what Benjamin sought to expose as fascist aestheticization. To discuss crucial differences, and thus to open up a framework in which it becomes possible to talk in a meaningful and differentiated way about the political uses and abuses of aura and experience under the condition of postmodernity, will be the task of the final two sections of this chapter.

David Harvey has suggested that the postmodern condition of advanced Western capitalist nations by and large reflects a political, social, and cultural response to a fundamentally new way of how capitalism works in the late twentieth century. The postmodern represents both a break with the regime of Fordist modes of standardized mass production and mass consumption and a foray into an era of "flexible accumulation" as the hegemonic principle of capitalist reproduction, an era "characterized by more flexible labour processes and markets, of geographical mobility and rapid shifts in consumption practices."[28] Inaugurated circa 1970, this new post-Fordist phase of capitalist accumulation brings forth the emergence of novel and highly diversified sectors of production, of unstable, heterogeneous markets, and of heated cycles of innovations. It also involves a new round of space/time compressions that shrink the temporal and spatial horizons of both private and public experiences and in so doing spread decision-making processes over an ever more global, variegated, and accelerated space. Understood as the successor of Fordist, modernist rigidity, the condition of postmodernity thus represents and reflects a fundamental disorganization of centralized and homogenous modes of capitalist production and consumption. Flexible accumulation disperses traditional capitalist relations and the concentration of capital; it displaces large production plants and surrounding cities in favor of diversified small-batch manufacturing sites, subcontracting firms at peripheral places, and a decentering of the urban lifeworld.[29] In response, post-Fordist societies observe the advent of new modalities of individualized and highly diversified commodity consumption. However precarious and ambiguous in nature, flexible accumulation cannot succeed without equipping individual consumers with a new kind of market authority that supersedes the standardized practices of Fordist mass consumption.

Fordist mass culture offered little choice between different media channels or offerings and thereby produced a relatively homogenous community of, however atomized, viewers or consumers. One of the reasons for the rapid success of TV was that it was able to offer private pleasures of seemingly public relevance. Situated in the homely shelter of the living room, everyone pretty much watched the same show at the same time and hence was able to experience isolated acts of cultural consumption as a quasi-communal affair. Fordist consumerism carried the burden of providing an always precarious mythology of social integration and democratic egality. It offered the image of a unified population pursuing the same goals and hunting for the same objects of desire: the pleasures of buying and window-shopping as the principal ticket to citizenship.

Post-Fordist culture, by way of contrast, is characterized by the workings of hybrid multimedia aggregates and by identities that are diversified and hardly ever consistent. Confronted with technologically mediated processes of temporal and spatial stretching, the relatively predictable consumer of Fordist mass culture converts into a symbolic poacher and cultural bricoleur who seizes heterogenous materials from different times and spaces, takes position in multiple temporalities at once, and assumes ever-shifting positionalities. Post-Fordist technoculture grafts the principle of flexible accumulation onto the exchange and acquisition of symbolic materials. In doing so, it nullifies what allowed the individual to experience Fordist consumer societies as imagined communities. Cultural technologies such as VCRs or Walkmans, fast-forward buttons or digital cameras, discharge the assumptions about homogenous time and space so central to the ideological effects of Fordist mass media: "One can literally rent another space and time when one borrows a videotape to watch on a VCR."[30] The integration of PC, telephone, TV, and video, the emergence of PC banking and shopping, the direct access to Internet archives and databanks, and the dazzle of new video games and virtual reality simulations, all point toward the arrival of a new kind of consumer whose continual selections result in a highly individualized (and commodified) use of an eminently diverse media landscape.

Benjamin understood mechanical reproduction as a stimulus for new forms of cultural authority: the newsboy who discussed the outcome of a bicycle race, for Benjamin, indicated the advent of a culture of experts thriving on the fact that Fordist mass media satisfy "modern man's legitimate claim to being reproduced" (ILL 232; GS 1:494). In the age of digital information and domestic cultural technologies such as VCRs, video cameras, and website editors, Benjamin's participatory utopia of cultural empowerment seems to have come to full fruition. Not only do we find ourselves as objects of visual or digital reproduction, we also seem to be in relative control over the very means and technologies that allow us to shape our iden-

tities and self-representations. In order to exhaust the multiplicity of opportunities and warrant the most effective accumulation of pleasure and
leisure, postmodern consumers need to know much more than simply how
to consume. Expertdom in fact has become a prerequisite of cultural survival today. Consumers need to know how to manipulate sophisticated
technologies and traverse various media channels at once. Furthermore,
they also need to know how to handle mounting pressures to reduce complexity, to make and mark distinctions and select between highly competi-
tive offerings, to forget about alternative options while consuming a
specific option, and to meet a dynamic inflation of demands and expectations.[31]

Yet even if postmodern culture seems to require us to become experts in
Benjamin's sense, it is not difficult to see that our contemporary life on
screen fundamentally differs from the kind of images and identities Benjamin hoped to see expertly circulated on the screens of Fordist mass culture. On the World Wide Web, for example, we construct a network
identity by composing and pasting words, images, and sounds drawn from
perplexingly global and inconsistent sources.[32] Experts surfing the Web fur-
nish their homes by fusing diverse materials, genres, styles, and idioms of
expression into one intrinsically decentered and infinite hypertext; there is
no actual limit for the number of links we allocate on a homepage as tokens
of our multiple interests and personae. Postmodern technoculture thus
couples its new forms of cultural authority to a multiplication of identities
and viewing positions that supersede the unified identity of Benjamin's
proletarian newsboy fascinated with proletarian spectator sports. Needless
to say, this diversification of cultural identities extends to the realm of
the political as well. Helmut Dubiel's "Mercedes-worker from Baden-
Württemberg, who is unionized yet also – as a member of an action group –
protests against a nearby Mercedes test course and who votes for the Christian Democratic Party because it promises lower taxation on factory cars"is
a good case in point here.[33] He not only indicates the accelerating refrac-
tions of the postmodern political consciousness, but also the fact that –
under the rule of flexible accumulation – political identities result from
an increasingly complex and by no means stable combination of various parameters and elements – parameters and elements that reflect competing
and hardly predictable compounds of social, economic, and cultural positionalities.

Fordist concepts of cultural production, consumption, and reception, then, no longer will do in order to theorize the ways in which individuals today make use of the hybridization of media channels and the pluralization of modes of expression. "Consumers in the classical sense appear antiquated in face of the new offerings."[34] If the concept of postmodernism is meant to signify more than simply a cultural fashion or a new aesthetic paradigm, then it ought to bring into view precisely what is different about the conditions of individual experience and the institutions of cultural consumption today; that is, to conceptualize the relationship between the emergence of highly strategic practices of symbolic appropriation, the progressive decentering and multiplication of identity, and the changes in the global economic system that make us live in a permanent elsewhere and elsewhen. Postmodern criticism, however, often tends to overlook possible complicities between today's flexible accumulation of hybrid identities, nonhierarchical differences, and heterogenous forms of agency, on the one hand, and the ways in which Western capitalism and commodification work on a global and local scale in the late twentieth century, on the other. Instead, it uncritically heroizes the centrifugal force of post-Fordist societies as part of a "fantastic unbinding of cultures, forms of life, styles, and world perspectives that today no longer simply encounter each other, but mutually open up to one another, penetrate each other in the medium of mutual interpretation, mix with one another, enter into hybrid and creative relationships, and produce an overwhelming pluralism, a decentered, hence obscure multiplicity, indeed a chaos of linked but contingent, nearly undecipherable sounds and texts."[35] As a result, particularly in its poststructuralist inflections, this form of criticism often all too quickly assigns subversive meanings to the fracturing of identity and the present roamings of cultural poachers, glossing over the fact that local acts of cultural empowerment do not necessarily result in inclusive articulations of resistance or opposition. What is important to keep in mind is that no carnivalistic unbinding of fixed traditions, unified identities, or Fordist media practices per se will yield the emancipatory effects many theorists attest to technoculture's bursting asunder of modern space, experience, and meaning. If the multiplication of cultural identities and the diversification of symbolic practices should not lead to a cacophony of highly fragmented image bits and sound bytes, but rather help enable politically relevant and focused processes of collective will-formation, then what is needed instead is the formation of public and counterpublic spheres that mediate between the global and the local, between the by no means synchronized forces of cultural, political, and economic stretching. Only if, in other words, the post-Fordist refraction of culture and its scenarios of virtual travel are linked to a successful institutionalization of communicative infrastructures that calibrate the conflicting dimensions of globalization[36] – only then will it be possible to safeguard forms of solidarity that empower individual and collective agents to make effective use of the logic of spatiotemporal displacement so pertinent to our age of digital information.

It is interesting to note in this context that in many instances the contemporary desire for auratic experiences expresses nothing other than the hope for structures of mediation that negotiate the global and the local, restore meaningful spaces to the exploded topographies of postmodern culture, secure forms of individual agency and mimetic nonintentionality, and thus find remedies for the loss of memory in our fantastically unbound culture of channel surfers. Whether cultivated in contemporary museum practices, the digital airlifting of nineteenth-century opera, or the wrapping of political monuments, postmodern aura indicates that the anarchic freedom of global poachers remains imaginary if they fail to develop an ethos of significance – that is to say, individual and collective structures of valorization that allow situated subjects to distinguish between narratives, images, sounds, and symbols of lesser and of greater importance. While having been thoroughly incorporated into the circuits of mass culture and digital information, aura today therefore often also signifies the however paradoxical and quixotic quest for a return of the real, a critical outcry against ever more inclusive scenarios of simulation.[37] As it aims at a transitory reenchantment of human perception and object relations, a discontinuous reinscription of aura can remind us of our need for experience in its most emphatic sense. It probes the economic and cultural hegemony of flexible accumulation, vocalizing residues of opposition to the universal dominance of exchange-values, to the devaluation of objects under the rule of global commodification. At a time when post-Fordist capitalist relations simultaneously shrink and expand the spatiotemporal dimensions of our lifeworlds in an unprecedented manner, the reinvention of auratic experiences offers a "testing ground for reflections on temporality and subjectivity, identity and alterity."[38] Instead of suturing the individual automatically into a false spectacle of collectivity and reconciliation, aura today brings into focus that a life without memory and without the thick materiality of sentient experience is not a life at all. It opens our eyes to the fact that armchair voyages through hyperspace and along electronic information superhighways – in spite of all their liberatory potentials – may ironically imprison meaning and freedom in an iron cage of false empowerment, of pseudo-individualization. As one among multiple other modes of mass cultural experience, the return of aura demonstrates the fact that contemporary popular culture may itself contain certain correctives to its own ideologies and practices, to the vanishing of history and memory into "terminal" perceptions that are endlessly replayed as film and video. Objecting to the dematerialization of experience in postmodernity, aura reminds us that any collision of heterogeneous spaces and conflicting temporalities may release us from oppressive traditions and monolithic identities only if we succeed in relating the symbolic material of diverse cultures to the experiential trajectories of sentient bodies and the materiality of everyday practice.

The syncretic blend of auratic charisma and mass appeal, of modernist rhetoric of defamiliarization and postmodern happening, in Christo's *Wrapped Reichstag* – to return to the opening discussion of this chapter – is a good example. A local event with global reverberations, Christo's *Wrapped Reichstag* evoked the charm of auratic and mimetic experiences in order to constitute what I would like to call a hybrid visual public sphere, one in which – unlike Habermas's classical model of the bourgeois public sphere – the body and its pleasures played an undeniable role. *Wrapped Reichstag*'s transitory aura opened up a variety of cultural spaces in which it became possible not only to negotiate past and present, the local and the global, but also the diverse itineraries of sensuality and cognition, corporeal experience and discursive intervention. Proliferated through various media channels at once and disseminated to highly heterogenous audiences, the aura of Christo's event promoted the visual to a force powerful enough to uncouple concepts of German national identity from the legacy of the nineteenth century, from the nationalistic and essentializing rhetoric of monolingual, ethnic, or cultural singularity. Undermining the iconic symbolism of nationalist discourse, *Wrapped Reichstag* appealed to auratic desires in order to transform a monument into a literal projection screen; the project's aura called forth competing images of past and present, bringing into focus the constructedness of history, truth, and identity. In doing so, Christo's intervention reminded us that among other things visual culture in the age of flexible accumulation – even as global spectacle and mass diversion – can delimit a site of division, difference, and contestation. To consider Christo's viewers with the help of Benjamin as duped by the auratic power of the project therefore fails to recognize the altered landscapes of experience, communication, and commodification in a post-Fordist information society. In the tradition of a long-standing Western ocularphobia, it also underestimates the potential virtues of the visual today to articulate experience, insight, and knowledge across given boundaries of public and private.[39] In readmitting auratic experiences through the backdoor of postauratic culture, *Wrapped Reichstag* exposed the very inadequacy of evaluating the intentional fabrication of aura today within a Benjaminian framework, to equate the workings of postmodern visual culture with the Nazi spectacle. In a time of accelerated amnesia and spatial displacement, the transitory aura of *Wrapped Reichstag* and its diverse post-hermeneutic appropriations, in certain respects, helped energize the formation of an ethos of significance. Far from resulting in a retrogressive aestheticization of politics, the project's aura made it possible for Germans to rethink what it means to be German in a globalized culture, to reevaluate critically the legacy of their past, and to reinsert the body and its pleasures into postnationalist negotiations of culture and community.

Given these fundamental changes in the nature of visual culture today, did Adorno, when criticizing Benjamin's undialectical demise of aura and defending the persistence of aesthetic experience, get it right both theoretically and historically? Does Christo's success indicate a curiously twisted and posthumous victory of Adorno over Benjamin? Does post-Fordist aura render Benjamin's artwork essay, the philosophy of mechanical reproduction, and the concomitant critique of the aestheticization of politics a past chapter of intellectual history?

There are good reasons to believe that Benjamin's critique of aura and the aestheticization of politics no longer provides what it originally was meant to offer: a critical yardstick that measures the political instrumentality of cultural expressions and practices. Surely, Benjamin's analysis of twentieth-century visual culture as a laboratory of spatiotemporal displacement is still useful in order to conceptualize the ways in which contemporary culture endorses and commodifies the postmodern regime of mobile virtual looking. At the same time, however, we cannot overlook radical changes in the structure of experience and its social organization separating us from Benjamin's time and reasoning. Whether they concern transformations in the production and social function of auratic perception, in the bearing of today's media channels on the formation of cultural authority, or in global capitalism's strategies of commodification, these historical differences, I would argue, should caution us not to draw any facile parallels between the media spectacles of the 1990s and what Benjamin called the aestheticization of politics in fascism. Thanks to fundamentally different modes of how we look and how we assume subject positions in the fields of visual culture, a postauratic refurbishing of aura today may result in quite different political effects than under the rule of fascism. Even when produced by advanced technologies, synthetic aura today therefore does not necessarily coincide with the (fascist) attempt to discipline distraction, anaesthetize sense perception, and obliterate the private body as a site of desire and experience. Contrary to Benjamin's assumption, aura, in other words, survived the gestalt of a full-fledged culture of mechanical reproduction, but it did so under conditions that also run counter to Adorno's indictment of postautonomous art as a sole repository of mass deception and manipulation. Neither Adorno's virulent critique of the Fordist culture industry and his heroization of the negativity of modernist art, nor Benjamin's one-sided valorization of postauratic art and his ambivalent charge against aesthetic experience, therefore, will do in order to provide keywords for theorizing postmodern consumption and amnesia. Each in its own way fusing historical-descriptive and normative lines of argumentation, the paradigmatic categories of Adorno and Benjamin respectively are progressively consumed by the very historical process they were meant to theorize. The point, therefore, is not to speculate about who may have won over whom, or – in the gesture of a Jim Collins[40] – check Benjamin and Adorno into the Grand Hotel Abyss of modernist theory, but rather to investigate what can be redeemed of Benjamin (and Adorno) for our own times; that is to say, how we can see ourselves in his critique of modern culture, and how we can envision his role under the postmodern conditions of flexible accumulation.

It is not difficult to see that there has never been a greater need to take critical issue with the nexus of cultural expressions, media technologies, and modes of political legitimation. Postmodern culture has bundled the various dimensions of representation – semiotic, aesthetic, and political – into a global grammar of commodity consumption, prioritizing the image over reality and promoting fun and diversion to the primary glue of what might hold society together. An unmediated Benjaminian perspective, however, will hardly help us reflect about the agendas and effects of current spectacles of simulation and simulacra. While the stage management and commodification of the political might have become the norm today, it would be grossly inaccurate to argue – like Benjamin – that the fusion of politics and consumption in the age of TV campaigns is coupled to projects of national rebirth through imperial warfare and ethnic cleansing. Media spectacles such as the Gulf War clearly replay under postmodern conditions aspects of what Benjamin meant when speaking of the aestheticization of politics. But we would level all historical distinctions if we rendered the antiseptic and strangely auratic presentation of warfare on CNN itself in a Benjaminian mode as the primary telos of postmodern politics. The ruminations of theorists such as Jean Baudrillard, on the other hand, theorists who make global commentaries on the postmodern spectacle their intellectual trademark, are of limited use for a critical understanding of how contemporary media appeal to and refigure dominant modes of perception. Instead of examining how postmodern subjects make use of cultural material in order to assume positionalities and situate themselves in however deformed fabrics of public and private life, Baudrillard simply declares that the logic of simulation has produced a new ontology. Baudrillard's declarations thus preclude necessary further reflections on how contemporary media – including the one of money – colonize traditional lifeworlds in order to change our ways of seeing. In claiming that the Gulf War has never taken place, or that Disneyland simply exists in order to hide "that it is the 'real' country, all of 'real' America that *is* Disneyland," Baudrillard in fact relapses to a curiously Fordist and text-oriented perspective that obscures how actual viewers – positioned in historically contingent viewing situations – make use of specific viewing events.[41] Reading the simulated gestalt of the contemporary spectacle as a work that contains all rules of its own appropriation, Baudrillard implies that the postmodern profusion of images not only entertains viewers, but produces a homogenous subject in the first place: it lures viewers into an imaginary totality and thus emplaces them in a fixed and standardized position; it prompts the spectator endlessly to replay childhood scenarios and traumas or simply to regress to the interiority of the womb. Similar to Guy Debord, Baudrillard describes the hyperreal society of simulation as a guardian of sleep and dreams, a spectacle that interpellates the incomplete individual into an imaginary subjectivity, a phantasmagoria of abundance, coherence, and collectivity. As if the participant owned no body and identity, no felt experience outside of the mediated presence of the event on screen, Baudrillard considers the appeal of the spectacular in late-capitalist societies as the very force that produces subjectivity to begin with, a kind of subjectivity that has always already forfeited any meaningful claim to autonomous agency, experience, and self-determination.

According to Benjamin's peculiar understanding, historical materialism – as applied to the realm of aesthetic theory – inquires into the technical and economic conditions motivating our attitudes toward beauty.[42] What we consider beautiful is a matter of historical contingencies. It reflects changing structures of experience, of the modes in which technologies of reproduction and exchange inflect our ways of seeing, feeling, remembering, knowing, and dreaming. Benjamin's artwork essay theorized individual and collective perceptions of beauty in a Fordist age of standardized mass production and mass consumption. The aestheticization thesis was meant to think through the political instrumentality of nineteenth-century conceptions of beauty as a means of integrating the Fordist mass into the social system of fascism. It hoped to conceptualize how fascism feeds on changing attitudes toward auratic and mimetic experience in order to carry out its counterrevolutionary projects of warfare and national rebirth. Fascism, following Benjamin's argument, aestheticizes politics not only because it circulates spellbinding images of political action seemingly untouched by the institutional and normative decentering of power in modernity, but also because it renders these images as the primary objects of aesthetic experience and pleasure in the twentieth century. Fascism is both a political and aesthetic project. It appeals to people's emotions and sensory forms of experience, but it at the same time aspires to neutralize the senses, negate particularity, and erase the body as a site of independent perceptions.

Benjamin's materialist insistence on the historical motivation of aesthetic experience should alert us not to apply his critical terminology in an unmediated fashion to the political managing of the visual in our post-Fordist age of digital information and flexible accumulation. Neither contemporary structures of sense perception nor those of individual and collective recollection are identical with those that Benjamin believed to be at the center of the fascist spectacle. To be sure, as I have argued earlier, Benjamin's notion of experience is clearly too narrow (and too gender biased) itself to remain fully valid even for the period he himself sought to examine. His thesis about the decay of aura is too monolithic to explicate the diverse and competing regimes of seeing and experience that mark the modern condition. But in spite of such conceptual bottlenecks, it is precisely his emphasis on the historically specific organization of individual pleasure and perception that provides us with a strong argument to counter both revisionist reconstructions of fascist aesthetics as mere style and iconography, and impetuous portrayals of contemporary visual culture as an uncanny relative of the fascist public sphere. In many respects much more of a critical historicist than he was willing to admit, Benjamin himself urges us to understand notions such as fascist aesthetics and political aestheticization in their historical context. Instead of inflating Benjamin's conceptual apparatus and speculating about what else might be fascist beside fascism, we fare much better if we employ his tools of criticism for the purpose of better understanding what exactly was considered beautiful under fascism – and by whom.

Such cautionary use, however, is by no means meant to strip Benjamin of his actuality. Even if our structures of experience have undergone crucial changes since the 1930s and thus render impossible the peculiar calibration of perception and power Benjamin observed in fascism, it is in Benjamin's emphatic insistence on experience itself that we may find the relevance of his reflections today. If we want to follow Benjamin's lead indeed, then any meaningful analysis of the nexus of power and the aesthetic today needs to meet strong intellectual and methodological demands, and transcend general remarks about the political as theater, the symbolic inventories of political representation, the rhetoric of metaphorical transfiguration, or the spectacular surfaces of pseudo-events. In critiquing the aestheticization of politics, Benjamin's aim was to show how political presentation interacts with historically contingent patterns of perception, and how imperatives of power and money may colonize the specific ways of what and how we see. Any theory of the postmodern spectacle learning from Benjamin, therefore, cannot do without a strong ethnographic component, one that is able to map from a phenomenological perspective the symbolic spaces and cultural practices of everyday life. Contrary to Adorno, who in his historical context was unable to see postautonomous art as a catalyst of meaningful activities, Benjamin encourages us to understand the everyday and popular as locations of continuing negotiations and interventions, of struggle and articulation. Unlike Adorno, Benjamin did not despair vis-à-vis what seems to have become the norm today: the commodification of all cultural practices. Instead, he was eager to conceptualize – however successfully – the popular dimension as a principally ambiguous and unstable juncture at which desire, fantasy, and knowledge could be articulated with the means of modern industrial culture themselves, through cultural practices that bypassed earlier channels of publicity and allowed for the emancipatory organization of vernacular and group-specific experiences, including those of alienation and speechlessness. In light of the postmodern amalgamation of high and low and the nearly full integration of economics and culture today, Benjamin's pragmatism remains a viable intellectual strategy. It teaches us that no talk about the aesthetic moment of the political can assume any validity today if it fails to account for how the postmodern proliferation of images interacts with historically specific patterns of everyday practice and perception, how sentient bodies today maneuver their ways through the endlessly refracted and progressively virtual spaces of culture in order to warrant the possibility of experience, and try to make and mark history.

NOTES

INTRODUCTION:
FASCISM, MASS CULTURE, AND THE AVANTE-GARDE

1. Don DeLillo, *White Noise* (New York: Penguin, 1985), 25–26.

2. Eric Rentschler, *The Ministry of Illusion: Nazi Cinema and Its Afterlife* (Cambridge: Harvard University Press, 1996), 223.

3. Susan Buck-Morss, "Aesthetics and Anaesthetics: Walter Benjamin's Artwork Essay Reconsidered," *New Formations* 20 (summer 1993): 123–43.

4. Georg Seeßlen, *Tanz den Adolf Hitler: Faschismus in der populären Kultur* (Berlin: Edition Tiamat, 1994), 14–20.

5. Simonetta Falasca-Zamponi, *Fascist Spectacle: The Aesthetics of Power in Mussolini's Italy* (Berkeley: University of California Press, 1997), 192.

6. DeLillo, *White Noise*, 13.

7. Charles S. Maier, foreword to *Reevaluating the Third Reich*, ed. Thomas Childers and Jane Caplan (New York: Holmes & Meier, 1993), xv.

8. Tim Mason, "Whatever Happened to 'Fascism'?" in Childers and Kaplan, *Reevaluating the Third Reich*, 257.

9. Roger Griffin, *The Nature of Fascism* (New York: St. Martin's, 1991), 26.

10. Stanley G. Payne, *A History of Fascism, 1914–1945* (Madison: University of Wisconsin Press, 1995), 6–7.

11. Umberto Eco, "Ur-Fascism," *New York Review of Books*, 22 June 1995, 13.

12. Michael Prinz and Rainer Zitelmann, eds., *Nationalsozialismus und Modernisierung* (Darmstadt: Wissenschaftliche Buchgesellschaft, 1991). Zitelmann has developed his controversial right-wing stance in further detail in *Hitler: Selbstverständnis eines Revolutionärs* (Stuttgart: Klett-Cotta, 1987) and "Nationalsozialismus und Moderne: Eine Zwischenbilanz," in *Übergänge: Zeitgeschichte zwischen Utopie und Machbarkeit*, ed. Werner Süß (Berlin: Duncker & Humblot, 1990), 195–204.

13. See, in particular, Uwe-Karsten Ketelsen, *Literatur und Drittes Reich* (Schernfeld: SH-Verlag, 1992); Jan Pieter Barbian, *Literaturpolitik im 'Dritten Reich': Institutiuonen, Kompetenzen, Betätigungsfelder* (Frankfurt am Main: Buchhändler-

Vereinigung, 1993); Ulrike Haß, *Militante Pastorale: Zur Literatur der anitmodernen Bewegungen im frühen 20. Jahrhundert* (Munich: Wilhelm Fink, 1993).

14. See, for most recent examples, Rentschler, *The Ministry of Illusion*; Karsten Witte, *Lachende Erben, Toller Tag: Filmkomödie im Dritten Reich* (Berlin: Vorwerk 8, 1995); Linda Schulte-Sasse, *Entertaining the Third Reich: Illusions of Wholeness in Nazi Cinema* (Durham: Duke University Press, 1996); David Bathrick, "Making a National Family with the Help of Radio: The Nazi 'Wunschkonzert,'" *Modernism/Modernity* 4.1 (1997): 115–28; and my own pieces on the Nazi Western, "Unsettling America: German Westerns and Modernity," *Modernism/Modernity* 2.3 (1995): 1–22, and "Siegfried Rides Again: Westerns, Technology, and the Third Reich," *Cultural Studies* 11.3 (October 1997): 418–42.

15. Dan Diner, "On Guilt Discourse and Other Narratives: Epistemological Observations regarding the Holocaust," *History and Memory* 9.1–2 (fall 1997): 301–20.

16. Diner, "On Guilt Discourse and Other Narratives": 312.

17. Daniel Jonah Goldhagen, *Hitler's Willing Executioners: Ordinary Germans and the Holocaust* (New York: Knopf, 1996).

18. See Michael P. Steinberg, "The Collector as Allegorist: Goods, Gods, and the Objects of History," in *Walter Benjamin and the Demands of History*, ed. Michael P. Steinberg (Ithaca: Cornell University Press, 1996), 88–118.

19. Falasca-Zamponi, *Fascist Spectacle*, 12.

20. Philippe Lacoue-Labarthe, *Heidegger, Art and Politics: The Fiction of the Political*, trans. Chris Turner (Oxford: Basil Blackwell, 1990), 77.

21. Lacoue-Labarthe, *Heidegger, Art and Politics*, 95.

22. Lacoue-Labarthe, *Heidegger, Art and Politics*, 56.

23. Lacoue-Labarthe, *Heidegger, Art and Politics*, 52.

24. Lacoue-Labarthe, *Heidegger, Art and Politics*, 77.

25. Lacoue-Labarthe, *Heidegger, Art and Politics*, 61.

26. Lacoue-Labarthe, *Heidegger, Art and Politics*, 2–3.

27. Robert C. Holub, *Crossing Borders: Reception Theory, Poststructuralism, Deconstruction* (Madison: University of Wisconsin Press, 1992), 178.

28. Rentschler, *The Ministry of Illusion*, 22.

29. Raymond Williams, *Culture and Society: 1780–1950* (1958; New York: Columbia University Press, 1983), xvi; see also Raymond Williams, *Marxism and Literature* (Oxford: Oxford University Press, 1977), 11–20.

30. Richard Wolin, "Kulchur Wars: The Modernism/Postmodernism Controversy Revisited," in *Labyrinths: Explorations in the Critical History of Ideas* (Amherst: University of Massachusetts Press, 1995), 21.

31. For a paradigmatic example of this argument, see Peter Ulrich Hein, *Die Brücke ins Geisterreich: Künstlerische Avantgarde zwischen Kulturkritik und Faschismus*

(Reinbek: Rowohlt, 1992).

32. Boris Groys, *The Total Art of Stalinism: Avant-Garde, Aesthetic Dictatorship, and Beyond*, trans. Charles Rougle (Princeton: Princeton University Press, 1992); originally published in German as *Gesamtkunstwerk Stalin* (Munich: Hanser, 1988).

33. Groys, *The Total Art of Stalinism*, 64–65.

34. Peter Bürger, *Theory of the Avant-Garde*, trans. Michael Shaw (Minneapolis: University of Minnesota Press, 1984).

35. Hal Foster, *The Return of the Real* (Cambridge: MIT Press, 1996), 8.

36. Russell A. Berman, "Consumer Society: The Legacy of the Avant-garde and the False Sublation of Aesthetic Autonomy," in *Modern Culture and Critical Theory: Art, Politics, and the Legacy of the Frankfurt School* (Madison: University of Wisconsin Press, 1989), 46.

37. Andrew Hewitt, *Fascist Modernism: Aesthetics, Politics, and the Avant-Garde* (Stanford: Stanford University Press, 1993), 21.

38. See Weber's famous "Zwischenbetrachtung," trans. as "Religious Rejections of the World and Their Directions," in *From Max Weber: Essays in Sociology*, ed. H. H. Geerth and C. Wright Mills (New York: Oxford University Press, 1946), 323–59.

39. Franz Dröge and Michael Müller, *Die Macht der Schönheit: Avantgarde und Faschismus oder Die Geburt der Massenkultur* (Hamburg: Europäische Verlagsanstalt, 1995), 91–123.

40. Jürgen Habermas, *The Philosophical Discourse of Modernity*, trans. Frederick G. Lawrence (Cambridge: MIT Press, 1987), 50.

41. Andreas Huyssen, *After the Great Divide: Modernism, Mass Culture, Postmodernism* (Bloomington: Indiana University Press, 1986).

42. See, for instance, Lambert Zuidervaart, *Adorno's Aesthetic Theory: The Redemption of Illusion* (Cambridge: MIT Press, 1991); Tom Huhn and Lambert Zuidervaart, eds., *The Semblance of Subjectivity: Essays in Adorno's Aesthetic Theory* (Cambridge: MIT Press, 1997); and Shierry Weber Nicholsen, *Exact Imagination, Late Work: On Adorno's Aesthetics* (Cambridge: MIT Press, 1997).

43. Peter Uwe Hohendahl, *Prismatic Thought: Theodor W. Adorno* (Lincoln: University of Nebraska Press, 1995), 119.

44. Huyssen, *After the Great Divide*, vii.

45. For more on the relation between classical critical theory and contemporary Anglo-American cultural studies, see Lutz P. Koepnick, "Negotiating Popular Culture: Wenders, Handke, and the Topographies of Cultural Studies," *German Quarterly* 69 (fall 1996): 381–400.

46. Russell A. Berman, "Cultural Criticism and Cultural Studies: Reconsidering the Frankfurt School," in *Cultural Studies of Modern Germany: History, Representation, and Nationhood* (Madison: University of Wisconsin Press, 1993), 23.

INTRODUCTION TO PART I

1. "A 'ruling organization' will be called 'political'insofar as its existence and order is continuously safeguarded within a given *territorial* area by the threat and application of physical force on the part of the administrative staff. A compulsory political organization with continuous operations will be called a 'state'insofar as its administrative staff successfully upholds the claim to the *monopoly* of the *legitimate* use of physical force in the enforcement of its order." Max Weber, *Economy and Society: An Outline of Interpretative Sociology*, trans. Ephraim Fischoff, Hans Gerth, et al., eds. Guenther Roth and Claus Wittich (New York: Bedminster Press, 1968), 54.

2. On the eighteenth- and nineteenth-century tradition of aesthetic politics in Germany, see Josef Chytry, *The Aesthetic State: A Quest in Modern German Thought* (Berkeley: University of California Press, 1989).

3. See Lutz P. Koepnick, "Simulating Simulation: Art and Modernity in *Faust II*," *Seminar: A Journal of Germanic Studies* 34.1 (February 1998): 1–25.

4. Karl Marx, "Der achtzehnte Brumaire des Louis Bonaparte," in Karl Marx and Friedrich Engels, *Studienausgabe: Geschichte und Politik 2*, ed. Iring Fetscher (Frankfurt am Main: Fischer, 1966), 34.

5. See Lutz P. Koepnick, "August Strindberg und die Ästhetik der Macht. Rekonstruktion einer Kritikstrategie," *Skandinavistik: Zeitschrift für Sprache, Literatur und Kultur der nordischen Länder* 22.2 (1992): 85–106.

6. Thomas Mann, *Betrachtungen eines Unpolitischen. Gesammelte Werke in Einzelbänden: Frankfurter Ausgabe*, ed. Peter de Mendelssohn (Frankfurt am Main: Fischer, 1983), 538.

7. Martin Jay, "'The Aesthetic Ideology' as Ideology; or, What Does It Mean to Aestheticize Politics?" *Cultural Critique* (1992): 43.

8. Susan Sontag, "Fascinating Fascism," *Under the Sign of Saturn* (New York: Vintage, 1981), 91.

1. BAROQUE DRAMA AND AUTONOMOUS POLITICS

1. See Bertolt Brecht's "Radiotheorie," *Gesammelte Werke in 20 Bänden* (Frankfurt am Main: Suhrkamp, 1967), 18:117–34.

2. Hans Heinz Holz, "Prismatisches Denken," in *Über Walter Benjamin*, ed. Theodor W. Adorno et al. (Frankfurt am Main: Suhrkamp, 1968), 62–110.

3. For the most important recent analyses of Benjamin's early aesthetics, see Michael W. Jennings, *Dialectical Images: Walter Benjamin's Theory of Literary Criticism* (Ithaca: Cornell University Press, 1987), 121–211; Uwe Steiner, *Die Geburt der Kritik aus dem Geist der Kunst: Untersuchungen zum Begriff der Kritik in den frühen*

Schriften Walter Benjamins (Würzburg: Königshausen & Neumann, 1989); Rainer Nägele, *Theater, Theory, Speculation: Walter Benjamin and the Scenes of Modernity* (Baltimore: Johns Hopkins University Press, 1991), 108–34; Klaus Garber, *Zum Bilde Walter Benjamins: Studien – Porträts – Kritiken* (Munich: Wilhelm Fink, 1992), 13–66.

4. Azade Seyhan, "Allegories of History: The Politics of Representation in Walter Benjamin," in *Image and Ideology in Modern/Postmodern Discourse*, ed. David B. Downing and Susan Bazargan (Albany: State University of New York Press, 1991), 237.

5. John Pizer, "History, Genre and 'Ursprung' in Benjamin's Early Aesthetics," *German Quarterly* 60.1 (1987): 75.

6. "Über 'Schein' " (GS 1: 831–33); "On Semblance" (SW 1: 223–25).

7. Friedrich Nietzsche, *The Birth of Tragedy and the Case of Wagner*, trans. Walter Kaufmann (New York: Vintage, 1967), 34. Unfortunatly, Kaufmann decided to translate "schöne Schein" with "beautiful illusion" rather than "appearance" or "semblance."

8. For a general study of Benjamin's appropriation and critique of Nietzsche, see Renate Reschke's article "Barbaren, Kult und Katastrophen: Nietzsche bei Benjamin. Unzusammenhängendes im Zusammenhang gelesen," in *Aber ein Sturm weht vom Paradiese her: Texte zu Walter Benjamin*, ed. Michael Opitz (Leipzig: Reclam, 1992), 303–39; Martha B. Helfer, "Benjamin and the Birth of Tragedy: The Trauerspiel Essays, 1916–1926," *Kodikas/Code/Ars Semiotica* 11.1–2 (1988): 179–93.

9. Nietzsche, *Birth of Tragedy*, 52.

10. Anthony J. Cascardi, "Comedia and Trauerspiel: On Benjamin and Calderon," *Comparative Drama* 16.1 (1982): 10.

11. William J. McGrath, *Dionysian Art and Populist Politics in Austria* (New Haven: Yale University Press, 1974).

12. "Schicksal und Charakter" (GS 2:171–79); "Fate and Character" (REF 304–11).

13. Samuel Weber, in "Genealogy of Modernity: History, Myth and Allegory in Benjamin's *Origin of the German Mourning Play*," *MLN* 106.3 (1991): 465–500, insists on the active moment operative within the final silence, the "Schweigen" of Benjamin's mythic heroes: "For 'silence'is a condition, a state: in English, one *is* silent, or at best, 'falls'silent. The Schweigen of the hero, by contrast, is performative; it is an *act of defiance*, even if it is not fully understood as such by the hero" (481–82). Benjamin, however, leaves no doubt that despite their sublime rebellion against the mythic law and order, the heroes of the ancient tragedy fail to overcome myth and indeed even reproduce it through their "performative" submission to silence at the end.

14. Gerhard Scheit, "Der Totenkopf als Messias? Ursprung und Modernität bei

Walter Benjamin und Georg Lukács," *Weimarer Beiträge: Zeitschrift für Literaturwissenschaft, Ästhetik und Kulturtheorie* 35.12 (1989): 1967.

15. Bernd Witte, *Walter Benjamin – Der Intellektuelle als Kritiker: Untersuchungen zu seinem Frühwerk* (Stuttgart: Metzler, 1976), 56.

16. During the last decade or so, academia has observed not only a scholarly reevaluation of Schmitt as a diagnostic of bourgeois democracy but also a number of fiery debates about Schmitt's intellectual impact on what for the longest time seemed to be his undoubted intellectual adversary: the Frankfurt School. To be sure, Ellen Kennedy's controversial 1986 essay about Schmitt and Habermas constructs intellectual affinities only at costs of misconstruing Habermas's own notion of democracy. However, Kennedy's argument indicates the dire need to shed more light on the confusing grey zone that separated and united Schmitt's critique of parliamentarism and the formation of critical theory during the 1920s and early 1930s. For more about the debate about affinities and differences between Schmitt and the Frankfurt School, see Ellen Kennedy, "Carl Schmitt und die 'Die Frankfurter Schule'. Deutsche Liberalismuskritik im 20. Jahrhundert," *Geschichte und Gesellschaft* 12 (1986): 380–419; and, as responses, Alfons Söllner, "Jenseits von Carl Schmitt. Wissenschaftsgeschichtliche Richtigstellungen zur politischen Theorie im Umkreis der 'Frankfurter Schule,' " *Geschichte und Gesellschaft* 12 (1986): 502–29; Ulrich K. Preuß, "Carl Schmitt und die Frankfurter Schule: Deutsche Liberalismuskritik im 20. Jahrhundert," *Geschichte und Gesellschaft* 13 (1987): 400–18; as well as Martin Jay, "Les extremes ne se touchent pas. Eine Erwiderung auf Ellen Kennedy," *Geschichte und Gesellschaft* 13 (1987): 542–58.

17. In a letter written to Schmitt as late as December 1930, Benjamin explicitly acknowledged the constitutive role of Schmitt's works. Sending a copy of his *Trauerspiel* study to Schmitt, Benjamin emphasizes "how much this book in its representation of the doctrine of sovereignty in the 17th century owes to you [Schmitt]" (GS 1:887). In addition, he highlights the correspondences between "my modes of research in the philosophy of art and yours in the philosophy of the state" (GS 1:887), with regard to Schmitt's most recent treatise on dictatorship (Carl Schmitt, *Die Diktatur: Von den Anfängen des modernen Souveränitätsgedankens bis zum proletarischen Klassenkampf*, 2nd ed. [Munich: Duncker & Humblot, 1928]). Norbert Bolz, in *Auszug aus der entzauberten Welt: Philosophischer Extremismus zwischen den Weltkriegen* (Munich: Wilhelm Fink, 1989), promises a philosophical discussion of Benjamin's letter (85–94), only, however, to present his readers with an uncritical picture of Schmittian elements in Benjamin. For more on the controversial status of Benjamin's *Trauerspiel* book among contemporary baroque scholars, see Klaus Garber, *Rezeption und Rettung: Drei Studien zu Walter Benjamin* (Tübingen: Max Niemeyer, 1987), 59–120; Hans-Jürgen Schings, "Walter Benjamin, das barocke

Trauerspiel und die Barockforschung," *Daß eine Nation die andere verstehen möge: Festschrift für Marian Szyrocki zu seinem 60. Geburtstag*, ed. Norbert Honsza and Hans-Gert Roloff (Amsterdam: Rodopi, 1988), 663–76; Uwe Steiner, "Allegorie und Allergie: Bemerkungen zur Diskussion um Benjamins Trauerspielbuch in der Barockforschung," *Daphnis: Zeitschrift für Mittlere Deutsche Literatur* 18.4 (1989): 641–701.

18. Pierre Bourdieu, *L'Ontologie politique de Martin Heidegger* (Paris: Editions de Minuit, 1988), 24.

19. Carl Schmitt, *Political Theology: Four Chapters on the Concept of Sovereignty*, trans. George Schwab (Cambridge: MIT Press, 1985), 5.

20. According to Jürgen Habermas, Schmitt's decisionism seeks "to separate democracy, which he conceives in terms of identity, from public discussion, which he attributes to liberalism" only to "lay the conceptual groundwork for detaching democratic will-formation from the universalist presuppositions of general participation, limiting it to an ethnically homogeneous substratum of the population, and reducing it to argument-free acclamation by immature masses." Jürgen Habermas, "The Horrors of Autonomy: Carl Schmitt in English," in *The New Conservatism: Cultural Criticism and the Historians' Debate*, ed. and trans. Shierry Weber Nicholsen (Cambridge: MIT Press, 1989), 139.

21. Schmitt, *Political Theology* 15.

22. Armin Adam, *Rekonstruktion des Politischen: Carl Schmitt und die Krise der Staatlichkeit 1912–1933* (Weinheim: VCH, Acta Humaniora, 1992), 28.

23. Carl Schmitt, *Politische Romantik* (Berlin: Duncker &Humblot, 1919), 115–52.

24. Richard Wolin, *The Politics of Being: The Political Thought of Martin Heidegger* (New York: Columbia University Press, 1990), 22–40.

25. Yaron Ezrahi, *The Descent of Icarus: Science and the Transformation of Contemporary Democracy* (Cambridge: Harvard University Press, 1990), 71.

26. See Reinhard Mehring, *Carl Schmitt zur Einführung* (Hamburg: Junius, 1992), 152.

27. David Pan, "Political Aesthetics: Carl Schmitt on Hamlet," *Telos: A Quarterly of Critical Thought* 72 (1987): 155.

28. Habermas, "The Horrors of Autonomy," 137.

29. John McCole, *Walter Benjamin and the Antinomies of Tradition* (Ithaca: Cornell University Press, 1993), 166: "Benjamin frankly admired the political theory of Carl Schmitt, which centered on the idea that sovereignty inheres in whoever can master the state of emergency. But this result, and the affinity with Schmitt, were extremely problematic for Benjamin, since they would collapse his position into the decisionism of the radical conservatives."

30. Jennings, *Dialectical Images*, 17.

31. Garber, *Zum Bilde Walter Benjamins*, 245.

32. For more on Benjamin and the inhuman, see Beatrice Hanssen, *Walter Benjamin's Other History: Of Stones, Animals, Human Beings, and Angels* (Berkeley: University of California Press, 1998).

33. The essays, lectures, and lecture notes recently published by Andrzej Warminski (Paul de Man, *Aesthetic Ideology* [Minneapolis: University of Minnesota Press, 1996]), in my view, have added little to what was known about the methodological direction and overall scope of de Man's unfinished book project, *Aesthetics, Rhetoric, Ideology*. Most of the texts collected in this volume reflect materials published in often much more comprehensive and accessible form before. Notwithstanding Warminski's hagiographic praise in the introduction, the volume ends up documenting the extent to which the critique of aesthetic ideologies, rather than signifying a decisive turn and critical intensification of de Man's thought prior to his death, has been central to his intellectual work ever since the 1950s.

34. Christopher Norris, *Paul de Man: Deconstruction and the Critique of Aesthetic Ideology* (New York: Routledge, 1988), 53.

35. Paul de Man, "Phenomenality and Materiality in Kant," in *Hermeneutics: Questions and Prospects*, eds. Gary Shapiro and Alan Sica (Amherst: University of Massachusetts Press, 1984), 124.

36. Paul de Man, "Aesthetic Formalization: Kleist's *Über das Marionettentheater*," *The Rhetoric of Romanticism* (New York: Columbia University Press, 1984), 264–65.

37. de Man, "Aesthetic Formalization," 290.

38. Hewitt, *Fascist Modernism*, 168–69.

2. Carnival, Industrial Culture, Politics of Authenticity

1. Max Horkheimer and Theodor W. Adorno, *Dialectic of Enlightenment*, trans. John Cumming (New York: Continuum, 1995), 123.

2. Horkheimer and Adorno, *Dialectic of Enlightenment*, 135.

3. Horkheimer and Adorno, *Dialectic of Enlightenment*, 132–33.

4. Peter Uwe Hohendahl, *Building a National Literature: The Case of Germany, 1830–1870*, trans. Renate Baron Franciscono (Ithaca: Cornell University Press, 1989), 307–51.

5. Hohendahl, *Building a National Literature*, 311.

6. Miriam Hansen, "*Schindler's List* Is Not *Shoah*: The Second Commandment, Popular Modernism, and Public Memory," *Critical Inquiry* 22.2 (winter 1996): 307.

7. Jürgen Habermas, *The Philosophical Discourse of Modernity*, trans. Frederick Lawrence (Cambridge: MIT Press, 1987), 216.

8. Russell A. Berman, *The Rise of the Modern German Novel: Crisis and Charisma* (Cambridge: Harvard University Press, 1986), 179–86.

9. Siegfried Kracauer, *From Caligari to Hitler: A Psychological History of the German Film* (Princeton: Princeton University Press, 1947), 55.

10. Marc Silberman, "Specular Presence and Historical Revolution: Ernst Lubitsch's *Passion*," in *German Cinema: Texts in Contexts* (Detroit: Wayne State University Press, 1995), 3–18.

11. For a detailed analysis of Lang's appropriation and alteration of Wagner's *Ring* for his *Nibelungen*-epic, see Klaus Kanzog, "Der Weg der Nibelungen ins Kino. Fritz Langs Film-Alternative zu Hebbel und Wagner," in *Wege des Mythos in der Moderne: Richard Wagner 'Der Ring des Nibelungen'*, ed. Dieter Borchmeyer (Munich: Deutscher Taschenbuch, 1987), 202–23.

12. Kracauer, *From Caligari to Hitler,* 272.

13. Peter Reichel, *Der schöne Schein des Dritten Reiches: Faszination und Gewalt des Faschismus* (Munich: Hanser, 1991), 155.

14. The simultaneity of spectacle and open violence, sensual spell and emotional integration, terror and aesthetics seems already inscribed to the movement's very name. Tied together with leather strings, the Roman rod bundles – called *fasces* – represented both symbols and instruments of domination. The Latin word *fascinare*, on the other hand, derives from the same etymological root, meaning "to bewitch" or "to allure." Fascism, then, aims at emotional bondage and subordination, primarily generated through a systematic bewitchment of reason and the human senses, through a calculated symbolism of power. A further aspect originates from a third extension of the linguistic origin: *fascinum*, the Latin word for the male sexual organ. For the fascist dedifferentiation of politics transcended simple issues of ideological seduction and mass illusion; up to, say, 1941, support and success of the Hitler and Mussolini regimes rested on pillars broader than the mere display of political erotics, the mere decoration of power through art. In truth, under the auspices of the *fascinosum*, art was transformed into a practical expression of power itself, a phallic triumph over the amorphous, chaotic forms of modern life.

15. Jeffrey Herf, *Reactionary Modernism: Technology, Culture, and Politics in Weimar and the Third Reich* (Cambridge: Cambridge University Press, 1984), 189–216.

16. Leonardo Quaresima, "Der Film im Dritten Reich: Moderne, Amerikanismus, Unterhaltungsfilm," *Montage/AV* 3.2 (1994): 12.

17. Rentschler, *The Ministry of Illusion*, 16.

18. Aside from Jeffrey Herf's study of technology and culture in the 1920s and 1930s and Peter Reichel's recent excellent publication, some of the more important works and anthologies about the aesthetic moment of fascism include Susan Son-

tag, "Fascinating Fascism," in *Under the Sign of Saturn* (New York: Farrar, Strauss, & Giroux, 1980), 73–105; Klaus Vondung, *Magie und Manipulation: Ideologischer Kult und politische Religion des Nationalsozialismus* (Göttingen: Vandenhoeck & Ruprecht, 1971); Horst Denkler and Karl Prümm, eds., *Die deutsche Literatur im Dritten Reich: Themen Traditionen, Wirkungen* (Stuttgart: Reclam, 1976); Rolf Schnell, ed., *Kunst und Kultur im deutschen Faschismus* (Stuttgart: Metzler, 1978); Berthold Hinz et al., eds. *Die Dekoration der Gewalt: Kunst und Medien im Faschismus* (Gießen: Anabas, 1979); Anson Rabinbach, "The Aesthetics of Production in the Third Reich," in *International Fascism: New Thoughts and New Approaches*, ed. George L. Mosse (London: Sage, 1979), 189–222; Reinhold Merker, *Die Bildenden Künste im Nationalsozialismus: Kulturideologie, Kulturpolitik, Kulturproduktion* (Cologne: Dumont, 1983); Ingemar Karlsson and Arne Ruth, *Samhället som teater: Estetik och politik i Tredje riket* (Stockholm: Liber, 1983); Saul Friedländer, *Kitsch und Tod: Der Widerschein des Nazismus* (Munich: Hanser, 1984).

19. Norbert Frei, *Der Führerstaat: Nationalsozialistische Herrschaft 1933 bis 1945* (Munich: Deutscher Taschenbuch, 1987), 167.

20. Siegfried Kracauer, "Das Ornament der Masse," in *Das Ornament der Masse: Essays* (Frankfurt am Main: Suhrkamp, 1977), 50–63.

21. Ernst Bloch, *Erbschaft dieser Zeit* (Frankfurt am Main: Suhrkamp, 1985), 70.

22. Herbert Marcuse, "Über den affirmativen Charakter der Kultur," in *Kultur und Gesellschaft I*, 13th ed. (Frankfurt am Main: Suhrkamp, 1980), 56–101.

23. Hans Heinz Holz, "Prismatisches Denken," in Adorno et al., eds. *Über Walter Benjamin*, 65.

24. For more about the editorial battles around the publication of Benjamin's exile essays, see Chryssoula Kambas, *Walter Benjamin im Exil: Zum Verhältnis von Literaturpolitik und Ästhetik* (Tübingen: Max Niemeyer, 1983), 158–62.

25. Kambas, *Walter Benjamin im Exil*, 81.

26. See Ansgar Hillach, "Der Anteil der Kultur an der Prägung faschistischer Herrschaftsmittel: Was leistet Walter Benjamins Diagnose des Faschismus," in *Walter Benjamin: Profane Erleuchtung und rettende Kritik*, ed. Norbert W. Bolz and Richard Faber, 2nd ed. (Würzburg: Königshausen & Neumann, 1985), 264.

27. Hillach, "Der Anteil der Kultur," 248.

28. Reichel, *Der schöne Schein des Dritten Reiches*, 207.

29. "Über die Art der Italiener, zu diskutieren" (GS 6:199).

30. Fritz Stern, *The Politics of Cultural Despair: A Study in the Rise of the German Ideology* (New York: Anchor, 1965).

31. Mikhail Bakhtin, *Problems of Dostoevsky's Poetics*, trans. Caryl Emerson (Minneapolis: University of Minnesota Press, 1984), 124.

32. See Carrie L. Asman, "Theater and Agon/Agon and Theater: Walter Benjamin and Florens Christian Rang," *MLN* 107.3 (1992): 606–24.

33. Florens Christian Rang, *Historische Psychologie des Karnevals*, ed. Lorenz Jäger (Berlin: Brinkmann & Bose, 1983), 23.

34. GS 1:1050.

35. Ansgar Hillach, "'Ästhetisierung des politischen Lebens': Benjamins faschismustheoretischer Ansatz – eine Rekonstruktion," in *"Links hatte noch alles sich zu enträtseln . . ." Walter Benjamin im Kontext*, ed. Burkhardt Lindner (Frankfurt am Main: Syndikat, 1978), 127–67.

36. Nietzsche, *The Case of Wagner*, 172.

37. Nietzsche, *The Case of Wagner*, 169.

38. Nietzsche, *The Case of Wagner*, 166.

39. Theodor W. Adorno, *In Search of Wagner*, trans. Rodney Livingstone (London: New Left Books, 1981), 31.

40. My use of this disinction here is inspired by Michael Steinberg's highly instructive analysis of the politics of the Salzburg Festival. See Michael P. Steinberg, *The Meaning of the Salzburg Festival: Austria as Theater and Ideology, 1890–1938* (Ithaca: Cornell University Press, 1990), 38–39.

41. Hillach, "'Ästhetisierung des politischen Lebens,'" 146–47.

42. Hillach, "'Ästhetisierung des politischen Lebens,'" 147.

43. Edmund Burke, *The Works of the Right Honourable Edmund Burke* (Oxford: Oxford University Press, 1906), 1:91–92.

44. Reichel, *Der schöne Schein des Dritten Reiches*, 222–31.

45. Wolfgang Welsch, "Adornos Ästhetik: Eine implizite Ästhetik des Erhabenen," in *Ästhetisches Denken* (Stuttgart: Reclam, 1990), 114–56.

46. A text of 1929 ("Einiges zur Volkskunst" [GS 6:187]) defines kitsch and its relation to art and folk art as follows: "Only the impoverished, emptied individual knows no other means by which to transform himself other than through pretense. Pretense seeks the arsenal of masks within us. Yet we are usually poor ones. In truth, the whole world is full of masks, and we in fact cannot imagine to what degree even the most significant pieces of furniture (e.g. a Romanesque armchair), were once such masks. Through the mask the individual sees out of the situation and creates his configurations in its core. It is the task of folk art to provide us with this mask and the space to create the configuration of our fate in its core. And only from this perspective can one say clearly and fundamentally what distinguishes folk art from art proper:

Art teaches to look inside things.

Folk art and kitsch allow us to see out of things."

47. See Herbert Marcuse, "Der Kampf gegen den Liberalismus in der totalitären Staatsauffassung," *Kultur und Gesellschaft* 1, 17–55; Wolin, *The Politics of Being*; and by the same author, *Labyrinths*, 103–41.

48. Alfred Baeumler, *Männerbund und Wissenschaft* (Berlin: Junker & Dünnhaupt, 1934), 109.

49. Baeumler, *Männerbund und Wissenschaft*, 108.

50. REF 277–300; GS 2:179–203.

51. "If the first is required to prove its worth in victory, the second is subject to the restriction that it may not set itself new ends. Police violence is emancipated from both conditions. It is lawmaking, for its characteristic function is not the promulgation of laws but the assertion of legal claims for any decree, and law-preserving, because it is at the disposal of these ends. The assertion that the ends of police violence are always identical or even connected to those of general law is entirely untrue. Rather, the 'law'of the police really marks the point at which the state, whether from impotence or because of the immanent connections within any legal system, can no longer guarantee through the legal system the empirical ends that it desires at any price to attain" (REF 286–87; GS 2:189).

52. "Über das Grauen I" (GS 6:75–77).

3. Aesthetic Dictatorship

1. Michael Geyer, "The State in National Socialist Germany," in *Statemaking and Social Movements: Essays in History and Theory*, ed. Charles Bright and Susan Harding (Ann Arbor: University of Michigan Press, 1984), 196; see also by the same author, "The Nazi State Reconsidered," in *Life in the Third Reich*, ed. Richard Bessel (Oxford: Oxford University Press, 1987), 57–68.

2. Geyer, "The State in National Socialist Germany," 210.

3. For a closer examination of Goebbels's novel and its quasi-biographical form as a diary, see Dieter Saalmann's essay, "Fascism and Aesthetics: Joseph Goebbels's Novel: A German Fate through the Pages of a Diary," *Orbis Litterarum* 41.3 (1986): 213–28.

4. Joseph Goebbels, *Michael: A Novel*, trans. Joachim Neugroschel (New York: Amok Press, 1987), 14.

5. Goebbels, *Michael*, 17.

6. In her article "Benjamin's Love Affair with Death," *New German Critique* 48 (1989): 63–86, Rey Chow highlights provocatively and in further detail the "troubling male subjectivity in Benjamin's texts" (65). From a feminist perspective, Chow challenges the notion of Benjamin as a champion of recent discourses about subversion, marginality, and otherness, showing striking ambiguities inherent in Ben-

jamin's often necrophilic construction of femininity, his desire for the inanimate. For different accounts of Benjamin's gender politics, see also Sigrid Weigel, *Topographien der Geschlechter: Kulturgeschichtliche Studien zur Literatur* (Reinbek: Rowohlt, 1990), 212–23; and Eva Geulen, "Toward a Genealogy of Gender in Walter Benjamin's Writing," *German Quarterly* 69.2 (1996): 161–80.

7. Paul Virilio, *Speed and Politics: An Essay on Dromology*, trans. Mark Polizzotti (New York: Semiotext(e), 1986), 115.

8. See Gerhard Bachleitner, "Der Kult des Authentischen," *Merkur: Deutsche Zeitschrift für Europäisches Denken* 39.7 (1985): 628–32.

9. John McCole has traced the origin and metamorphoses of the concept of "Geist" in Benjamin's work in his study *Walter Benjamin and the Antinomies of Tradition*, 35–70. Emerging in Benjamin's earliest work to demarcate the visionary role of the youth movement against the established institutions, the category of "Geist" will reappear in his mature postwar work as well; yet what Benjamin's will salvage is rather the concept's ideological force than its original content.

10. For critical introductory studies of the literature of the turn of the century, see Christa Bürger, Peter Bürger, Jochen Schulte-Sasse, eds., *Naturalismus, Ästhetizismus* (Frankfurt am Main: Suhrkamp, 1979).

11. See Ralph-Rainer Wuthenow, *Muse, Maske, Meduse: Europäischer Ästhetizismus* (Frankfurt am Main: Suhrkamp, 1978), 103.

12. See Peter Bürger, *Theory of the Avant-Garde*, trans. Michael Shaw (Minneapolis: University of Minnesota Press, 1984), 35–54. Given the complex social positioning of the art-for-art's-sake movement, Benjamin considers turn-of-the-century aestheticism as more than mere political escapism. By turning away and sealing itself off from bourgeois society, aestheticism reveals *ex negativo* the truth about the situation of art under the aegis of modern capitalism. In his famous essay on surrealism (1929), Benjamin writes: "Art for art's sake was scarcely ever to be taken literally; it was almost always a flag under which sailed a cargo that could not be declared because it still lacked a name" (REF 183–84; GS 2:301). According to Benjamin, aestheticism constituted a premature attack on bourgeois society and its principles of utility, and for this reason only did it remain ensnared in the very system it aspired to overhaul. Only the surrealist challenge of both aesthetic autonomy and bourgeois society enlightened the aestheticst self-misunderstanding, thereby constituting a more mature assault on the commercialization of art in modernity. For the importance of surrealism for Benjamin's overall theory of modernity and rendition of the social function of art, see Josef Fürnkäs, *Surrealismus als Erkenntnis: Walter Benjamin – Weimarer Einbahnstraße und Pariser Passagen* (Stuttgart: Metzler, 1988); and Margaret Cohen, *Profane Illumination: Walter Benjamin and the Paris of Surrealist Revolution* (Berkeley: University of California Press, 1993).

13. Oscar Wilde, *The Picture of Dorian Gray* (New York: Modern Library/Random House, 1992), xv–xvi.

14. "The concept of artistic technique is a fairly recent product. It was unknown as late as the period of the French Revolution, during which the aesthetic domination of nature was well on its way to becoming conscious of itself. While the name may have been lacking, the thing itself was certainly familiar at the time. Artistic technique is not a phenomenon of pragmatic adaption to an age which avidly labelled itself 'technological,' as if productive forces alone, viewed in abstraction from relations of production, determined the structure of an age. In cases where aesthetic technology seeks directly to translate science into art instead of looking for technical innovations, art misses the boat." Theodor W. Adorno, *Aesthetic Theory*, trans. C. Lenhardt (London: Routledge & Kegan Paul, 1984), 87.

15. On the obscure status of the manifesto, see the editor's comment in GS 1:1055. Even though Tiedemann suggests that the quotation was borrowed from a French newspaper translation, he reports that Marinetti's manifesto does not appear in any bibliography or iconography about the futurist movement. One can hardly avoid asking oneself – somewhat heretical, as it were – whether Benjamin made the whole thing up by himself. What is additionally puzzling is that this unidentified Marinetti quote stands out rather uniquely in the context of Benjamin's overall body of writing. Benjamin discusses neither Marinetti nor Italian fascism in any other text in further detail. See also Russell A. Berman, "The Aestheticization of Politics: Walter Benjamin on Fascism and the Avant-Garde," in *Modern Culture and Critical Theory*, 36.

16. Jeffrey T. Schnapp, *Staging Fascism: 18BL and the Theater of Masses for Masses* (Stanford: Stanford University Press, 1996), 90.

17. Andreas Huyssen, "The Vamp and the Machine: Fritz Lang's Metropolis," in *After the Great Divide*, 70.

18. For more on the modern discourse on man as machine and its fascist variants, see Anson Rabinbach, *The Human Motor: Energy, Fatigue, and the Origins of Modernity* (New York: Basic Books, 1990).

19. The origin of this aestheticist desire to efface the otherness of nature may be located in Charles Baudelaire's essays about the painter Constantin Guys, in particular in Baudelaire's apology for female makeup during the 1850s. Here, Baudelaire sought to unhinge the aesthetic principle of mimesis and prepare the ground for the voyage of aesthetic modernism into antimimetic realms of representation. For Baudelaire, the woman who uses all sorts of tricks to efface the ugly traces of nature in her face became an allegory for the venture of the artist to create a work of art. Yet turn-of-the-century aestheticism recasts Baudelaire's exclusion of nature into a prin-

ciple, not only of artistic production, but of life in general. According to the doctrines of *l'art pour l'art* and its spiritual nephew *Jugendstil*, "[a]rt is not only supposed to deflect the gaze from reality, but rather to displace it. Reality is supposed to transform through art into appearance, aesthetic appearance ought to become the highest reality" (Hartmut Scheible, *Literarischer Jugendstil in Wien: Eine Einführung* [Munich: Artemis, 1984], 19).

20. Jeffrey Herf, *Reactionary Modernism: Technology, Culture, and Politics in Weimar and the Third Reich* (Cambridge: Cambridge University Press, 1984).

21. Peter Adam, *Art of the Third Reich* (New York: Harry N. Abrams, 1988), 9. I will return to these controversies around the historicization of Nazi art in part 2.

22. Berthold Hinz, "'Entartete Kunst' und 'Kunst im Dritten Reich,'" in *Kunst und Macht im Europa der Diktaturen 1930 bis 1945*, ed. Dawn Ades et al. (London: Hayward Gallery, 1996), 332.

23. Karen A. Fiss, "Der deutsche Pavillion," *Kunst und Macht*, 110.

24. Wilfried van der Will, "Culture and the Organization of National Socialist Ideology 1933 to 1945," in *German Cultural Studies: An Introduction*, ed. Rob Burns (Oxford: Oxford University Press, 1995), 131–32.

25. Chryssoula Kambas suggests that one should understand Benjamin's surprising interest in fascisms other than German National Socialism in relation to his exile situation in Paris and his general views about the strategic function of literary politics. See Chryssoula Kambas, *Walter Benjamin im Exil: Zum Verhältnis von Literaturpolitik und Ästhetik* (Tübingen: Max Niemeyer, 1983), 16–80.

26. For an analysis of the intellectual relationship between Benjamin and Gide, see Chryssoula Kambas, "'Indem wir uns scheiden, erblicken wir uns selbst': André Gide, Walter Benjamin und der deutsch-französische Dialog," in *"Was nie geschrieben wurde, lesen": Frankfurter Benjamin-Vorträge*, ed. Lorenz Jäger and Thomas Regehly (Bielefeld: Aisthesis, 1992), 132–56.

27. I am using Norbert Frei's historical categories here as developed in his *Der Führerstaat: Nationalsozialistische Herrschaft 1933 bis 1945* (Munich: Deutscher Taschenbuch, 1987).

28. Herbert Marcuse, "Über den affirmative Charakter der Kultur," 56–101; for a critical comparison of Benjamin's and Marcuse's mode of cultural critique, see Jürgen Habermas, "Consciousness-Raising or Redemptive Criticism: The Contemporaneity of Walter Benjamin," *On Walter Benjamin: Critical Essays and Recollections*, ed. Gary Smith (Cambridge: MIT Press, 1988), 90–128; and as a response, Peter Bürger, "Benjamins 'rettende Kritik': Vorüberlegungen zum Entwurf einer kritischen Hermeneutik," *Germanische-Romanische Monatsschrift* 23 (1973): 198–210.

29. See the introduction to part 2 as well as chapter 7.

30. Max Weber, *Economy and Society: An Outline of Interpretive Sociology*, trans. Ephraim Fischoff, Hans Gerth et al., ed. Guenther Roth and Claus Wittich (New York: Bedminster Press, 1968), 243.

31. Weber, *Economy and Society*, 243–44.

32. The term "superoperetta" is from Kracauer, *From Caligari to Hitler*, 208.

33. Weber, *Economy and Society*, 241.

34. Sabine Hake, "Chaplin Reception in Weimar Germany," *New German Critique* 51 (1990): 90.

35. Siegfried Kracauer, "Chaplin in Berlin," in *Zeitgenosse Chaplin*, ed. Klaus Kreimeier (Berlin: Oberbaumverlag, 1987), 114; quoted in Hake, "Chaplin Reception in Weimar Germany," 88.

36. Andrew Hewitt, *Political Inversions: Homosexuality, Fascism, and the Modernist Imaginary* (Stanford: Stanford University Press, 1996), 38–78.

4. MEDUSIAN POLITICS

1. Goebbels, *Michael*, 83.

2. Ezrahi, *The Descent of Icarus*, 73.

3. Eric L. Santner, *Stranded Objects: Mourning, Memory, and Film in Postwar Germany* (Ithaca: Cornell University Press, 1990), 123.

4. See, for example, Neil Postman, *Amusing Ourselves to Death: Public Discourse in the Age of Show Business* (New York: Viking, 1985).

5. Rentschler, *The Ministry of Illusion*, 22.

6. Silberman, *German Cinema*, 52.

7. Rentschler, *The Ministry of Illusion*, 16–19.

8. Miriam Hansen, "Benjamin, Cinema and Experience: 'The Blue Flower in the Land of Technology,'" *New German Critique* 40 (winter 1987): 182.

9. "Stifter" (GS 2:608–10; SW 1:111–13).

10. Jean-Louis Baudry, "Ideological Effects of the Basic Cinematographic Apparatus," in *Film Theory and Criticism*, ed. Gerald Mast, Marshall Cohen, and Leo Braudy. 4th ed. (New York: Oxford University Press, 1992), 302–12; Christian Metz, *The Imaginary Signifier: Psychoanalysis and the Cinema* (Bloomington: Indiana University Press, 1982).

11. Baudry, "Ideological Effects of the Basic Cinematographic Apparatus," 31.

12. Norbert Bolz, "Schwanengesang der Gutenberg-Galaxis," in *Allegorie und Melancholie*, ed. Willem van Reijen (Frankfurt am Main: Suhrkamp, 1992), 237–58.

13. Siegfried Kracauer, *Theory of Film: The Redemption of Physical Reality* (1960; New York: Oxford University Press, 1965), 46–59.

14. David Bordwell, *The Cinema of Eisenstein* (Cambridge: Harvard University Press, 1993), 43.

15. Sigmund Freud, "Das Medusenhaupt," in *Gesammelte Werke* (London: Imago, 1941), 17:45–48.

16. Freud, *Gesammelte Werke* 17:47.

17. Freud, *Gesammelte Werke* 17:48.

18. See Eisenstein's 1923 essay "The Montage of Attractions," in which he very precisely anticipates Benjamin's theory of tactile reception. Accordingly, film must overcome the perceptual resistance of the normal spectator by administering a series of shocks, acts of visual violence that crack the affectual indifference of the viewer and thus allow for comprehensive physiological rather than exclusively optical modes of response. Attacking what he considers Dziga Vertov's implicit aestheticism, Eisenstein writes: "It is not a Cine-Eye that we need but a Cine-Fist"(Bordwell, *The Cinema of Eisenstein*, 116). What is ballistics to Benjamin is fist fight to Eisenstein.

19. "Kleine Geschichte der Photographie," (GS 2:368–85).

20. On Benjamin and photography, see Eduardo Cadava, "Words of Light: Theses on the Photography of History," in *Fugitive Images: From Photography to Video*, ed. Patrice Petro (Bloomington: Indiana University Press, 1995), 221–44; and by the same author, *Words of Light: Theses on the Photography of History* (Princeton: Princeton University Press, 1997).

21. Susan Sontag, *On Photography* (New York: Dell, 1977), 15.

22. Sontag, *On Photography*, 71.

23. Friedrich Nietzsche, *Unzeitgemäße Betrachtungen. Werke*, ed. Karl Schlechta (Frankfurt am Main: Ullstein, 1983), 1:225–29.

24. Laura Mulvey, "Visual Pleasure and Narrative Cinema," in *Issues in Feminist Film Criticism*, ed. Patricia Evens (Bloomington: Indiana University Press, 1990), 31.

25. "The first, scopophilic, arises from the pleasure in using another person as an object of sexual stimulation through sight. The second, developed through narcissism and the constitution of the ego, comes from identification with the image seen. . . . The first is a function of the sexual instincts, the second of ego libido. . . . Both are formative structures, mechanisms not meaning. In themselves they have no signification, they have to be attached to an idealization. Both pursue aims in indifference to perceptual reality, creating the imagized, eroticized concept of a world that forms the perception of the subject and makes a mockery of empirical objectivity" (Mulvey, "Visual Pleasure and Narrative Cinema," 32).

26. Thomas Elsaesser, "Primary Identification and the Historical Subject: Fassbinder and Germany," in *Narrative, Apparatus, Ideology*, ed. Philip Rosen (New York: Columbia University Press, 1986), 545.

27. Schulte-Sasse, *Entertaining the Third Reich*, 117.

28. "Die Ferne und die Bilder" (GS 4:427).

29. Gaylyn Studlar, *In the Realm of Pleasure: Von Sternberg, Dietrich, and the Masochistic Aesthetic* (New York: Columbia University Press, 1988).

30. Gilles Deleuze, *Masochism: An Interpretation of Coldness and Cruelty* (New York: George Braziller, 1971).

31. "In Lacanian theory, the mirror phase emergence of individual subjectivity is associated with pleasurable identificatory looking, while Freud's account of the castration complex also depends on a strategy of looking. In spite of the substantial contribution these theories have made to film scholarship, there has been a tendency in feminist work on film to accept these theories as 'truth' and to ignore both their phallocentrism and the determinism that their prescriptive application often suggests" (Studlar, *In the Realm of Pleasure*, 3).

32. Following Studlar's argument, the von Sternberg/Dietrich productions in particular incorporate this masochistic dimension of cinematic spectatorship into the diegetic text itself. In Sternberg's highly artificial universes, reality seems suspended, replaced, reflected in iconic modes of representation. Based on "dreamlike chiaroscuro and decorative excess" (Gaylyn Studlar, "Masochism and the Perverse Pleasures of the Cinema," in *Movies and Methods*, ed. Bill Nichols [Berkeley: University of California Press, 1985], 2:607), Sternberg's films translate reality into a unique "heterocosm," a parallel world of self-reflexive aesthetic purification into which the pleasure of masochist submission are inscribed.

33. Siegfried Kracauer describes modes of iconic representation in *Triumph of the Will* as follows: "Like many faces and objects, isolated architectural details are frequently shot against the sky. These particular close shots, typical not only of *Triumph of the Will*, seem to assume the function of removing things and events from their own environment into strange and unknown space. The dimensions of that space, however, remain entirely undefined. It is not without symbolic meaning that the features of Hitler often appear before clouds." Kracauer, *From Caligari to Hitler*, 302.

34. In *Triumph of the Will*, for example, the indulgence in endless movement ultimately only serves, as Kracauer wrote in continuation of Benjamin's argument, to symbolize "the readiness of the masses to be shaped and used at will by their leader. The emphasis on these living ornaments can be traced to the intention of captivating the spectator with their aesthetic qualities and leading him to believe in the solidity of the swastika world" (Kracauer, *From Caligari to Hitler*, 302). To be sure, Riefenstahl rigorously explores the technological possibilities of mobile cameras to conjure an endless series of impressive *tableaux vivants*; but while she is panning, tilting, and tracking her cameras, the spectator is struck by the impression "that be-

fore our eyes palpable life becomes an apparition" (Kracauer, *From Caligari to Hitler*, 302).

35. Teresa de Lauretis, "Fellini's 9½," in *Technologies of Gender: Essays on Theory, Film, and Fiction* (Bloomington: Indiana University Press, 1987), 98.

36. David Bordwell, "The Classical Hollywood Style," in *The Classical Hollywood Cinema: Film Style and Mode of Production to 1960*, ed. David Bordwell, Kristin Thompson, and Janet Staiger (New York: Columbia University Press, 1985), 73.

37. For Hegel, the differentiation of scientific reason and of postreligious concepts of truth in the modern age rendered philosophy, instead of art, the highest medium of knowledge and insight: "Thought and reflection," Hegel argues in his *Aesthetics*, "have outstripped the beautiful arts" (Georg Wilhelm Friedrich Hegel, *Ästhetik*, ed. Friedrich Bassenge [Berlin: Das europäische Buch/VVA, 1985], 22). Modern scientific knowledge seeks to arrive at universal abstractions, laws, and rules; art, by contrast, fails to satisfy this peculiar modern desire for universality because it is dedicated to the representation of particulars in the realm of beautiful appearance. Outdone by the marvels of scientific reasoning, art therefore constitutes, according to Hegel, a practice of the past, one that survives only by mourning nostalgically the loss of its former prominence.

38. See Bordwell, *The Cinema of Eisenstein*, 111–38, 163–98.

39. Sergei Eisenstein, "The Cinematographic Principle and the Ideogram," in *Film Form: Essays in Film Theory*, trans. Jay Leyda (San Diego: Harcourt, Brace, Jovanovich, 1949), 30.

40. Bordwell, *The Cinema of Eisenstein*, 191.

41. Carl Mayer, initially collaborating with Ruttmann, withdrew from the production because of political disagreements with what he considered Ruttmann's surface approach. Paul Rotha reports: "The film as Ruttmann made it was far from Mayer's conception. Its surface approach was what Mayer had tried to avoid. He and Ruttmann agreed to differ" (Paul Rotha, "It's in the Script," *World Film News* [September 1938]: 205; quoted in Kracauer, *From Caligari to Hitler*, 184). See also Anton Kaes, "Film in der Weimarer Republik: Motor der Moderne," *Geschichte des deutschen Films*, ed. Wolfgang Jacobsen, Anton Kaes, and Hans Helmut Prinzler (Stuttgart: Metzler, 1993), 65–67.

42. Kracauer, *From Caligari to Hitler*, 187.

43. Bordwell, "The Classical Hollywood Style," 69.

44. André Bazin, "The Evolution of the Language of Cinema," in *What Is Cinema?* trans. Hugh Gray (Berkeley: University of California Press, 1967), 1:35–36.

45. For different accounts on the affinity between Benjamin and Brecht, see Hannah Arendt, *Walter Benjamin, Bertolt Brecht: Zwei Essays* (Munich: Piper, 1971); Burkhardt Lindner, "Brecht/Benjamin/Adorno: Über Veränderungen der Kunst-

produktion im wissenschaftlich-technischen Zeitalter," *Text und Kritik: Sonderband Bertolt Brecht* (1972): 13–26; and Rolf Tiedemann, "Brecht oder Die Kunst, in anderer Leute Köpfe zu denken," in *Dialektik im Stillstand: Versuche zum Spätwerk Walter Benjamins* (Frankfurt am Main: Suhrkamp, 1983), 42–73. Significantly, it was not until 1968 that Adorno, highly critical about the affinities between Brecht and Benjamin during the 1930s, reported a remark by Benjamin "that with the reproduction essay he sought to overtrump Brecht's radicalism"(Theodor W. Adorno, *Über Walter Benjamin*, ed. Rolf Tiedemann [Frankfurt am Main: Suhrkamp, 1970], 95). Adorno's and Benjamin's Suhrkamp editor Rolf Tiedemann has continued Adorno's attempt to reestablish distance between the "crude thinker" Brecht and the "philosopher" Benjamin: lamenting Benjamin's lack of critical distance to Brecht, Tiedemann claims polemically in his *Studien zur Philosophie Walter Benjamins* (Frankfurt am Main: Suhrkamp, 1973) that Benjamin aspired "the position of an authorized exegetic" (112), misinformed about the implications of his own philosophy.

46. Dieter Wellershoff, *Die Auflösung des Kunstbegriffs* (Frankfurt am Main: Suhrkamp, 1974), 87.

47. Bertolt Brecht, *Arbeitsjournal*, ed. Werner Hecht (Frankfurt am Main: Suhrkamp, 1973), 1:16 (capitalization as in the original).

48. Michael Löwy, *Redemption and Utopia: Jewish Libertarian Thought in Central Europe*, trans. Hope Heany (London: Athlone Press, 1992), 6.

49. Marleen Stoessel,*Aura: Das vergessene Menschliche. Zu Sprache und Erfahrung bei Walter Benjamin* (Munich: Hanser, 1983), 15.

50. Stoessel,*Aura*, 57–63.

51. John Ellis, *Visible Fictions* (London: Routledge, 1982); quoted in Mast, Cohen, and Braudy, *Film Theory*, 343.

52. Ellis, *Visible Fictions*, 347.

53. It is interesting to note in this context that while Benjamin was writing his artwork essay, the Nazis were heavily involved in exploring the possibilities of television as a tool of mass manipulation. As proclaimed as early as September 1935, television was seen as a highly promising technology to transport every German to the Nuremberg mass rallies or, conversely, "to carry the image of the Führer to all Germans'hearts"(Heiko Zeutschner, *Die braune Mattscheibe: Fernsehen im Nationalsozialismus* [Hamburg: Rotbuch, 1995], 91). For more on Nazi television, see Erwin Reiss, *"Wir senden Frohsinn": Fernsehen unterm Faschismus* (Berlin: Elefanten, 1979); Siegfried Zielinski,*Audiovisionen: Kino und Fernsehen als Zwischenspiele in der Geschichte* (Reinbek: Rowohlt, 1989), 98–174; and William Uricchio, ed., *Die Anfänge des deutschen Fernsehens: Kritische Annäherungen an die Entwicklung bis 1945* (Tübingen: Max Niemeyer, 1991).

54. Anne Friedberg, *Window Shopping: Cinema and the Postmodern* (Berkeley: University of California Press, 1993), 136–43.

55. Heinz Paetzold, *Neomarxistische Ästhetik: Teil 1: Bloch, Benjamin* (Düsseldorf: Schwann, 1974), 166.

56. Miriam Hansen, "Early Silent Cinema: Whose Public Sphere?" *New German Critique* 29 (spring/summer 1983): 180. I will return to these questions when reconsidering Benjamin's theories of visual perception from the vista of postmodern experience in chapter 8.

5. VISUAL CULTURE AND THE POLITICS OF PHANTASMAGORIA

1. Karl Marx, "Ökonomisch-philosophische Manuskripte aus dem Jahre 1844," in *Werke. Ergänzungsband 1* (Berlin: Dietz, 1973), 541–42.

2. In a letter written in October 1935, Benjamin introduced his critique of fascism as an integral moment of his ongoing *Arcades Project*. The artwork essay and its epilogue, Benjamin wrote, define a point of reference from which to speak about the past and, as importantly, to transcend the spells of the present: "As far as I am concerned, I am endeavoring to direct my telescope through the fog of blood toward a mirage of the nineteenth century which I try to depict with the kind of features it will display in a coming age, an age liberated from magic. Of course, I have to build this telescope myself first and in the course of this endeavor I have found a number of fundamental axioms for a materialistic theory of art for the first time ever. Presently, I am occupied with discussing them in a short programmatic text" (GS 5:1151).

3. Wolfgang Liebeneiner, "Die Harmonie von Bild, Wort und Musik im Film," *Film-Kurier*, 13 March 1939: 5.

4. Wolfgang Schivelbusch, *Geschichte der Eisenbahnreise: Zur Industrialisierung von Raum und Zeit im 19. Jahrhundert* (Munich: Hanser, 1977), 134–37.

5. Georg Simmel, "Die Großstädte und das Geistesleben," in *Brücke und Tor: Essays* (Stuttgart: Koehler, 1957), 228.

6. Markus Fischer, *Augenblicke um 1900: Literatur, Philosophie, Psychoanalyse und Lebenswelt zur Zeit der Jahrhundertwende* (Frankfurt am Main: Peter Lang, 1986).

7. Simmel, "Die Großstädte und das Geistesleben," 229.

8. For more on Simmel, Benjamin, and their corresponding projects to think through the logic of fragmentation inherent to modernity, see David Frisby, *Fragments of Modernity: Theories of Modernity in the Work of Simmel, Kracauer and Benjamin* (Cambridge: MIT Press, 1986).

9. Schivelbusch, *Geschichte der Eisenbahnreise,* 51–61. Consider Ralph Waldo Emerson's 1836 description of a coach ride in which the philosopher ingeniously describes the forms and ramifications of industrialized perception – that is, the "unrealizing" optics of railway travel: "A man who seldom rides, needs only to get into a coach and traverse his own town, to turn the street into a puppet-show. The men, the women, – talking, running, bartering, fighting, – the earnest mechanic, the lounger, the beggar, the boys, the dogs, are unrealized at once, or, at least wholly detached from all relation to the observer, and seen as apparent, not substantial beings. What new thoughts are suggested by seeing a face of country quite familiar, in the rapid movement of the railroad car! Nay, the most wonted objects, (make a very slight change in the point of vision,) please us most." Ralph Waldo Emerson, "Nature," *Selected Essays,* ed. Larzer Ziff (New York: Penguin Books, 1982), 64.

10. I will discuss Benjamin's approriation of psychoanalysis in the artwork essay in chapter 8. On Benjamin, Freud, and trauma, see several of the essays collected in Cathy Caruth, ed., *Trauma: Explorations in Memory* (Baltimore: Johns Hopkins University Press, 1995).

11. Sigmund Freud, *The Basic Writings,* trans. A. A. Brill (New York: Modern Library, 1938), 490.

12. Sigmund Freud, "Notiz über den 'Wunderblock,' " in *Studienausgabe* (Frankfurt am Main: Fischer, 1975), 3:363–69.

13. Edward W. Said, *Culture and Imperialism* (New York: Alfred A. Knopf, 1993).

14. "Karl Kraus" (REF 239–73; GS 2:334–67).

15. McCole, *Walter Benjamin and the Antinomies of Tradtion.*

16. Karl Marx, *Werke* (Berlin: Dietz, 1983), 23:86.

17. Jonathan Crary, *Techniques of the Observer: On Vision and Modernity in the Nineteenth Century* (Cambridge: MIT Press, 1992), 24.

18. See Lutz P. Koepnick, "August Strindberg und die Ästhetik der Macht. Rekonstruktion einer Kritikstrategie," *Skandinavistik: Zeitschrift für Sprache, Literatur und Kultur der nordischen Länder* 22.2 (1992): 85–106.

19. Schnapp, *Staging Fascism,* 2.

20. Susan Buck-Morss, *The Dialectics of Seeing: Walter Benjamin and the Arcades Project* (Cambridge: MIT Press, 1989), 312.

21. This biological and racial conception of language is at the center of Marcel Beyer's recent novel *Flughunde* (Frankfurt am Main: Suhrkamp, 1995), a novel narrating the fate of a sound technician during the Nazi period.

22. Victor Klemperer, *LTI: Tagebuch eines Philologen* (Berlin: Aufbau-Verlag, 1949), 29.

23. Alice Yaeger Kaplan, *Reproductions of Banality: Fascism, Literature, and French Intellectual Life* (Minneapolis: University of Minnesota Press, 1986), 155.

24. Baeumler, *Männerbund und Wissenschaft*, 132–33.

25. "The first railroad cars were designed like stage coaches, and the first electric light bulbs were shaped like gas flames. Newly processed iron was used for ornament rather than structural supports, shaped into leaves, or made to resemble wood. Industrially produced utensils were decorated to resemble flowers, fauna, seashells, and Greek and Renaissance antiques" (Buck-Morss, *The Dialectics of Seeing*, 111).

26. "Kapitalismus als Religion," (sw 1:288–91; GS 6:100–103).

27. I borrow here from Clifford Geertz's description of he traditional idea of the sacred in "primitive" societies in his essay "Ethos, World View, and the Analysis of Sacred Symbolism," *The Interpretation of Cultures* (New York: Basic Books, 1973), 126.

28. I will discuss the mythic and mimetic subtext of Benjamin's theory of mechanical reproduction in further detail in chapter 8.

29. Quoted in Dieter Bartetzko, *Zwischen Zucht und Ekstase: Zur Theatralik der NS-Architektur* (Berlin: Gebr. Mann, 1985), 55.

6. Perseus's Paradox

1. Jacob Burckhardt, *Force and Freedom: Reflections on History*, ed. James Hastings Nichols (New York: Pantheon Books, 1943), 275.

2. Hayden White, *Metahistory: The Historical Imagination in Nineteenth-Century Europe* (Baltimore: Johns Hopkins University Press, 1973), 41.

3. Rainer Maria Rilke, "Requiem für Wolf Graf von Kalckreuth," in *Werke* (Frankfurt am Main: Insel, 1984), 1.2:420.

4. Krista R. Greffrath, *Metaphorischer Materialismus: Untersuchungen zum Geschichtsbegriff Walter Benjamins* (Munich: Wilhelm Fink, 1981).

5. For inquiries into the epistemological underpinnings and ramifications of Benjamin's theory of "dialectical images," see Buck-Morss, *The Dialectics of Seeing*, 216–252; Jennings, *Dialectical Images*, 15–41; McCole, *Walter Benjamin and the Antinomies of Tradition*, 287–95.

6. Norbert W. Bolz, "Politische Kritik. Zum Streit um Walter Benjamin," *Frankfurter Hefte* 35 (1980): 64.

7. For critical evaluations of Benjamin the hermeneutician, see Peter Bürger, "'Benjamins rettende Kritik'. Vorüberlegungen zum Entwurf einer kritischen Hermeneutik," *Germanisch-Romanische Monatsschrift* 23 (1973): 198–210; Harro Müller, "Materialismus und Hermeneutik: Zu Benjamins späten theoretischen Schriften," *Studien zur Entwicklung einer materialen Hermeutik*, ed. Ulrich Nassen (Munich: Wilhelm Fink, 1979), 212–33; Heinrich Kaulen, *Rettung und Destruktion: Untersuchungen zur Hermeneutik Walter Benjamins* (Tübingen: Max Niemeyer, 1987).

8. Kaulen, *Rettung und Destruktion*, 133.

9. Theodor W. Adorno, *Über Walter Benjamin* (Tiedemann, 1970), 26.

10. Louis Aragon, *Nightwalker (Le Paysan de Paris)*, trans. Frederick Brown (Englewood Cliffs: Prentice-Hall, 1970), 52–53.

11. Rolf Tiedemann, *Dialektik im Stillstand: Versuche zum Späwerk Walter Benjamins* (Frankfurt am Main: Suhrkamp, 1983), 132.

12. Gershom Scholem, "Walter Benjamin und sein Engel," in *Zur Aktualität Walter Benjamins: Aus Anlaß des 80. Geburtstags von Walter Benjamin*, ed. Siegfried Unseld (Frankfurt am Main: Suhrkamp, 1972), 87–138; Rolf Tiedemann, *Dialektik im Stillstand*, 99–142.

13. Tiedemann, *Dialektik im Stillstand*, 103.

14. For more on Benjamin and astronomy as well as Benjamin's debt to Blanqui's study of astronomical images, see the discussion in Cadava, *Words of Light*.

15. Tiedemann, *Dialektik im Stillstand*, 101.

16. Jürgen Habermas, "Consciousness-Raising or Rescuing Critique," in *On Walter Benjamin: Critical Essays and Recollections*, 122.

17. Tiedemann, *Dialektik im Stillstand*, 101.

18. Theodor W. Adorno, "Introduction to Benjamin's *Schriften*," in Smith, *On Walter Benjamin: Critical Essays and Recollections*, 11.

19. Martin Jay, *Downcast Eyes: The Denigration of Vision in Twentieth-Century French Thought* (Berkeley: University of California Press, 1993), 21–148.

20. Barbara Maria Stafford, *Good Looking: Essay on the Virtue of Images* (Cambridge: MIT Press, 1996), 20–41.

21. Ovid, *The Metamorphoses*, trans. Mary M. Innes (Harmondsworth, UK: Penguin Books, 1955), 115.

22. Ovid, *The Metamorphoses*, 115.

23. See Lars Gustafsson, *Bernard Foys tredje rockad: Kriminalroman och rekonstruktion av Les Fleurs du mal av Charles Baudelaire* (Stockholm: Norstedts, 1986), 345–46.

INTRODUCTION TO PART 2

1. Andrew Hewitt, *Fascist Modernism: Aesthetics, Politics, and the Avant-Garde* (Stanford: Stanford University Press, 1993), 3.

2. *Die Macht der Bilder* (released in the United States as *The Wonderful Horrible Life of Leni Riefenstahl*).

3. Christoph Stölzl, "Vorwort," in *Kunst und Macht*, 9.

4. Michael P. Steinberg, "Introduction: Benjamin and the Critique of Allegorical Reason," in Steinberg, *Walter Benjamin and the Demands of History*, 18.

7. FASCIST AESTHETICS REVISITED

1. Quoted in Karlheinz Schmeer, *Die Regie des öffentlichen Lebens im Dritten Reich* (Munich: Pohl, 1956), 168.

2. For a sample of recent studies examining the relative heterogeneity of Nazi culture, see Detlev J. K. Peukert, *Inside Nazi Germany: Conformity, Opposition, and Racism in Everyday Life* (New Haven: Yale University Press, 1987); Otto Weber, *Tausend ganz normale Jahre: Ein Fotoalbum des gewöhnlichen Faschismus* (Nördlingen: Greno, 1987); Uwe Westphal, *Werbung im Dritten Reich* (Berlin: Transit, 1989); Reichel, *Der schöne Schein*; Michael H. Kater, *Different Drummers: Jazz in the Culture of Nazi Germany* (Oxford: Oxford University Press, 1992); Udo Pini, *Leibeskult und Liebeskitsch: Erotik im Dritten Reich* (Munich: Klinkhardt & Biermann, 1992); Michael Geyer, "Resistance as Ongoing Project: Visions of Order, Obligations to Strangers, Struggles for Civil Society," *Journal of Modern History* 64, supplement (December 1992): 217–41; Knud Wolffram, *Tanzdielen und Vergnügungspaläste: Berliner Nachtleben in den dreißiger und vierziger Jahren* (Berlin: Edition Hentrich, 1992); Winfried Nerdinger, ed., *Bauhaus-Moderne im Nationalsozialismus: Zwischen Anbiederung und Verfolgung* (Munich: Prestel, 1993); Childers and Caplan, *Reevaluating the Third Reich*; Franz Ritter, ed., *Heinrich Himmler und die Liebe zum Swing* (Leipzig: Reclam, 1994); Heiko Zeutschner, *Die braune Mattscheibe: Fernsehen im Nationalsozialismus* (Hamburg: Rotbuch, 1995); Erhard Schütz, "Zur Modernität des 'Dritten Reiches,'" *Internationales Archiv für Sozialgeschichte der Literatur* 20.1 (1995): 116–36, and by the same author, "Das 'Dritte Reich' als Mediendiktatur. Medienpolitik und Modernisierung in Deutschland 1933 bis 1945," *Monatshefte* 87.2 (summer 1995): 129–50; Rentschler, *The Ministry of Illusion*.

3. Rentschler, *The Ministry of Illusion*, 22.

4. Hans Dieter Schäfer, *Das gespaltene Bewußtsein: Deutsche Kultur und Lebenswirklichkeit 1933–1945* (Munich: Hanser, 1981), 143; see also by the same author, "Amerikanismus im Dritten Reich," in Prinz and Zitelmann, *Nationalsozialismus und Modernisierung*, 199–215.

5. Jürgen Habermas, *Legitimationsprobleme im Spätkapitalismus* (Frankfurt am Main: Suhrkamp, 1973), 68.

6. Theodor W. Adorno, "On Popular Music," in *On Record: Rock, Pop, and the Written Word*, ed. Simon Frith and Andrew Goodwin (London: Routledge, 1990), 308.

7. Bathrick, "Making a National Family with the Radio": 125.

8. Fredric Jameson, "Reification and Utopia in Mass Culture," in *Signatures of the Visible* (New York: Routledge, 1992), 34.

9. David Bathrick, "Inscribing History, Prohibiting and Producing Desire: Fassbinder's *Lili Marleen*," *New German Critique* 63 (fall 1994): 48.

10. Guy Debord, *Society of the Spectacle* (Detroit: Black and Red, 1983), #29.

11. Peter Labanyi, "Images of Fascism: Visualization and Aestheticization in the Third Reich," in *The Burden of German History 1919–45*, ed. Michael Laffan (London: Methuen, 1988), 172.

12. Labanyi, "Images of Fascism," 172.

13. Geyer, "The State in National Socialist Germany," 214.

14. Geyer, "The State in National Socialist Germany," 215.

15. For two recent and penetrating discussions of the figure of "mimesis" in Frankfurt School thought, see Martin Jay, "Mimesis and Mimetology: Adorno and Lacoue-Labarthe," in Huhn and Zuidervaart, *The Semblance of Subjectivity*, 29–54; Shierry Weber Nicholsen, "*Aesthetic Theory*'s Mimesis of Walter Benjamin," in Nicholsen, *Exact Imagination, Late Work*, 137–80.

16. Heinz-Dieter Kittsteiner, "The Allegory of the Philosophy of History in the Nineteenth Century," in Steinberg, *Walter Benjamin and the Demands of History*, 60; see also by the same author, "Walter Benjamin's Historicism," *New German Critique* 39 (fall 1986): 179–215.

17. Kittsteiner, "The Allegory of the Philosophy of History," 60.

18. Huyssen, *After the Great Divide*.

19. Jameson, "Reification and Utopia in Mass Culture," 34.

20. Peukert, *Inside Nazi Germany*, 196.

21. Horkheimer and Adorno, *Dialectic of Enlightenment*, 184–85.

22. See Schütz, "Das 'Dritte Reich' als Mediendiktatur," 129.

23. Labanyi, "Images of Fascism," 172–73.

24. Ian Kershaw, *Der Hitler-Mythos: Volksmeinung und Propaganda im Dritten Reich* (Stuttgart: Deutsche Verlags-Anstalt, 1980); *The 'Hitler Myth': Image and Reality in the Third Reich* (Oxford: Oxford University Press, 1987); "Hitler and the Germans," in *Life in the Third Reich*, ed. Richard Bessel (Oxford: Oxford University Press, 1987), 41–55; "Hitlers Popularität. Mythos und Realität im Dritten Reich," in *Herrschaftsalltag im Dritten Reich: Studien und Texte*, ed. Hans Mommsen and Susanne Willems (Düsseldorf: Schwann, 1988), 24–52.

25. Kershaw, "Hitler and the Germans," 41.

26. For more, see my "Allegory and Power: Walter Benjamin and the Politics of Representation," *Soundings: An Interdisciplinary Journal* 79.1–2 (1996): 59–78, in particular 62–66.

27. Kershaw, "Hitler and the Germans," 47.

28. Baeumler, *Männerbund und Wissenschaft*, 108.

29. See also chapter 3.

30. Max Weber, *Economy and Society: An Outline of Interpretative Sociology*, trans.

Ephraim Fischoff, Hans Gerth, et al., ed. Guenther Roth and Claus Wittich (New York: Bedminster Press, 1968), 241.

31. "The rational organization of labor leads necessarily to the repression of traditionalism and the denial of individual satisfaction. Civilization's progress may accomplish grand feats, but it prohibits personal contentment and erodes the power of cultural structures to provide orientation in everyday life. Against the background of the increasingly meaningless culture of Wilhelmine Germany, Weber suggests that only a thorough transformation of values might guarantee social coherence. Such an act belongs properly to the province of the charismatic leader." Berman, *The Rise of the Modern German Novel*, 41.

32. Kershaw, "Hitlers Popularität," 25.

33. Kershaw, "Hitler and the Germans," 54.

34. Horkheimer and Adorno, *Dialectic of Enlightenment*, 236.

35. John Fiske, *Understanding Popular Culture* (London: Routledge, 1989), 143.

36. Kershaw, "Hitlers Popularität," 47.

37. For a comprehensive documentation of the products of the 1986 historians' debate, see the special issue of *New German Critique* 44 (spring/summer 1988). For a critical evaluation of the postunification revision of German national history, see the various essays in Jürgen Habermas, *Die Normalität einer Berliner Republik: Kleine Politische Schriften VIII* (Frankfurt am Main: Suhrkamp, 1995).

38. Charles S. Maier, foreword to Childers and Kaplan, *Reevaluating the Third Reich*, xiii.

39. Rainer Zitelmann, "Die totalitäre Seite der Moderne," in Prinz and Zitelmann, *Nationalsozialismus und Modernisierung*, 19.

40. John Czaplicka, Andreas Huyssen, and Anson Rabinbach, "Cultural History and Cultural Studies," *New German Critique* 65 (spring/summer 1995): 9.

41. Peuckert, *Inside Nazi Germany*, 241.

8. BENJAMIN'S ACTUALITY

1. Anne Friedberg, "Cinema and the Postmodern Condition," in *Viewing Positions: Ways of Seeing Film*, ed. Linda Williams (New Brunswick: Rutgers University Press, 1995), 60; see also Friedberg's more comprehensive study, *Window Shopping*.

2. Rey Chow, "Where Have All the Natives Gone?" in *Displacements: Cultural Identities in Question*, ed. Angelika Bammer (Bloomington: Indiana University Press, 1994), 140.

3. See the various essays gathered in Victor Burgin, *In/Different Spaces: Place and Memory in Visual Culture* (Berkeley: University of California Press, 1996).

4. Hans Jürgen Syberberg, *Vom Unglück und Glück der Kunst in Deutschland nach dem letzten Kriege* (Munich: Matthes & Seitz, 1990), 50.

5. For a more thorough version of this argument, see my "Rethinking the Spectacle: History, Visual Culture, and German Unification," in *Zeitenwende/Wendezeiten: Ein halbes Jahrhundert deutsche Literatur (1945–1995)*, ed. Robert Weninger and Brigitte Rossbacher (Tübingen: Stauffenburg, 1997).

6. George L. Mosse, *The Nationalization of the Masses: Political Symbolism and Mass Movements in Germany from the Napoleonic Wars to the Third Reich* (Ithaca: Cornell University Press, 1975), 47–72.

7. See, for example, Thomas Meyer, "Repräsentativästhetik und politische Kultur," in *Kunst, Symbolik und Politik: Die Reichstagsverhüllung als Denkanstoß*, ed. Ansgar Klein et al. (Leverkusen: Leske & Budrich, 1995), 317–24.

8. Jim Collins, *Architectures of Excess: Cultural Life in the Information Age* (New York: Routledge, 1995), 25.

9. Andreas Huyssen, "Monumental Seduction," *New German Critique* 69 (fall 1996): 187.

10. Martin Jay has critically examined Benjamin's early theory of prelapsarian experience in a presentation at the symposium "The Future of Critical Theory: A Reassessment," Cornell University, April 1998.

11. "A Child's View of Color" (SW 1:51).

12. Heide Schlüpmann, "Kinosucht," *Frauen und Film* 33 (October 1982): 45–52.

13. Miriam Hansen, "Early Silent Cinema: Whose Public Sphere?," *New German Critique* 29 (spring/summer 1983): 180.

14. Horkheimer and Adorno, *Dialectic of Enlightenment*, 135.

15. Shierry Weber Nicholsen, "Adorno and Benjamin, Photography and the Aura," in *Exact Imagination, Late Work*, 181–225.

16. Adorno, "On Popular Music," 308.

17. Theodor W. Adorno, "On the Fetish-Character in Music and the Regression of Listening," in *The Essential Frankfurt School Reader*, ed. Andrew Arato and Eike Gebhardt (New York: Urizen Books, 1978), 280.

18. Theodor W. Adorno, "Transparencies on Film," *New German Critique* 24/25 (fall/winter 1981/82): 202.

19. Adorno, "Transparencies on Film": 202.

20. Patrice Petro, *Joyless Streets: Women and Melodramatic Representation in Weimar Germany* (Princeton: Princeton University Press, 1989).

21. Petro, *Joyless Streets*, 76.

22. Petro, *Joyless Streets*, 67.

23. Miriam Hansen, "Benjamin, Cinema and Experience: 'The Blue Flower in the Land of Technology,'" *New German Critique* 40 (winter 1987): 202.

24. Siegfried Kracauer, "Cult of Distraction," in *The Mass Ornament: Weimar Essays*, trans. Thomas Y. Levin (Cambridge: Harvard University Press, 1995), 327.

25. The notion cinema-of-attraction, as developed by Tom Gunning, provides a valuable concept describing modes of representation and address that precede the dominance of narrative in mainstream film; it conceptualizes modes of specularization that address the audience directly in order to elicit excitement and curiosity. See Tom Gunning, "The Cinema of Attraction(s)," *Wide Angle* 8.3–4 (1986): 63–70; see also Gunning's essay "An Aesthetic of Astonishment: Early Film and the (In)credulous Spectator," *Art & Text* 34 (1989): 31–45.

26. Hansen, "Benjamin, Cinema and Experience," 209.

27. John B. Thompson, *Ideology and Modern Culture* (Cambridge: Basil Blackwell, 1990), 16–17.

28. David Harvey, *The Condition of Postmodernity: An Enquiry into the Origins of Cultural Change* (Oxford: Basil Blackwell, 1989), 124.

29. Peter U. Hohendahl, *Prismatic Thought: Theodor W. Adorno* (Lincoln: University of Nebraska Press, 1995), 145.

30. Friedberg, "Cinema and the Postmodern Condition," 74; see also, Iain Chambers, "The Aural Walk," in *Migrancy, Culture, Identity* (London: Routledge, 1994), 49–53.

31. See Gerhard Schulze, *Die Erlebnisgesellschaft: Kultursoziologie der Gegenwart* (Frankfurt am Main: Campus, 1992), 33–89.

32. See Sherry Turkle, *Life on the Screen: Identity in the Age of the Internet* (New York: Simon & Schuster, 1995).

33. Helmut Dubiel, *Ungewißheit und Politik* (Frankfurt am Main: Suhrkamp, 1994), 90.

34. Gerhard Schulze, "Das Medienspiel," in *Kulturinszenierungen*, ed. Stefan Müller-Doohm and Klaus Neumann-Braun (Frankfurt am Main: Suhrkamp, 1995), 370.

35. Jürgen Habermas, "What Theories Can Accomplish – and What They Can't," in *The Past as Future*, trans. Max Pensky (Lincoln: University of Nebraska Press, 1994), 119.

36. Anthony Giddens, *The Consequences of Modernity* (Stanford: Stanford University Press, 1990), 55–78.

37. Hal Foster, *The Return of the Real* (Cambridge: MIT Press, 1996).

38. Andreas Huyssen, "Escape from Amnesia: The Museum as Mass Medium," in *Twilight Memories: Marking Time in a Culture of Amnesia* (New York: Routledge, 1995), 16.

39. Jay, *Downcast Eyes*; Barbara Maria Stafford, *Good Looking: Essays on the Virtue of Images* (Cambridge: MIT Press, 1996).

40. Jim Collins, *Uncommon Cultures: Popular Culture and Post-Modernism* (New York: Routledge, 1989), 1–27.

41. Jean Baudrillard, "La Guerre du Golfe n'a pas eu lieu," *Libération* (29 March 1991); Jean Baudrillard, *Simulacra and Simulation*, trans. Sheila Faria Glaser (Ann Arbor: University of Michigan Press, 1994), 12.

42. Steinberg, "The Collector as Allegorist," 107.

INDEX

Adam, Peter, 98–99
Adorno, Theodor W.: *Aesthetic Theory*, 24–25, 77, 78; on American mass culture, 55–58, 189, 198–99, 200; contrasted with Benjamin, 37, 113, 116, 237; criticisms of Benjamin by, 95, 166, 171, 218, 220–23, 225, 233, 234, 258 n.45; *Dialectic of Enlightenment*, 56, 208; *In Search of Wagner*, 72–73, 102–3; *Zeitschrift für Sozialforschung*, 63
aesthetic autonomy: Adorno's defense of, 24–25, 55–58, 102–3, 221–22, 233–34, 237; Benjamin's defense of, 37–40, 86–90; dismissal of, in fascist art, 103–4; historical approach to, 17, 29, 53–54, 143–44, 184; nineteenth-century erosion of, 72–73, 93–97, 182–83; Sontag's defense of, 32–33; surrealist attack on, 18–23, 251 n.12. *See also* aestheticism; aesthetic politics; autonomous politics; autonomy
aesthetic experience: Adorno's faith in survival of, 55, 220–21, 233; Benjamin's postaesthetic theory of, 91, 126, 148–49, 218–20, 234; high status of, in German intellectual tradition, 29; mechanical reproduction of, 60, 143–44, 220, 223; political spectacle as, 2, 51, 74, 98; Schmitt's conflation of, with politics, 44–45
aestheticism: avant-garde challenge to, 18–19, 20; Benjamin's attack on, 39–40, 79, 172–74, 226, 251 n.12; Eisenstein's attack on, 255 n.18; fascist, 14–18, 53, 90–91, 93–98, 100–101, 103–4, 105, 107, 111; origins of, 252 n.19; relationship to aesthetic politics of, 3, 31
aestheticization thesis. *See* aesthetic politics
aesthetic politics: basic problems of, 3–4,

30–33, 35–36; in Benjamin's early work, 36–50; Benjamin's later conception of, 139–40, 141–44, 164–65, 191–95, 198–201, 205–6; contemporary debate on, 1–9, 14–18, 24–26, 180–86, 187–89, 206–9, 213–18, 226–38; critique of Benjamin's conception of, 11–14, 22–24, 113–14, 135–39, 178–80, 189–91, 209–12, 223–26; dedifferentiation in, 1, 83–84, 104–5, 247 n.14; effect of fascism on Benjamin's conception of, 50–52, 53, 57–59, 63–82, 86, 89–98, 102–4; gender bias in Benjamin's account of, 33–34, 106–8, 117–29, 171–74; history of concept of, 29–30, 42–45, 62–63. *See also* mass culture; phantasmagoria; spectacle
aesthetics: Benjamin's early, 37–40, 86–91; Benjamin's materialist, 50–51, 62–63, 137–38, 142, 165, 235–38, 259 n.2; traditional, 49–50, 53–55, 75–77, 257 n.37. *See also* aesthetic autonomy; aesthetic experience; aestheticism; aesthetic politics; fascist aesthetics
allegory: Benjamin's use of, 166–71, 173–74; commodity as, 194–99, 199–200, 203; emancipatory power of, 41, 48, 79, 101, 149
Althusser, Louis, 116
anti-Semitism, 10–11, 35, 61, 85
Aragon, Louis, 166
Arcades Project (Benjamin), 4, 41, 114, 139; theoretical framework of, 142–44, 155–56, 160–61, 166, 191–92, 193, 200, 259 n.2
"Art and Power" (1996 art exhibition), 181–84
artistic technique, 94–95, 97
l'art pour l'art. See aestheticism